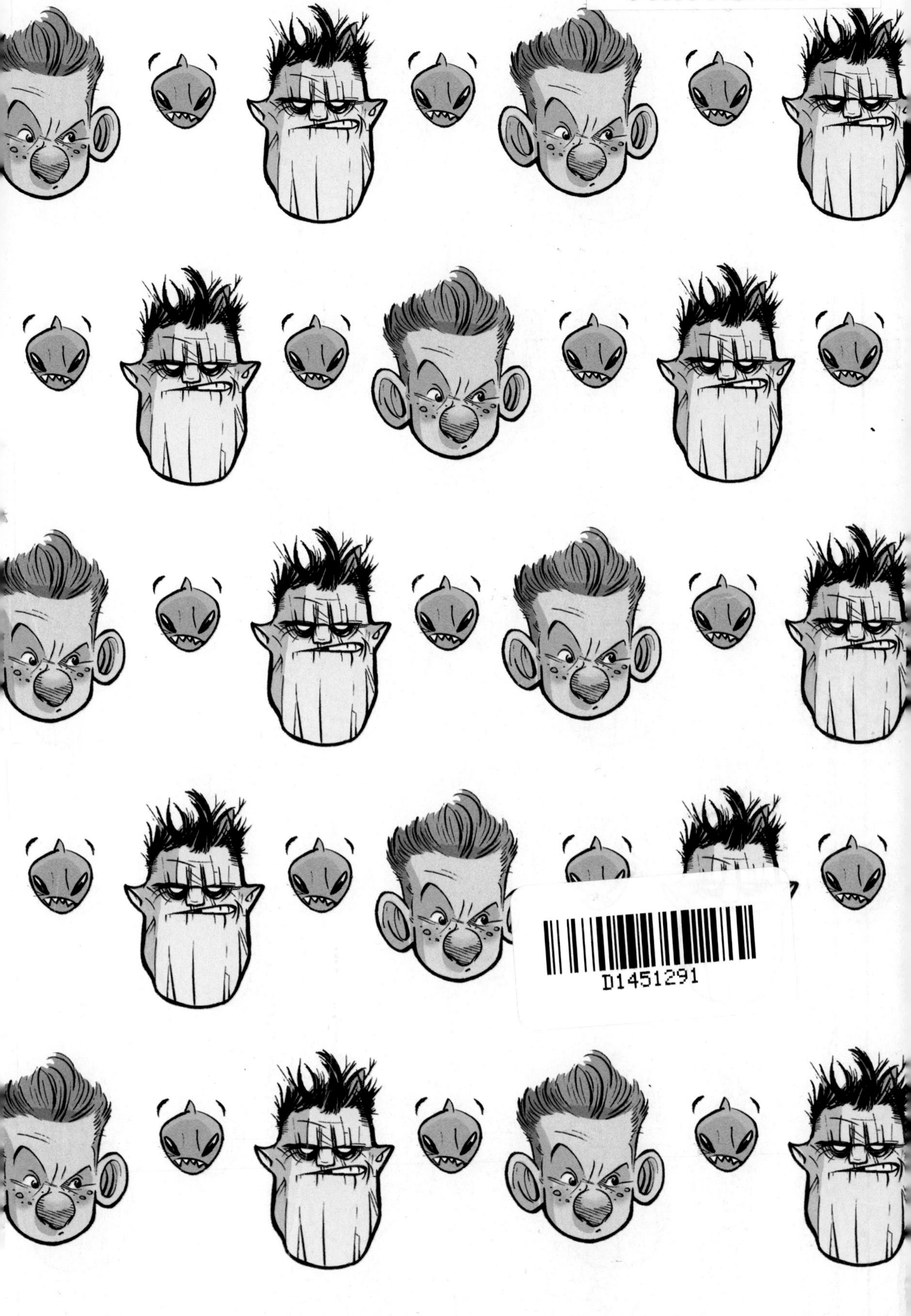

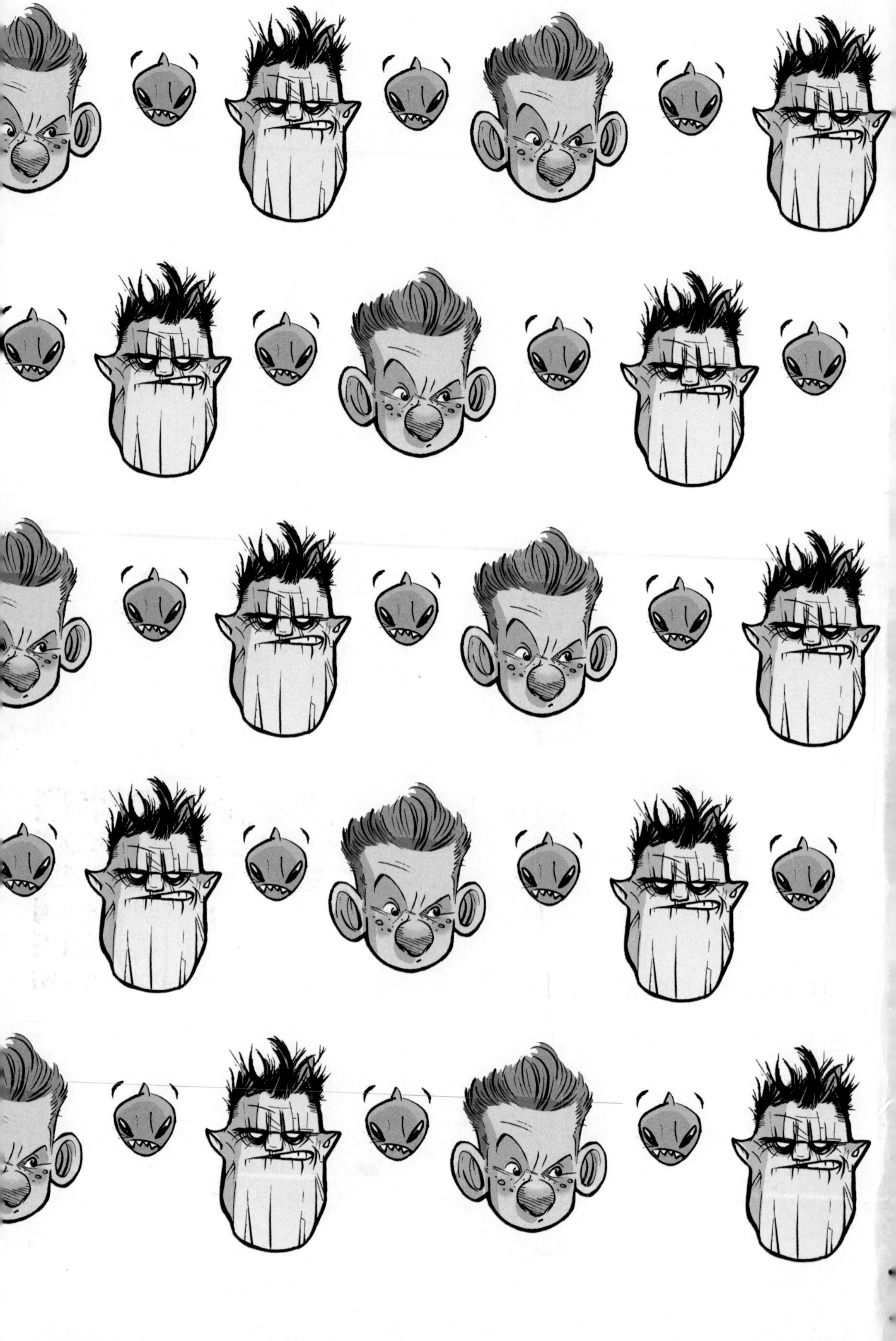

BIZARRO

WRITTEN BY **HEATH CORSON** ART BY **GUSTAVO DUARTE**

GUEST ART BY **BILL SIENKIEWICZ KELLEY JONES MICHELLE MADSEN FRANCIS MANAPUL**

FÁBIO MOON GABRIEL BÁ DARWYN COOKE RAFAEL ALBUQUERQUE TIM SALE & DAVE STEWART

COLOR BY **PETE PANTAZIS LEE LOUGHRIDGE** LETTERS BY **TOM NAPOLITANO**

COVER ART BY **GUSTAVO DUARTE**

SUPERMAN CREATED BY **JERRY SIEGEL & JOE SHUSTER** BY SPECIAL ARRANGEMENT WITH THE JERRY SIEGEL FAMILY

EDDIE BERGANZA Editor – Original series
ANDREW MARINO JEREMY BENT Assistant Editors – Original Series
JEB WOODARD Group Editor – Collected Editions
ROBIN WILDMAN Editor – Collected Edition
STEVE COOK Design Director – Books
LOUIS PRANDI Publication Design

BOB HARRAS Senior VP – Editor-in-Chief, DC Comics

DIANE NELSON President
DAN DIDIO and JIM LEE Co-Publishers
GEOFF JOHNS Chief Creative Officer
AMIT DESAI Senior VP – Marketing & Global Franchise Management
NAIRI GARDINER Senior VP – Finance
SAM ADES VP – Digital Marketing
BOBBIE CHASE VP – Talent Development
MARK CHIARELLO Senior VP – Art, Design & Collected Editions
JOHN CUNNINGHAM VP – Content Strategy
ANNE DEPIES VP – Strategy Planning & Reporting
DON FALLETTI VP – Manufacturing Operations
LAWRENCE GANEM VP – Editorial Administration & Talent Relations
ALISON GILL Senior VP – Manufacturing & Operations
HANK KANALZ Senior VP – Editorial Strategy & Administration
JAY KOGAN VP – Legal Affairs
DEREK MADDALENA Senior VP – Sales & Business Development
JACK MAHAN VP – Business Affairs
DAN MIRON VP – Sales Planning & Trade Development
NICK NAPOLITANO VP – Manufacturing Administration
CAROL ROEDER VP – Marketing
EDDIE SCANNELL VP – Mass Account & Digital Sales
COURTNEY SIMMONS Senior VP – Publicity & Communications
JIM (SKI) SOKOLOWSKI VP – Comic Book Specialty & Newsstand Sales
SANDY YI Senior VP – Global Franchise Management

BIZARRO

DC Comics, 2900 West Alameda Avenue, Burbank, CA 91505
Printed by RR Donnelley, Owensville, MO, USA. 12/30/15. First Printing.
ISBN: 978-1-4012-5971-6

Library of Congress Cataloging-in-Publication Data is available.

PEFC Certified

Printed on paper from
sustainably managed
forests and controlled
sources

PEFC/29-31-75   www.pefc.org

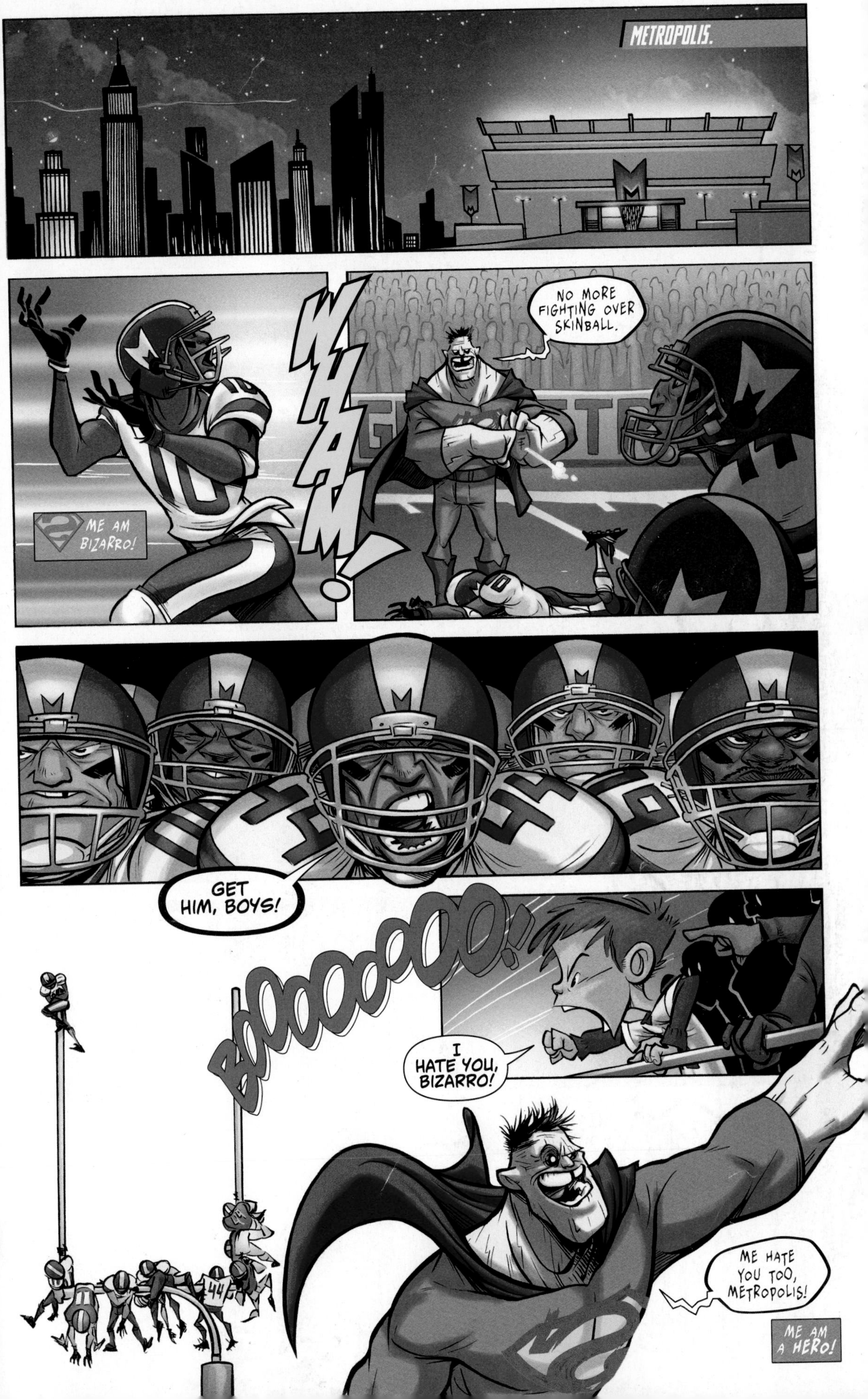
METROPOLIS.
ME AM BIZARRO!
WHAM!
NO MORE FIGHTING OVER SKINBALL.
GET HIM, BOYS!
BOOOOOOOOO!
I HATE YOU, BIZARRO!
ME HATE YOU TOO, METROPOLIS!
ME AM A HERO!

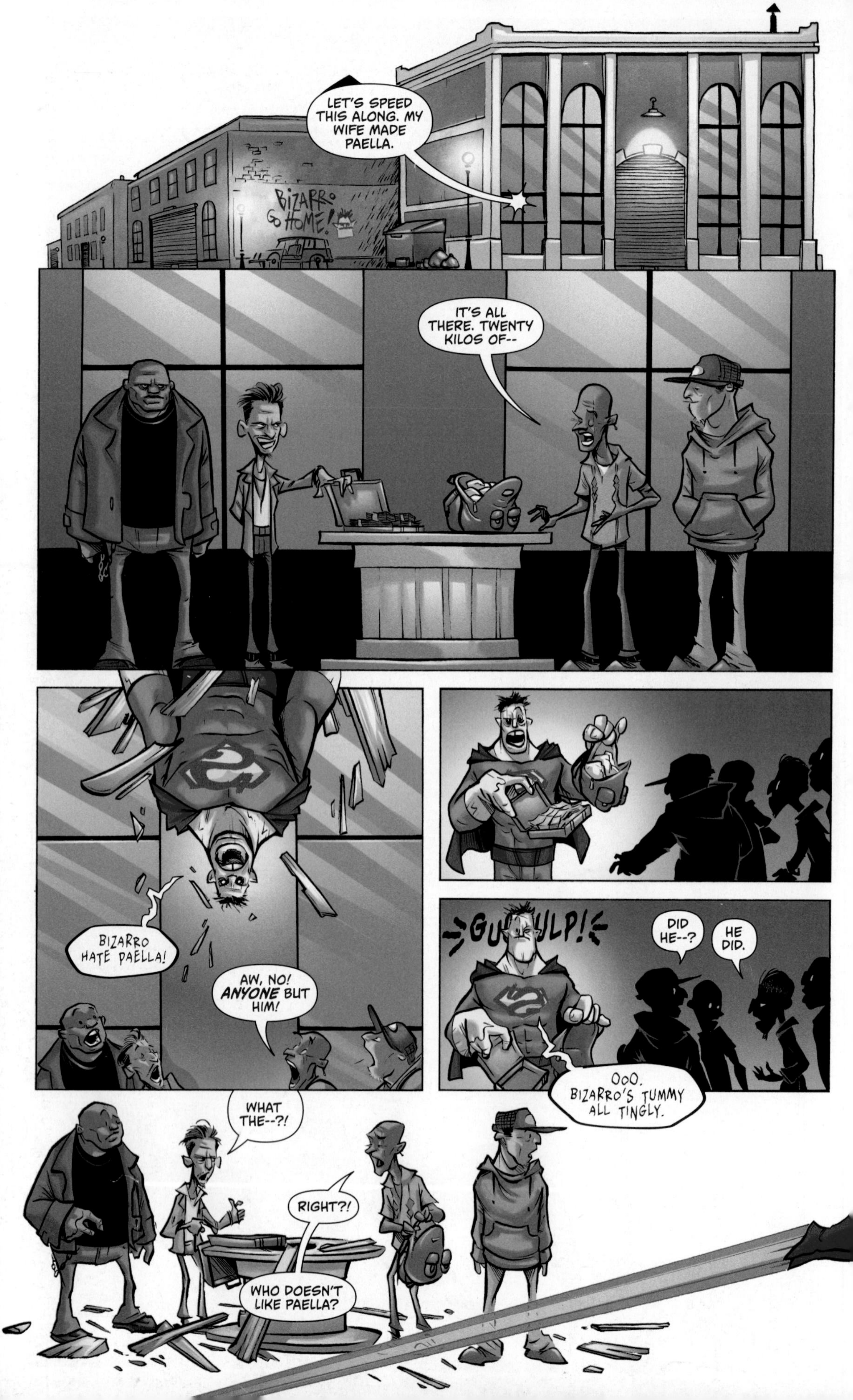
LET'S SPEED THIS ALONG. MY WIFE MADE PAELLA.
BIZARRO GO HOME!
IT'S ALL THERE. TWENTY KILOS OF--
BIZARRO HATE PAELLA!
AW, NO! ANYONE BUT HIM!
GULP!
DID HE--?
HE DID.
OOO. BIZARRO'S TUMMY ALL TINGLY.
WHAT THE--?!
RIGHT?!
WHO DOESN'T LIKE PAELLA?

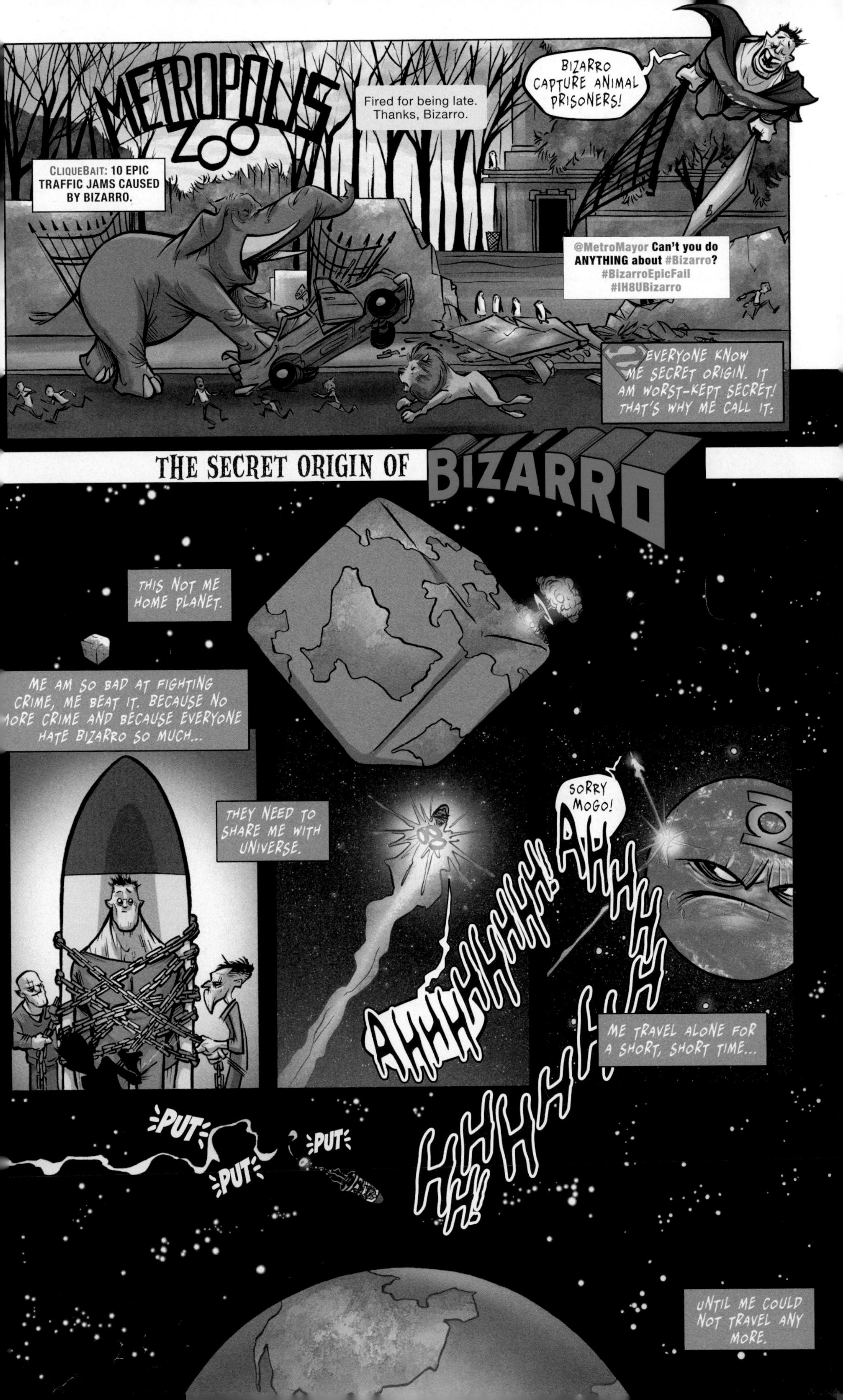
METROPOLIS ZOO
CLIQUEBAIT: 10 EPIC TRAFFIC JAMS CAUSED BY BIZARRO.
Fired for being late. Thanks, Bizarro.
BIZARRO CAPTURE ANIMAL PRISONERS!
@MetroMayor Can't you do ANYTHING about #Bizarro? #BizarroEpicFail #IH8UBizarro
EVERYONE KNOW ME SECRET ORIGIN. IT AM WORST-KEPT SECRET! THAT'S WHY ME CALL IT:
THE SECRET ORIGIN OF BIZARRO
THIS NOT ME HOME PLANET.
ME AM SO BAD AT FIGHTING CRIME, ME BEAT IT. BECAUSE NO MORE CRIME AND BECAUSE EVERYONE HATE BIZARRO SO MUCH...
THEY NEED TO SHARE ME WITH UNIVERSE.
SORRY MOGO!
AHHHHHHHH! AHHHHHHHHHHHHHHHH!
ME TRAVEL ALONE FOR A SHORT, SHORT TIME...
PUT PUT PUT
UNTIL ME COULD NOT TRAVEL ANY MORE.

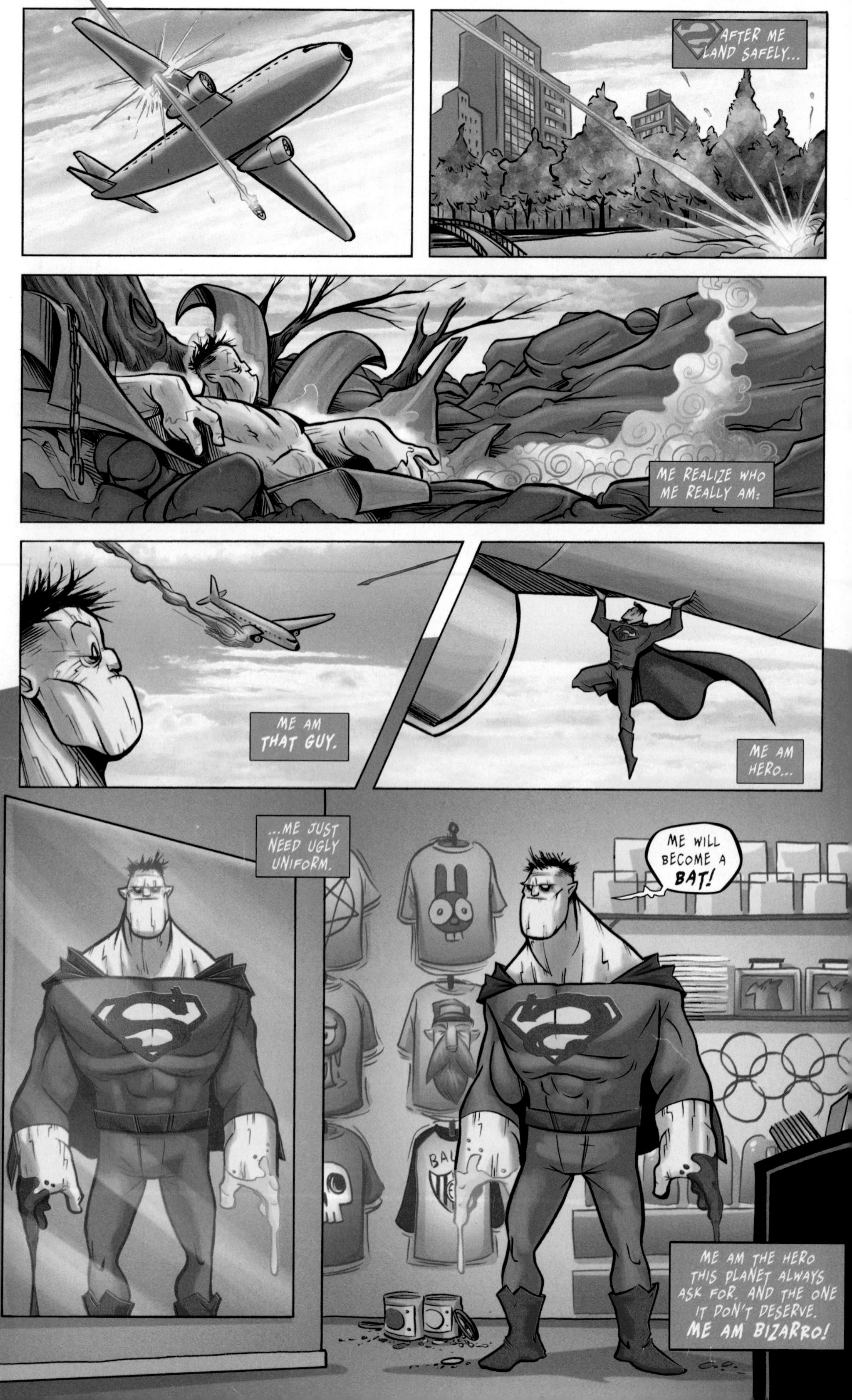
AFTER ME LAND SAFELY...
ME REALIZE WHO ME REALLY AM:
ME AM THAT GUY.
ME AM HERO...
...ME JUST NEED UGLY UNIFORM.
ME WILL BECOME A BAT!
ME AM THE HERO THIS PLANET ALWAYS ASK FOR. AND THE ONE IT DON'T DESERVE. ME AM BIZARRO!

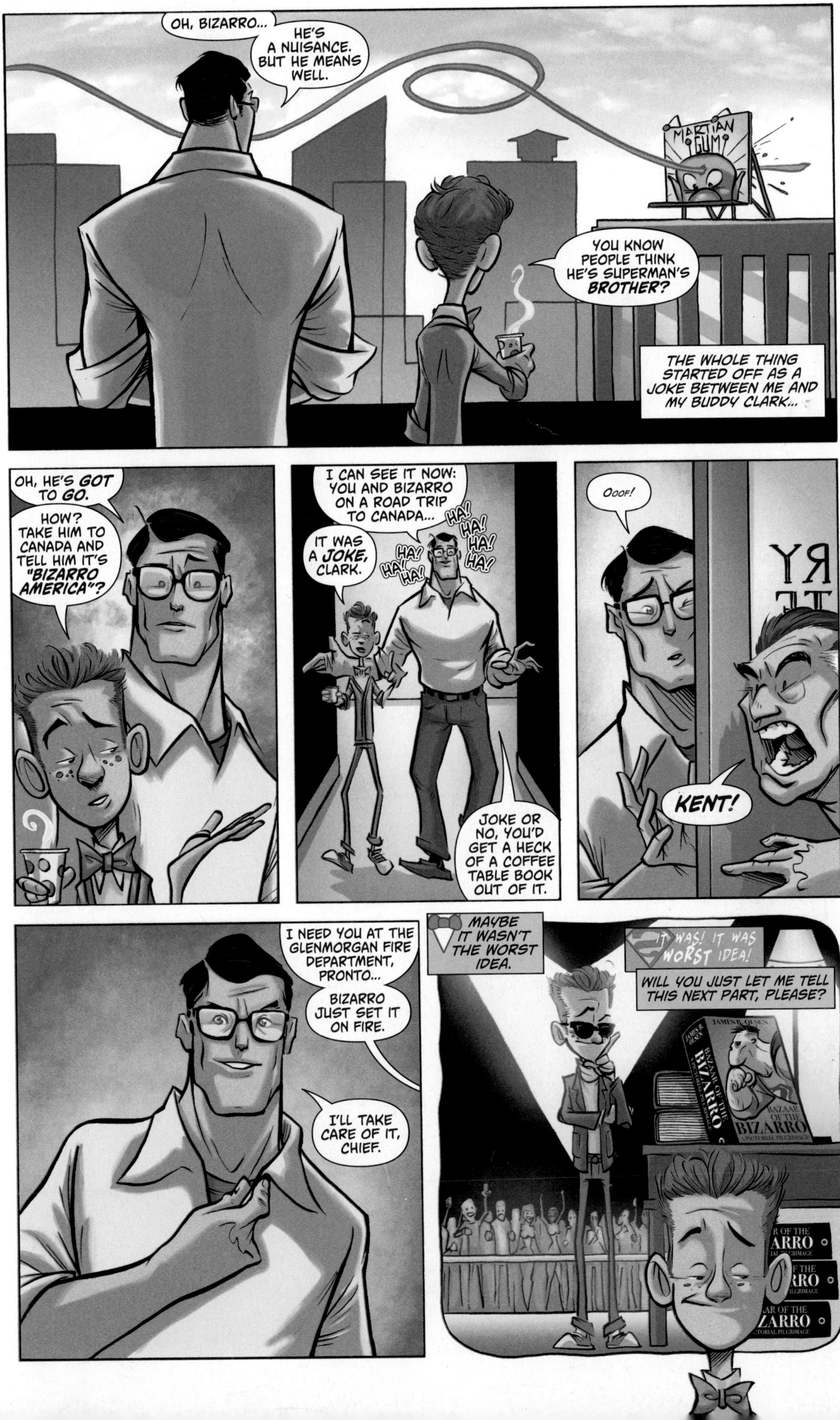
OH, BIZARRO...
HE'S A NUISANCE. BUT HE MEANS WELL.
MARTIAN GUM
YOU KNOW PEOPLE THINK HE'S SUPERMAN'S BROTHER?
THE WHOLE THING STARTED OFF AS A JOKE BETWEEN ME AND MY BUDDY CLARK...
OH, HE'S GOT TO GO.
HOW? TAKE HIM TO CANADA AND TELL HIM IT'S "BIZARRO AMERICA"?
I CAN SEE IT NOW: YOU AND BIZARRO ON A ROAD TRIP TO CANADA...
HA! HA! HA! HA!
IT WAS A JOKE, CLARK.
HA! HA! HA!
JOKE OR NO, YOU'D GET A HECK OF A COFFEE TABLE BOOK OUT OF IT.
OOOF!
KENT!
I NEED YOU AT THE GLENMORGAN FIRE DEPARTMENT, PRONTO...
BIZARRO JUST SET IT ON FIRE.
I'LL TAKE CARE OF IT, CHIEF.
MAYBE IT WASN'T THE WORST IDEA.
IT WAS! IT WAS WORST IDEA!
WILL YOU JUST LET ME TELL THIS NEXT PART, PLEASE?
BAZAAR OF THE BIZARRO
A PICTORIAL PILGRIMAGE

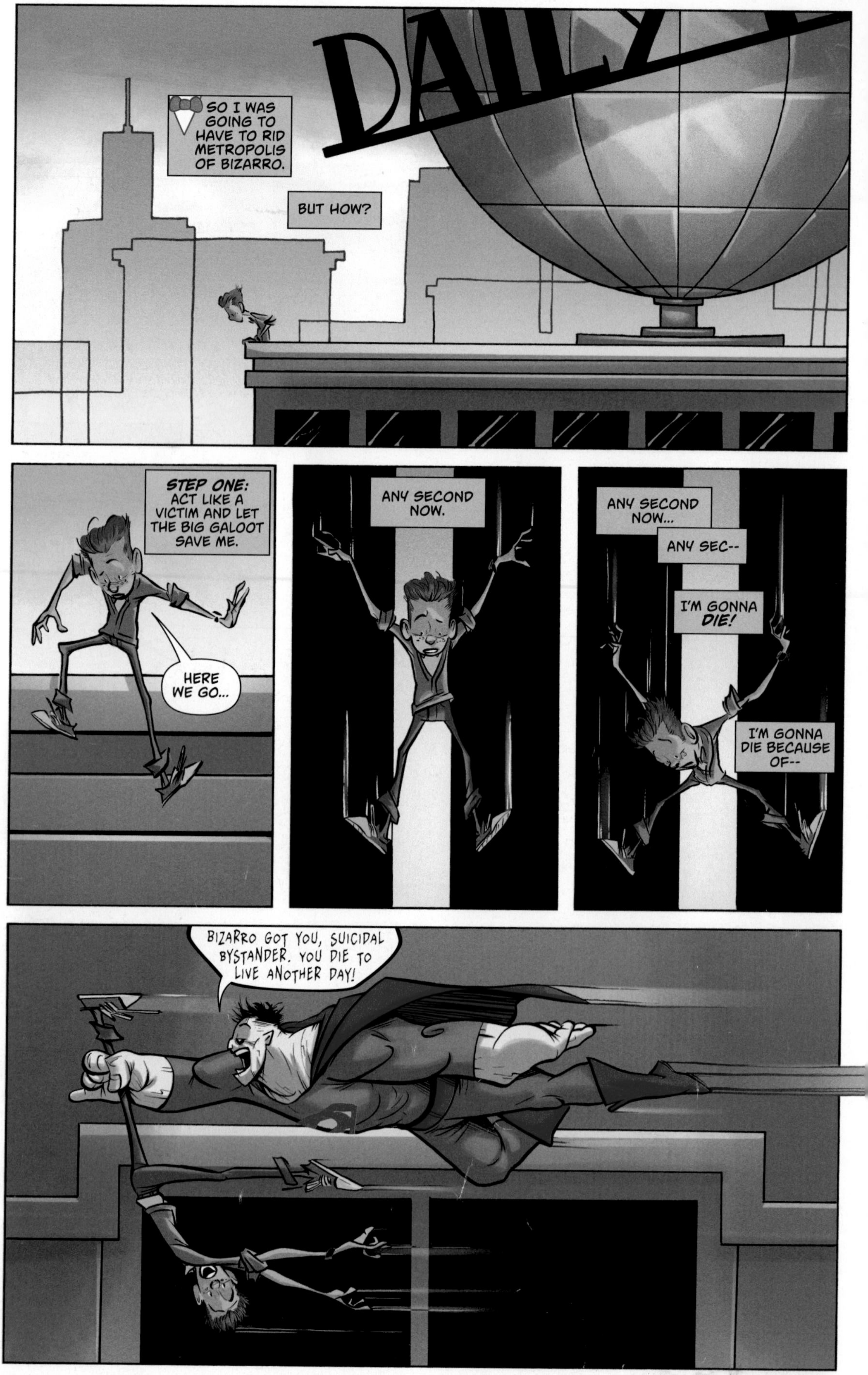
SO I WAS GOING TO HAVE TO RID METROPOLIS OF BIZARRO.
BUT HOW?
STEP ONE: ACT LIKE A VICTIM AND LET THE BIG GALOOT SAVE ME.
HERE WE GO...
ANY SECOND NOW.
ANY SECOND NOW...
ANY SEC--
I'M GONNA DIE!
I'M GONNA DIE BECAUSE OF--
BIZARRO GOT YOU, SUICIDAL BYSTANDER. YOU DIE TO LIVE ANOTHER DAY!

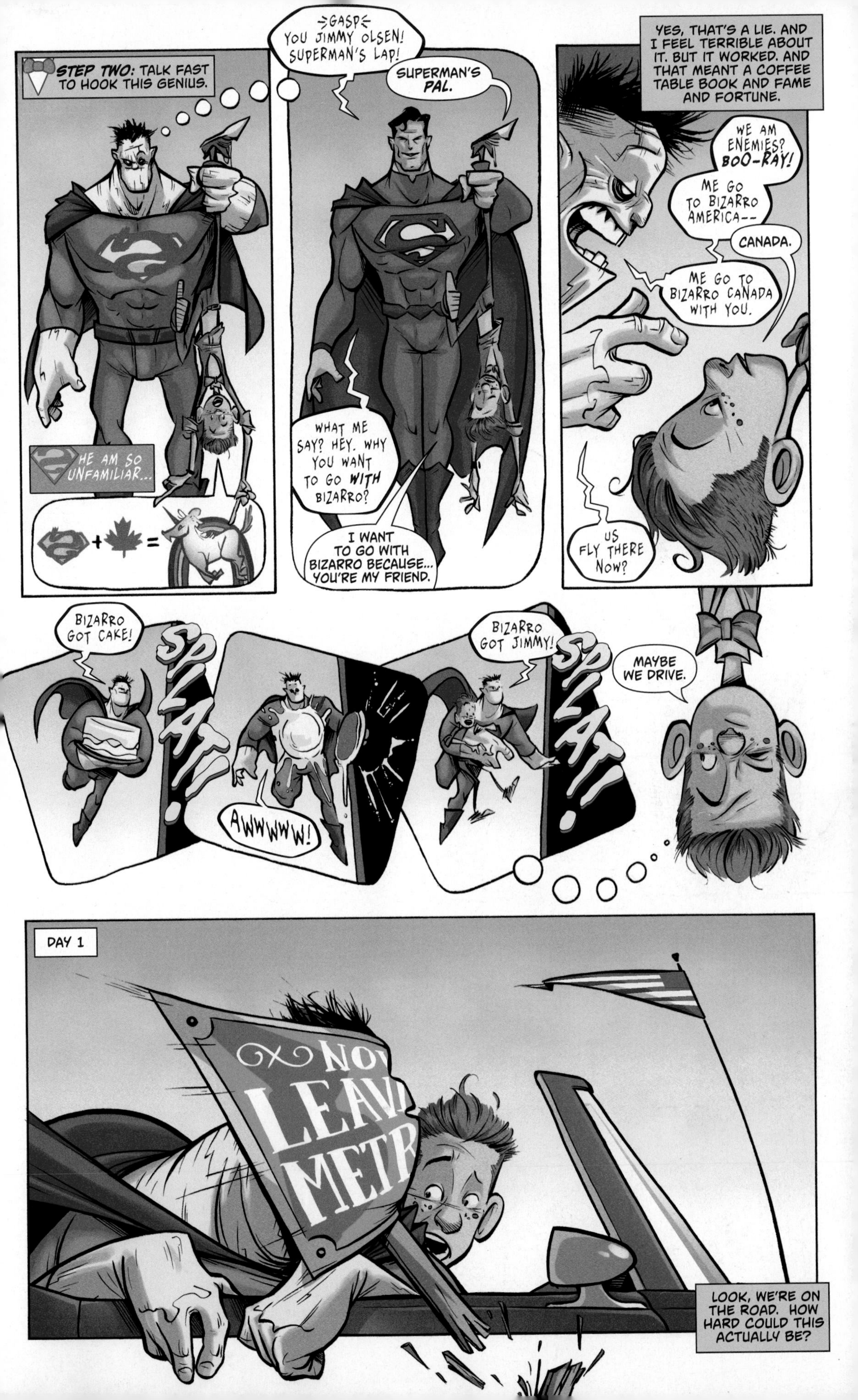
STEP TWO: TALK FAST TO HOOK THIS GENIUS.
HE AM SO UNFAMILIAR...
GASP YOU JIMMY OLSEN! SUPERMAN'S LAP!
SUPERMAN'S PAL.
WHAT ME SAY? HEY. WHY YOU WANT TO GO WITH BIZARRO?
I WANT TO GO WITH BIZARRO BECAUSE... YOU'RE MY FRIEND.
YES, THAT'S A LIE. AND I FEEL TERRIBLE ABOUT IT. BUT IT WORKED. AND THAT MEANT A COFFEE TABLE BOOK AND FAME AND FORTUNE.
WE AM ENEMIES? BOO-RAY!
ME GO TO BIZARRO AMERICA--
CANADA.
ME GO TO BIZARRO CANADA WITH YOU.
US FLY THERE NOW?
BIZARRO GOT CAKE!
SPLAT!
AWWWWW!
BIZARRO GOT JIMMY!
SPLAT!
MAYBE WE DRIVE.
DAY 1
NOW LEAVI METR
LOOK, WE'RE ON THE ROAD. HOW HARD COULD THIS ACTUALLY BE?

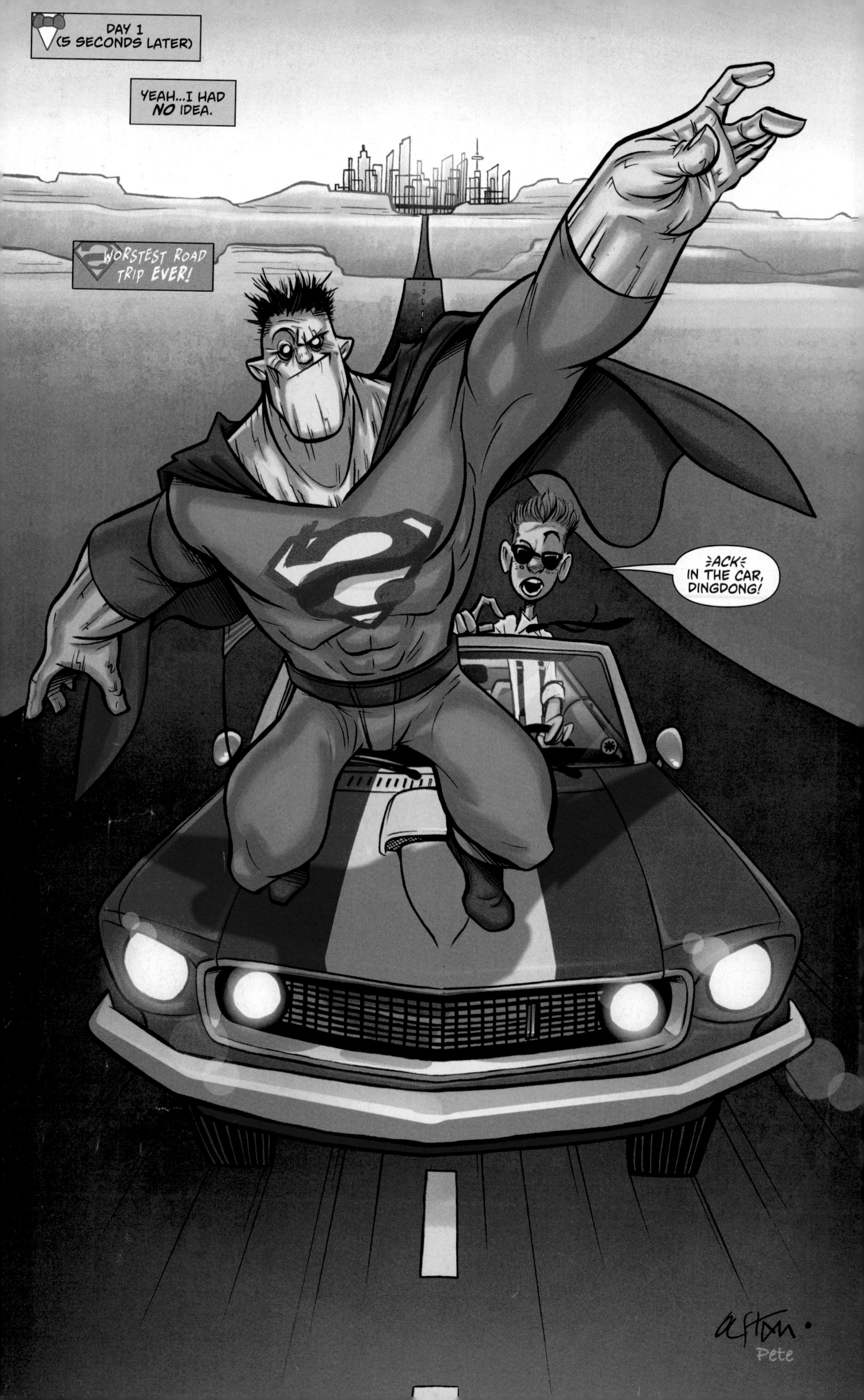

DAY 1 (5 SECONDS LATER)
YEAH...I HAD NO IDEA.
WORSTEST ROAD TRIP EVER!
ACK IN THE CAR, DINGDONG!
afton
Pete

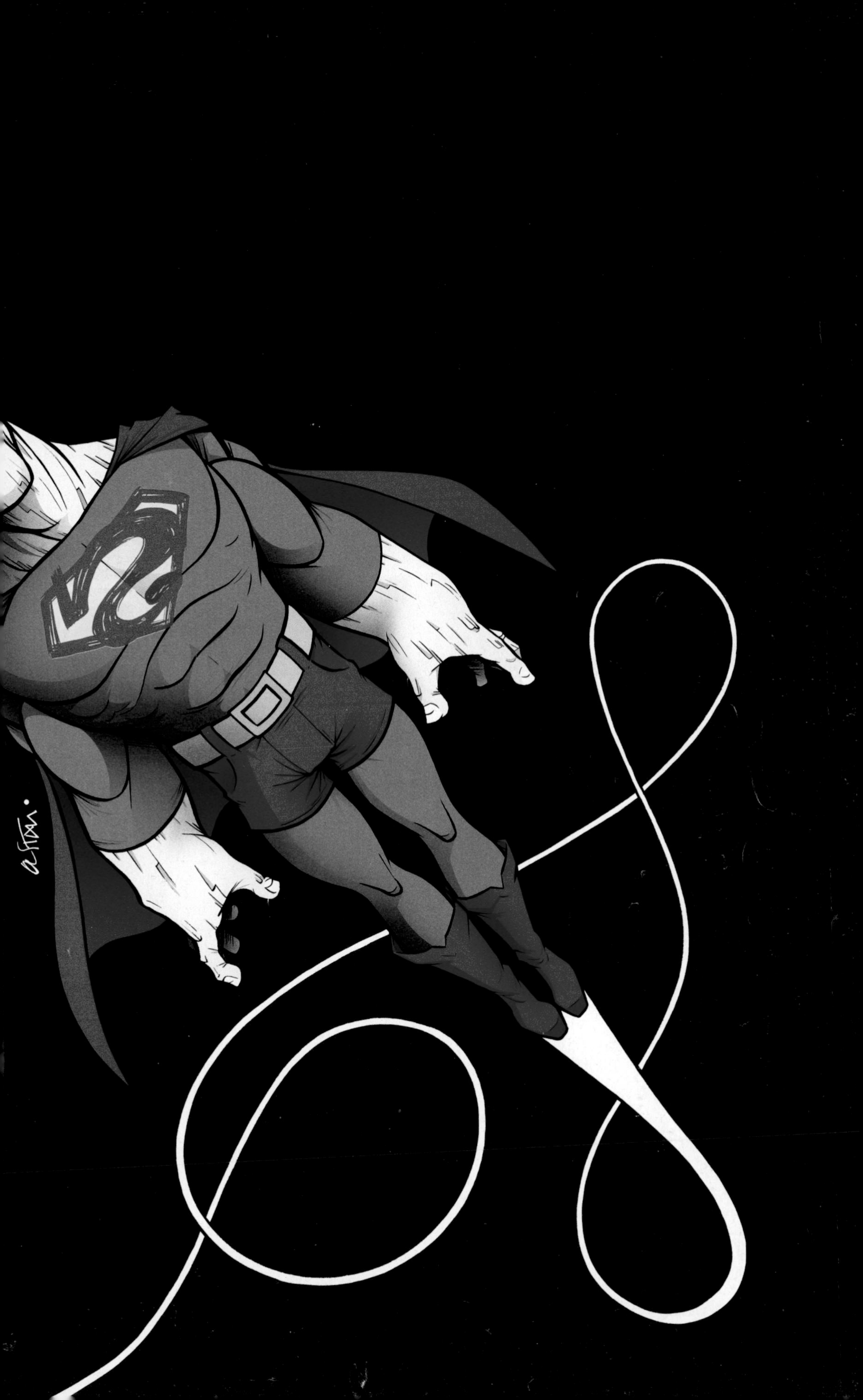

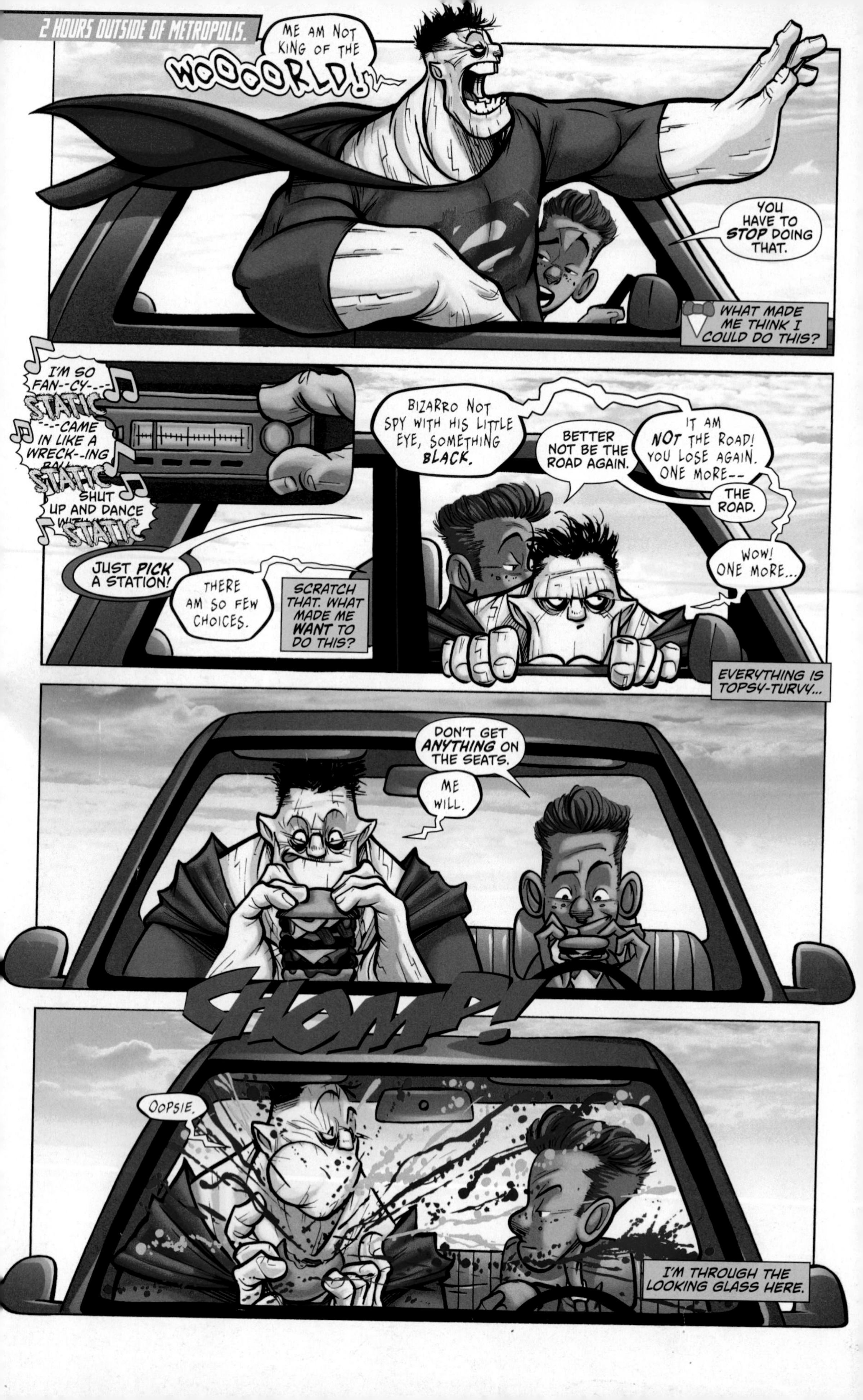
2 HOURS OUTSIDE OF METROPOLIS.
ME AM NOT KING OF THE WOOOORLD!
YOU HAVE TO STOP DOING THAT.
WHAT MADE ME THINK I COULD DO THIS?
I'M SO FAN--CY---
STATIC
---CAME IN LIKE A WRECK--ING
STATIC
SHUT UP AND DANCE
STATIC
JUST PICK A STATION!
THERE AM SO FEW CHOICES.
SCRATCH THAT. WHAT MADE ME WANT TO DO THIS?
BIZARRO NOT SPY WITH HIS LITTLE EYE, SOMETHING BLACK.
BETTER NOT BE THE ROAD AGAIN.
IT AM NOT THE ROAD! YOU LOSE AGAIN. ONE MORE--
THE ROAD.
WOW! ONE MORE...
EVERYTHING IS TOPSY-TURVY...
DON'T GET ANYTHING ON THE SEATS.
ME WILL.
CHOMP!
OOPSIE.
I'M THROUGH THE LOOKING GLASS HERE.

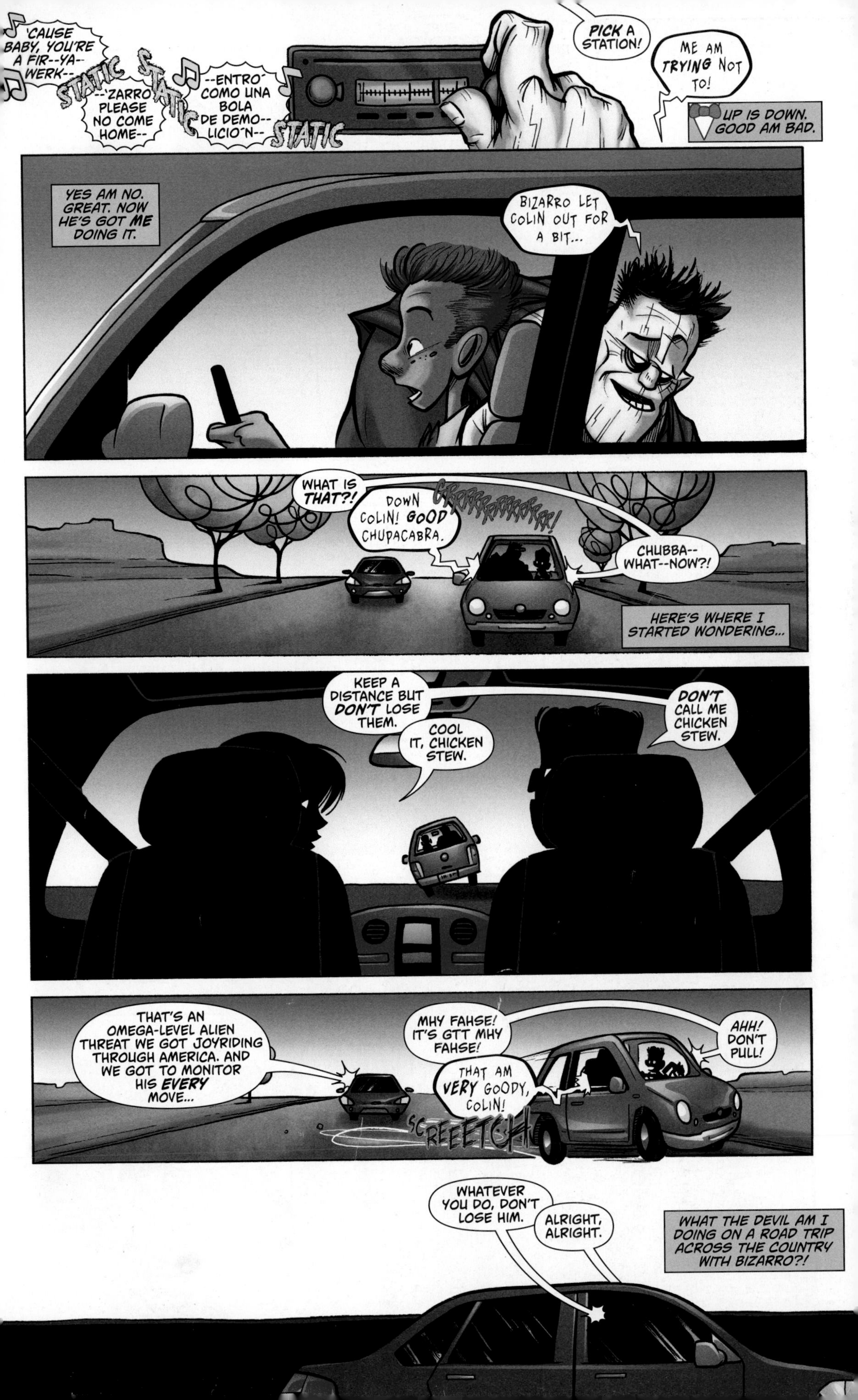
'CAUSE BABY, YOU'RE A FIR--YA--WERK--
STATIC
--'ZARRO PLEASE NO COME HOME--
STATIC
--ENTRO COMO UNA BOLA DE DEMO--LICIO´N--
STATIC
PICK A STATION!
ME AM TRYING NOT TO!
UP IS DOWN. GOOD AM BAD.
YES AM NO. GREAT. NOW HE'S GOT ME DOING IT.
BIZARRO LET COLIN OUT FOR A BIT...
WHAT IS THAT?!
DOWN COLIN! GOOD CHUPACABRA.
GRRRRRRRRRRRRRR!
CHUBBA--WHAT--NOW?!
HERE'S WHERE I STARTED WONDERING...
KEEP A DISTANCE BUT DON'T LOSE THEM.
DON'T CALL ME CHICKEN STEW.
COOL IT, CHICKEN STEW.
THAT'S AN OMEGA-LEVEL ALIEN THREAT WE GOT JOYRIDING THROUGH AMERICA. AND WE GOT TO MONITOR HIS EVERY MOVE...
MHY FAHSE! IT'S GTT MHY FAHSE!
AHH! DON'T PULL!
THAT AM VERY GOODY, COLIN!
SCREEETCH
WHATEVER YOU DO, DON'T LOSE HIM.
ALRIGHT, ALRIGHT.
WHAT THE DEVIL AM I DOING ON A ROAD TRIP ACROSS THE COUNTRY WITH BIZARRO?!

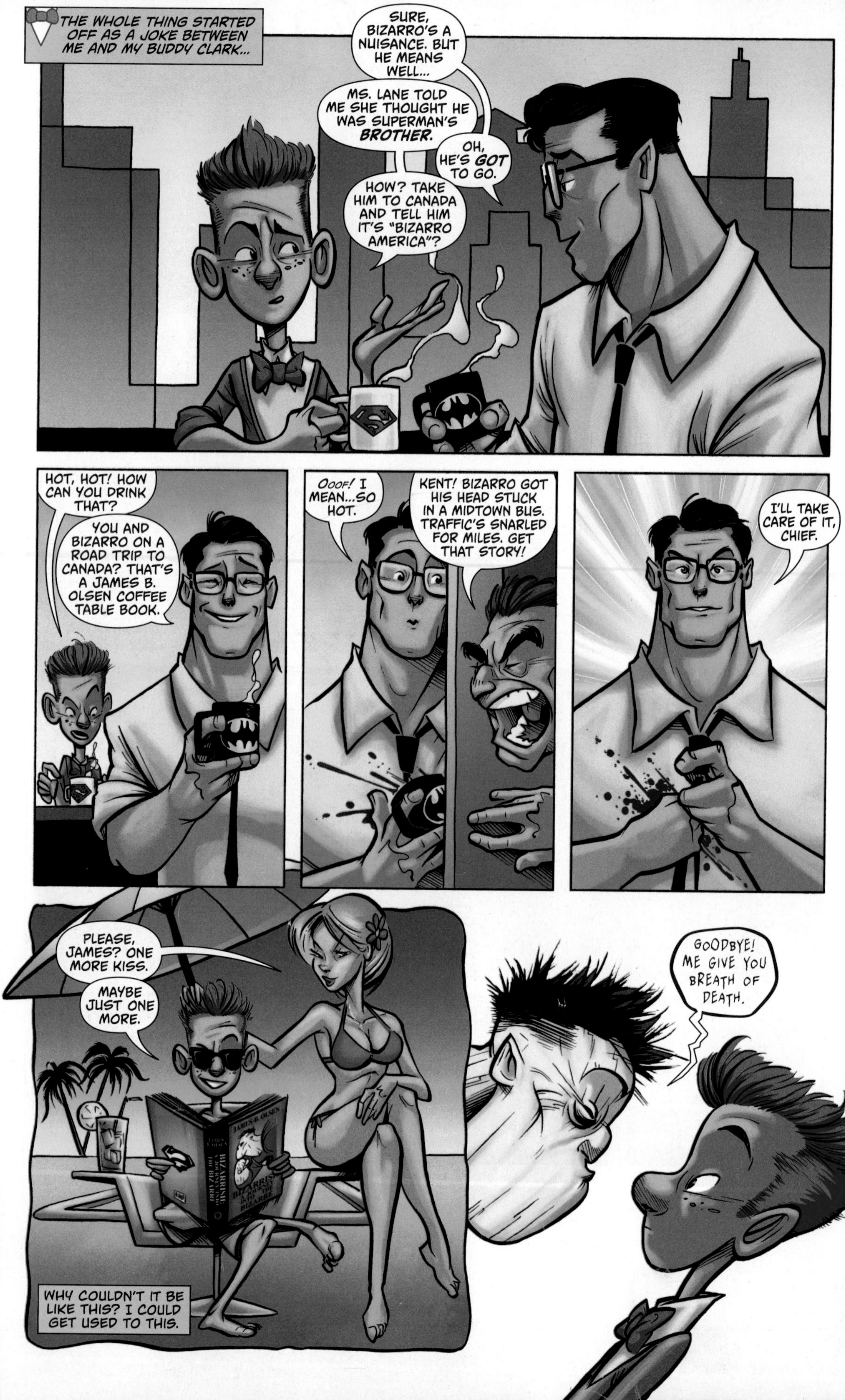
THE WHOLE THING STARTED OFF AS A JOKE BETWEEN ME AND MY BUDDY CLARK...
SURE, BIZARRO'S A NUISANCE. BUT HE MEANS WELL...
MS. LANE TOLD ME SHE THOUGHT HE WAS SUPERMAN'S **BROTHER.**
OH, HE'S ***GOT*** TO GO.
HOW? TAKE HIM TO CANADA AND TELL HIM IT'S "BIZARRO AMERICA"?
HOT, HOT! HOW CAN YOU DRINK THAT?
YOU AND BIZARRO ON A ROAD TRIP TO CANADA? THAT'S A JAMES B. OLSEN COFFEE TABLE BOOK.
OOOF! I MEAN...SO HOT.
KENT! BIZARRO GOT HIS HEAD STUCK IN A MIDTOWN BUS. TRAFFIC'S SNARLED FOR MILES. GET THAT STORY!
I'LL TAKE CARE OF IT, CHIEF.
PLEASE, JAMES? ONE MORE KISS.
MAYBE JUST ONE MORE.
JAMES B. OLSEN
WHY COULDN'T IT BE LIKE THIS? I COULD GET USED TO THIS.
GOODBYE! ME GIVE YOU BREATH OF DEATH.

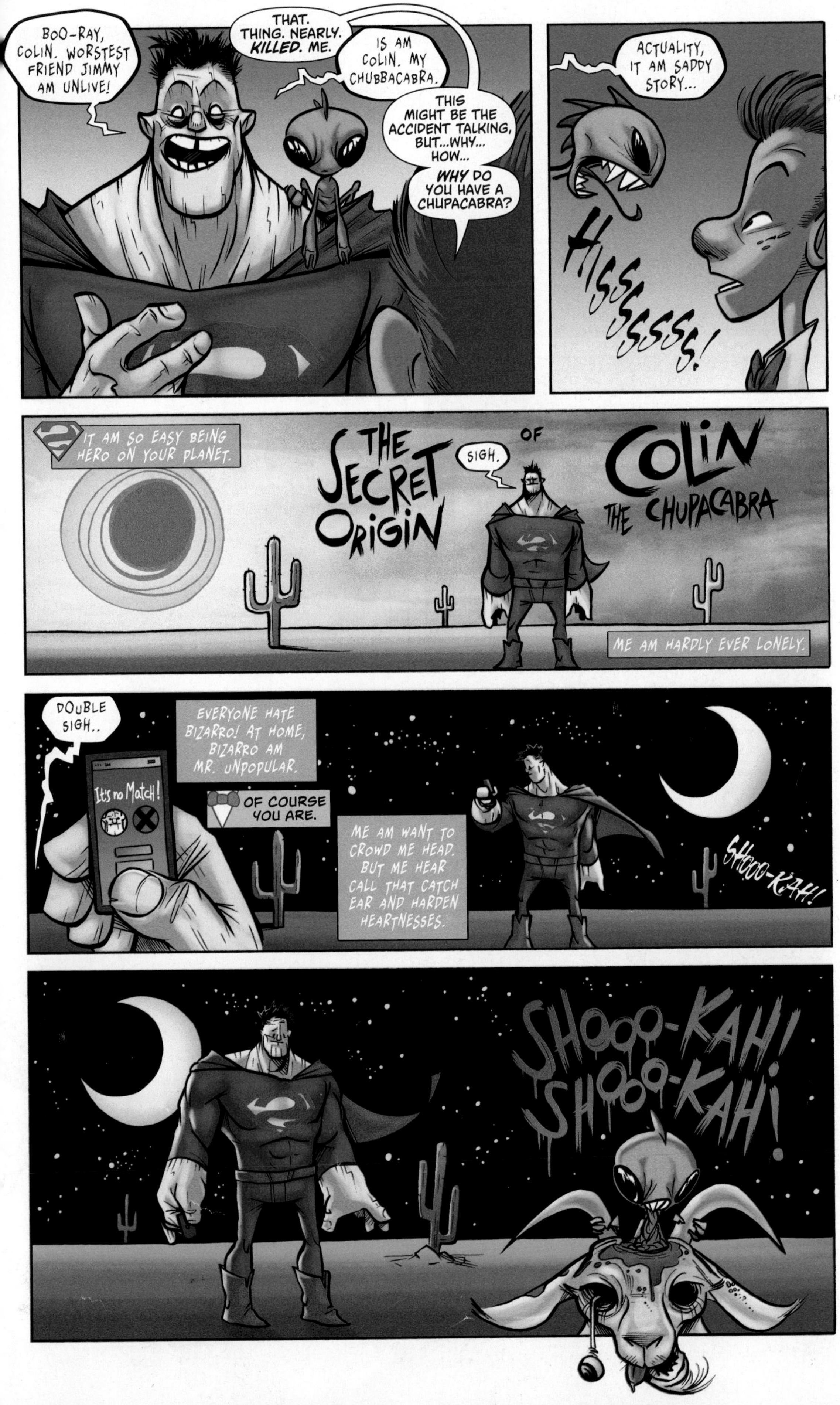
BOO-RAY, COLIN. WORSTEST FRIEND JIMMY AM UNLIVE!
THAT. THING. NEARLY. KILLED. ME.
IS AM COLIN. MY CHUBBACABRA.
THIS MIGHT BE THE ACCIDENT TALKING, BUT...WHY... HOW... WHY DO YOU HAVE A CHUPACABRA?
ACTUALITY, IT AM SADDY STORY...
HISSSSSSSS!
IT AM SO EASY BEING HERO ON YOUR PLANET.
THE SECRET ORIGIN OF COLIN THE CHUPACABRA
SIGH.
ME AM HARDLY EVER LONELY.
DOUBLE SIGH..
EVERYONE HATE BIZARRO! AT HOME, BIZARRO AM MR. UNPOPULAR.
It's no Match!
OF COURSE YOU ARE.
ME AM WANT TO CROWD ME HEAD. BUT ME HEAR CALL THAT CATCH EAR AND HARDEN HEARTNESSES.
SHOOO-KAH!
SHOOO-KAH! SHOOO-KAH!

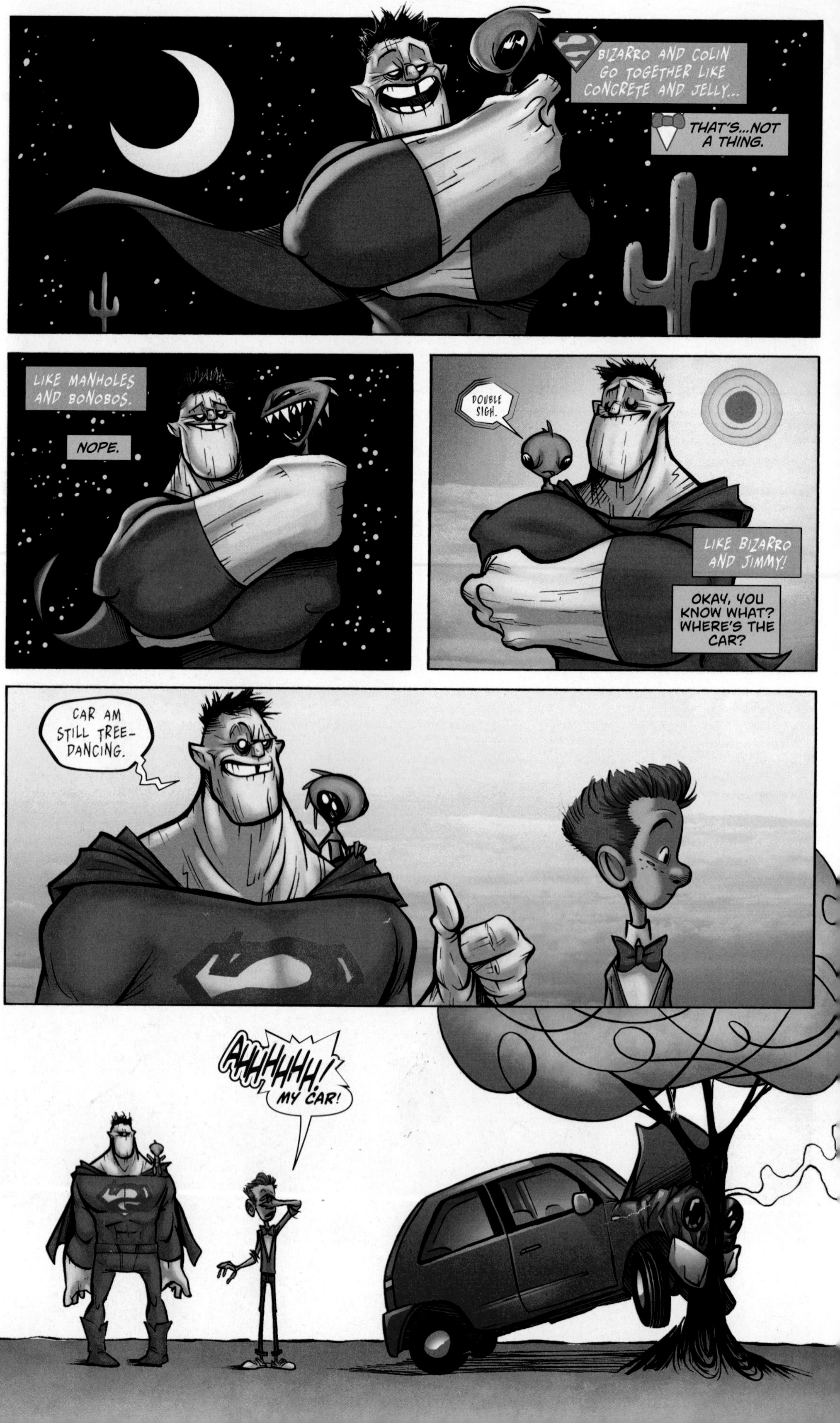
BIZARRO AND COLIN GO TOGETHER LIKE CONCRETE AND JELLY...
THAT'S...NOT A THING.
LIKE MANHOLES AND BONOBOS.
NOPE.
DOUBLE SIGH.
LIKE BIZARRO AND JIMMY!
OKAY, YOU KNOW WHAT? WHERE'S THE CAR?
CAR AM STILL TREE-DANCING.
AHHHHHH! MY CAR!

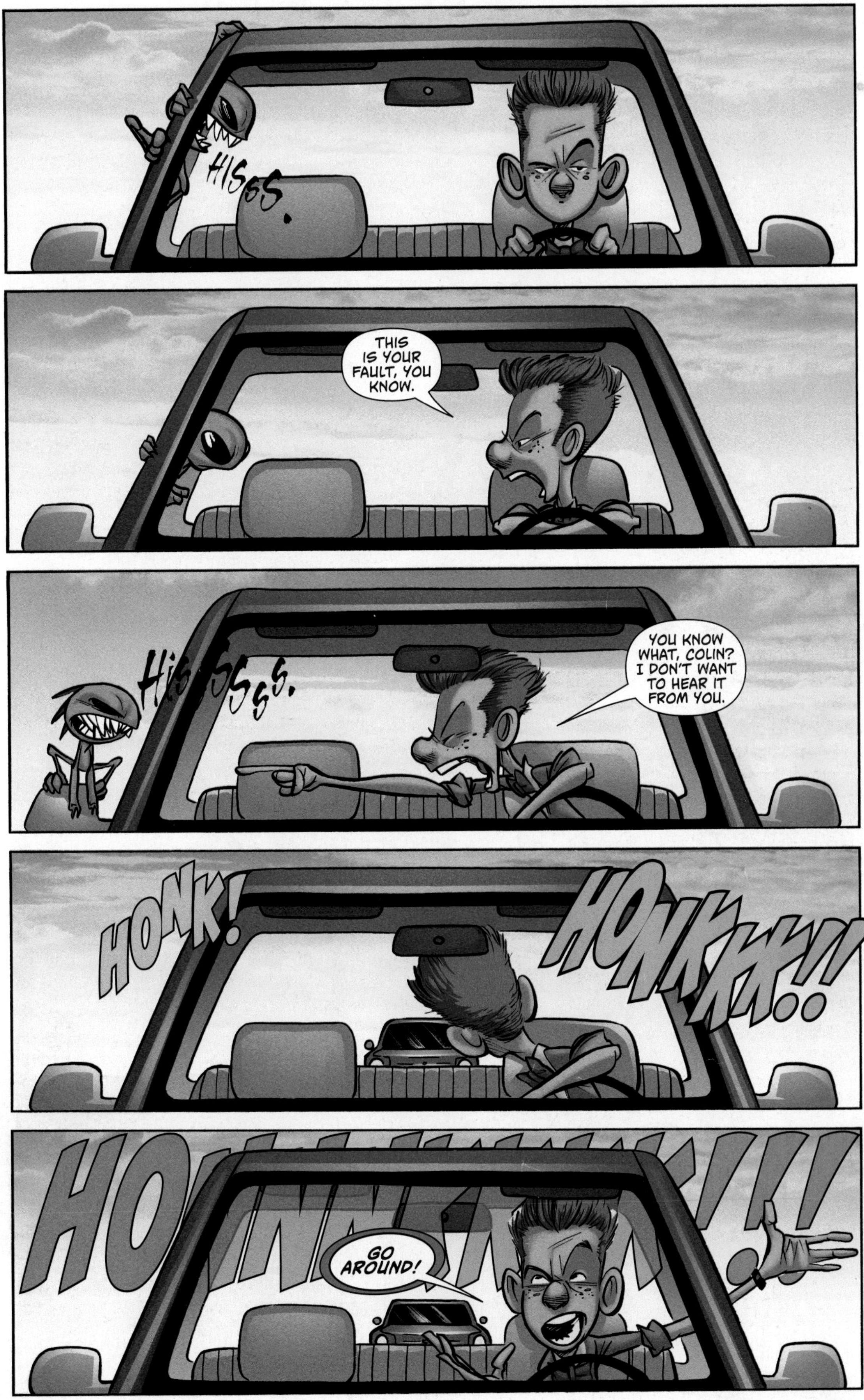
HISSS.
THIS IS YOUR FAULT, YOU KNOW.
HISSSSS.
YOU KNOW WHAT, COLIN? I DON'T WANT TO HEAR IT FROM YOU.
HONK!
HONKKK!!
GO AROUND!

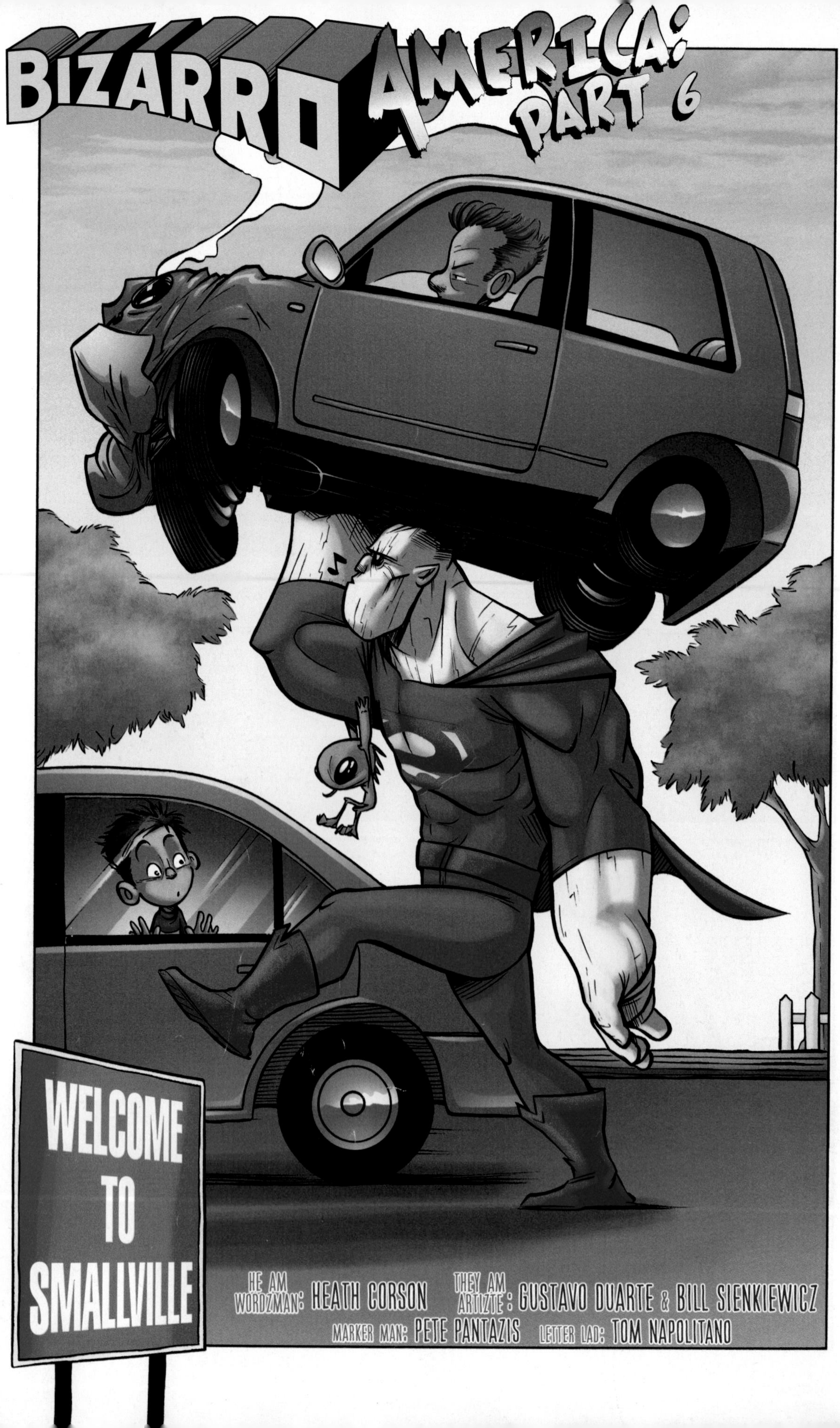

BIZARRO AMERICA: PART 6
WELCOME TO SMALLVILLE
HE AM WORDZMAN: HEATH CORSON
THEY AM ARTIZTE: GUSTAVO DUARTE & BILL SIENKIEWICZ
MARKER MAN: PETE PANTAZIS
LETTER LAD: TOM NAPOLITANO

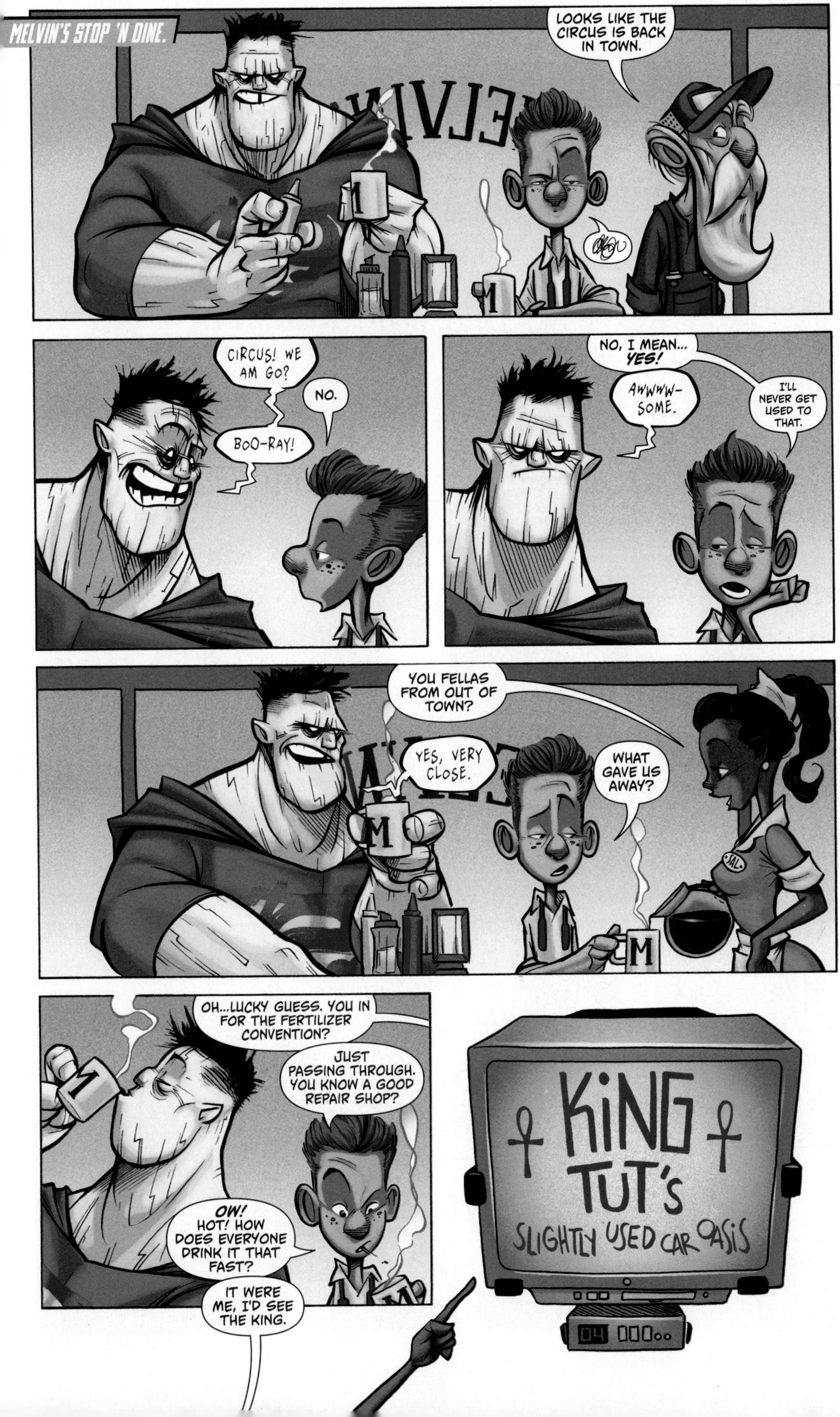
MELVIN'S STOP 'N DINE.
LOOKS LIKE THE CIRCUS IS BACK IN TOWN.
CIRCUS! WE AM GO?
NO.
BOO-RAY!
NO, I MEAN... YES!
AWWWW-SOME.
I'LL NEVER GET USED TO THAT.
YOU FELLAS FROM OUT OF TOWN?
YES, VERY CLOSE.
WHAT GAVE US AWAY?
SAL
OH...LUCKY GUESS. YOU IN FOR THE FERTILIZER CONVENTION?
JUST PASSING THROUGH. YOU KNOW A GOOD REPAIR SHOP?
OW! HOT! HOW DOES EVERYONE DRINK IT THAT FAST?
IT WERE ME, I'D SEE THE KING.
KiNG TUT's SLIGHTLY USED CAR OASIS

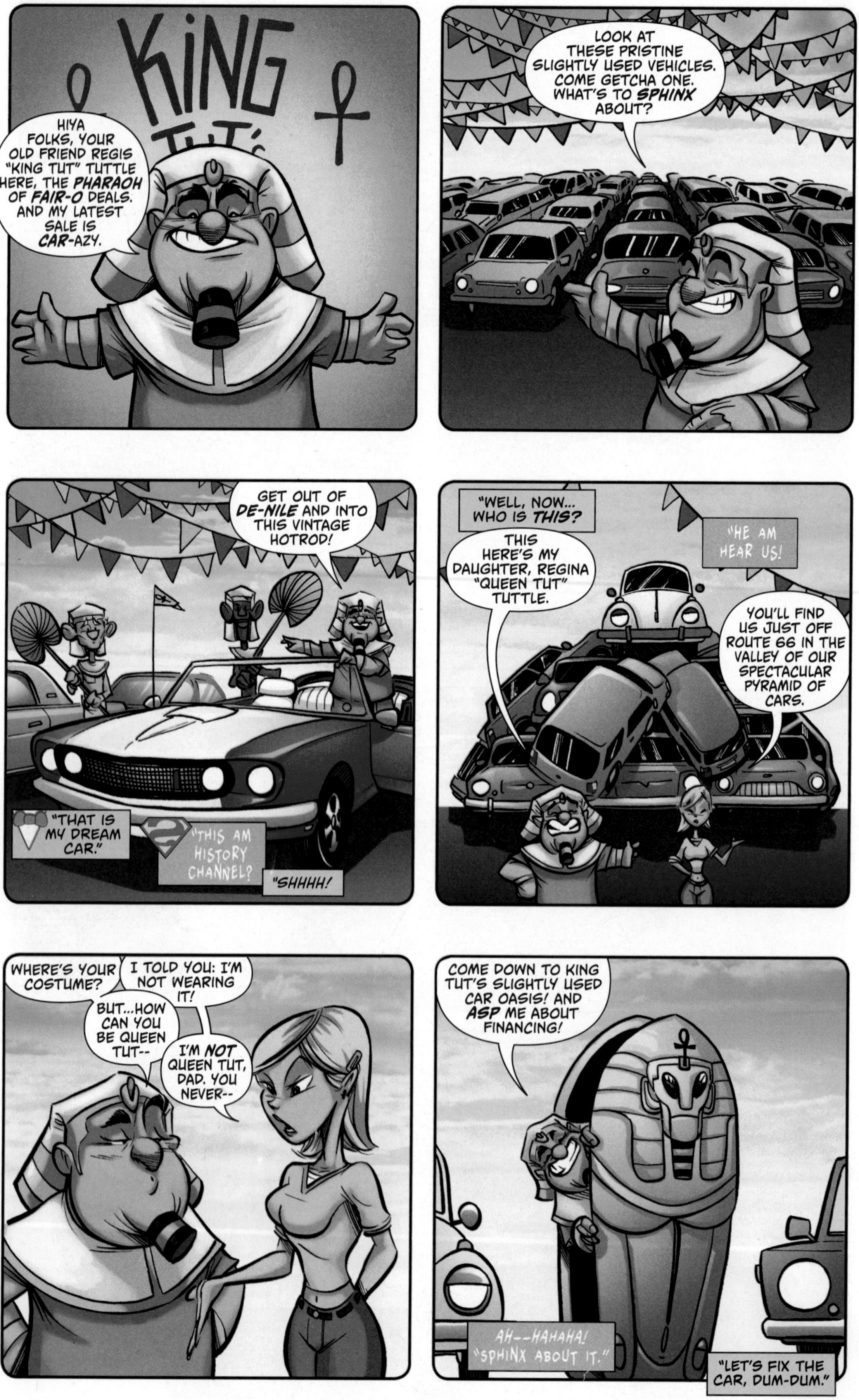
KING TUT'S
HIYA FOLKS, YOUR OLD FRIEND REGIS "KING TUT" TUTTLE HERE, THE PHARAOH OF FAIR-O DEALS. AND MY LATEST SALE IS CAR-AZY.
LOOK AT THESE PRISTINE SLIGHTLY USED VEHICLES. COME GETCHA ONE. WHAT'S TO SPHINX ABOUT?
GET OUT OF DE-NILE AND INTO THIS VINTAGE HOTROD!
"THAT IS MY DREAM CAR."
"THIS AM HISTORY CHANNEL?
"SHHHH!
"WELL, NOW... WHO IS THIS?
THIS HERE'S MY DAUGHTER, REGINA "QUEEN TUT" TUTTLE.
"HE AM HEAR US!
YOU'LL FIND US JUST OFF ROUTE 66 IN THE VALLEY OF OUR SPECTACULAR PYRAMID OF CARS.
WHERE'S YOUR COSTUME?
I TOLD YOU: I'M NOT WEARING IT!
BUT...HOW CAN YOU BE QUEEN TUT--
I'M NOT QUEEN TUT, DAD. YOU NEVER--
COME DOWN TO KING TUT'S SLIGHTLY USED CAR OASIS! AND ASP ME ABOUT FINANCING!
AH--HAHAHA! "SPHINX ABOUT IT."
"LET'S FIX THE CAR, DUM-DUM."

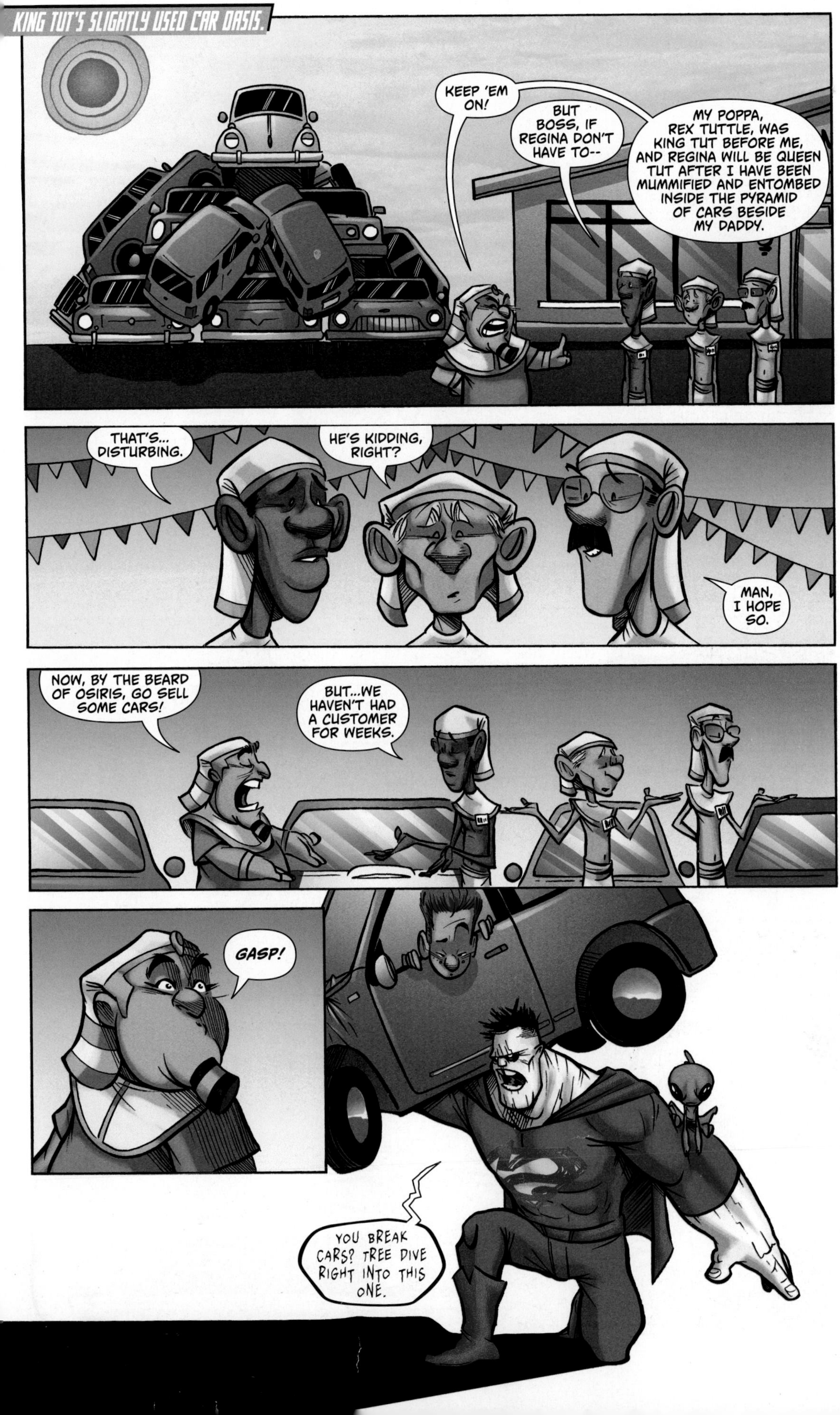
KING TUT'S SLIGHTLY USED CAR OASIS.
KEEP 'EM ON!
BUT BOSS, IF REGINA DON'T HAVE TO--
MY POPPA, REX TUTTLE, WAS KING TUT BEFORE ME, AND REGINA WILL BE QUEEN TUT AFTER I HAVE BEEN MUMMIFIED AND ENTOMBED INSIDE THE PYRAMID OF CARS BESIDE MY DADDY.
THAT'S... DISTURBING.
HE'S KIDDING, RIGHT?
MAN, I HOPE SO.
NOW, BY THE BEARD OF OSIRIS, GO SELL SOME CARS!
BUT...WE HAVEN'T HAD A CUSTOMER FOR WEEKS.
GASP!
YOU BREAK CARS? TREE DIVE RIGHT INTO THIS ONE.

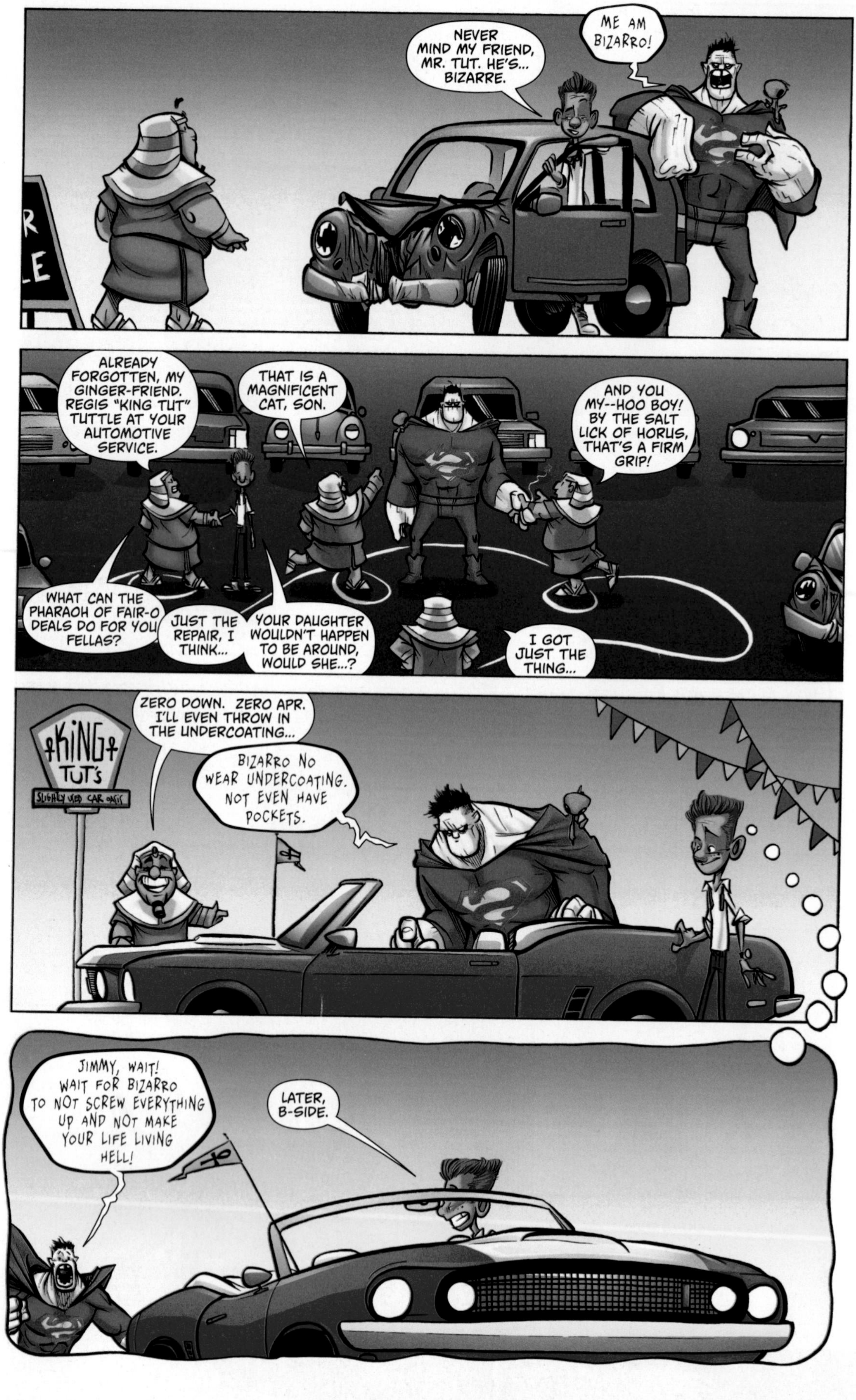
NEVER MIND MY FRIEND, MR. TUT. HE'S... BIZARRE.
ME AM BIZARRO!
ALREADY FORGOTTEN, MY GINGER-FRIEND. REGIS "KING TUT" TUTTLE AT YOUR AUTOMOTIVE SERVICE.
THAT IS A MAGNIFICENT CAT, SON.
AND YOU MY--HOO BOY! BY THE SALT LICK OF HORUS, THAT'S A FIRM GRIP!
WHAT CAN THE PHARAOH OF FAIR-O DEALS DO FOR YOU FELLAS?
JUST THE REPAIR, I THINK...
YOUR DAUGHTER WOULDN'T HAPPEN TO BE AROUND, WOULD SHE...?
I GOT JUST THE THING...
KING TUT'S
SLIGHTLY USED CAR OASIS
ZERO DOWN. ZERO APR. I'LL EVEN THROW IN THE UNDERCOATING...
BIZARRO NO WEAR UNDERCOATING. NOT EVEN HAVE POCKETS.
JIMMY, WAIT! WAIT FOR BIZARRO TO NOT SCREW EVERYTHING UP AND NOT MAKE YOUR LIFE LIVING HELL!
LATER, B-SIDE.

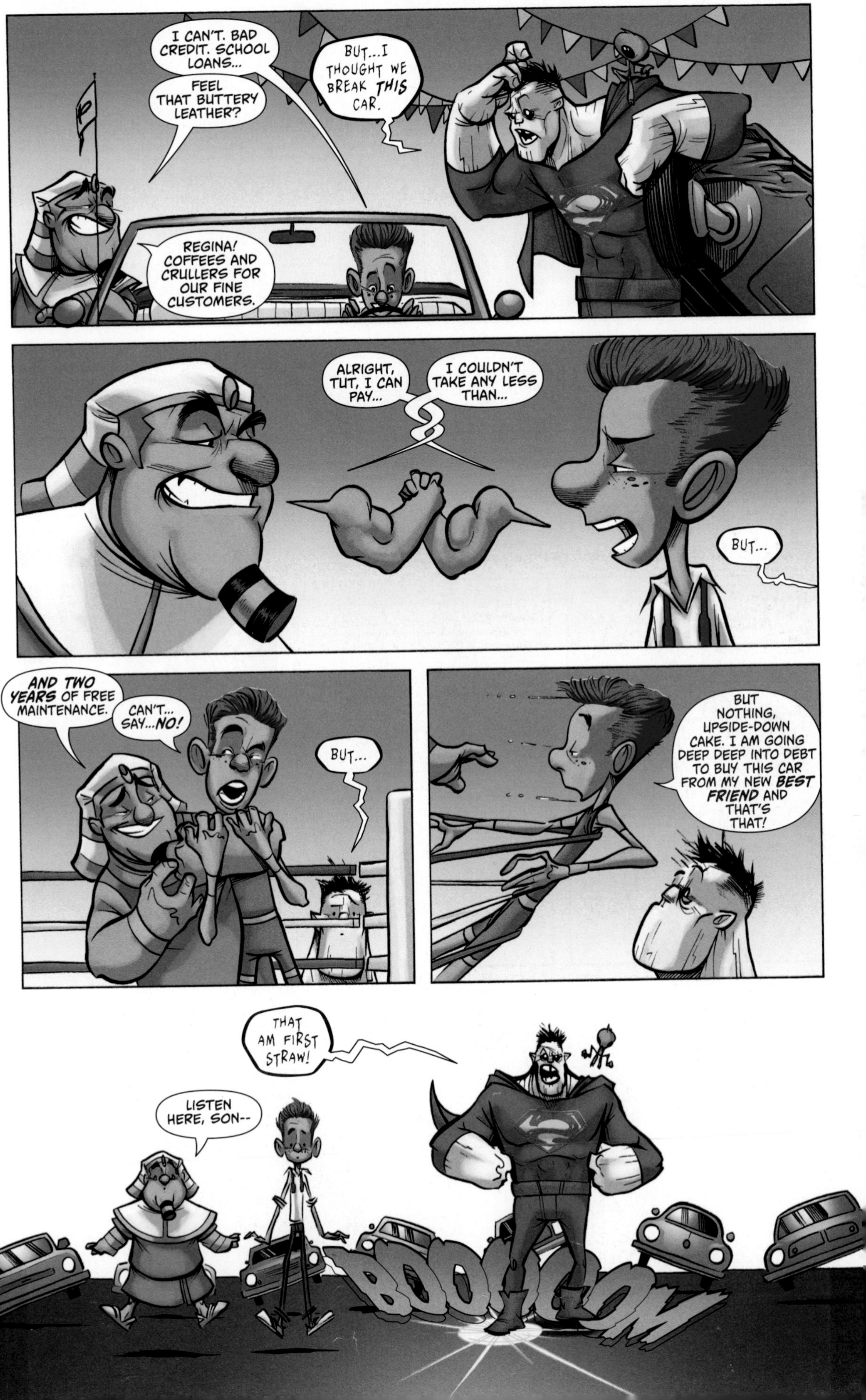
I CAN'T. BAD CREDIT. SCHOOL LOANS...
FEEL THAT BUTTERY LEATHER?
BUT...I THOUGHT WE BREAK THIS CAR.
REGINA! COFFEES AND CRULLERS FOR OUR FINE CUSTOMERS.
ALRIGHT, TUT, I CAN PAY...
I COULDN'T TAKE ANY LESS THAN...
BUT...
AND TWO YEARS OF FREE MAINTENANCE.
CAN'T... SAY...NO!
BUT...
BUT NOTHING, UPSIDE-DOWN CAKE. I AM GOING DEEP DEEP INTO DEBT TO BUY THIS CAR FROM MY NEW BEST FRIEND AND THAT'S THAT!
THAT AM FIRST STRAW!
LISTEN HERE, SON--

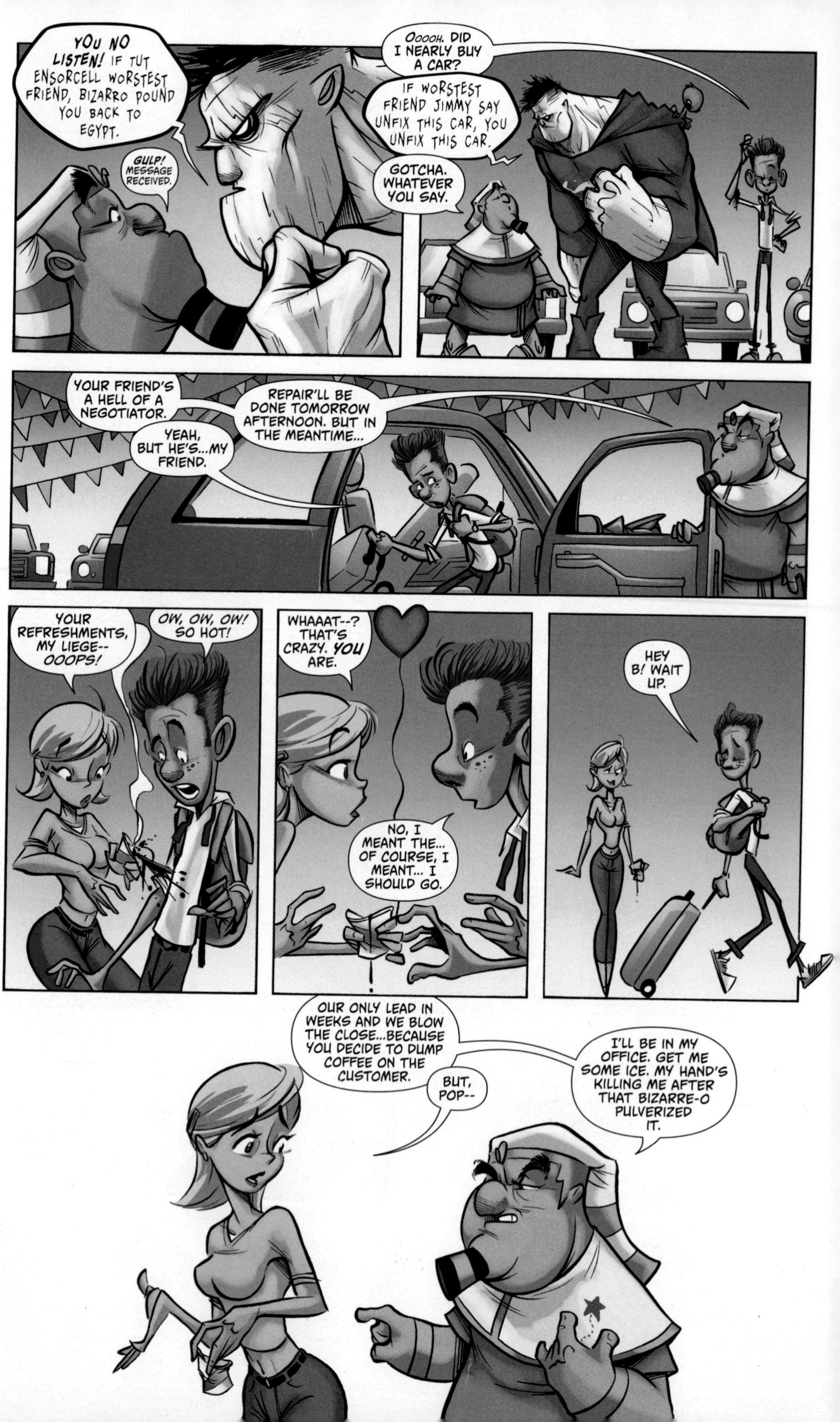

YOU NO LISTEN! IF TUT ENSORCELL WORSTEST FRIEND, BIZARRO POUND YOU BACK TO EGYPT.
GULP! MESSAGE RECEIVED.
OOOOH. DID I NEARLY BUY A CAR?
IF WORSTEST FRIEND JIMMY SAY UNFIX THIS CAR, YOU UNFIX THIS CAR.
GOTCHA. WHATEVER YOU SAY.
YOUR FRIEND'S A HELL OF A NEGOTIATOR.
REPAIR'LL BE DONE TOMORROW AFTERNOON. BUT IN THE MEANTIME...
YEAH, BUT HE'S...MY FRIEND.
YOUR REFRESHMENTS, MY LIEGE-- OOOPS!
OW, OW, OW! SO HOT!
WHAAAT--? THAT'S CRAZY. YOU ARE.
NO, I MEANT THE... OF COURSE, I MEANT... I SHOULD GO.
HEY B! WAIT UP.
OUR ONLY LEAD IN WEEKS AND WE BLOW THE CLOSE...BECAUSE YOU DECIDE TO DUMP COFFEE ON THE CUSTOMER.
BUT, POP--
I'LL BE IN MY OFFICE. GET ME SOME ICE. MY HAND'S KILLING ME AFTER THAT BIZARRE-O PULVERIZED IT.

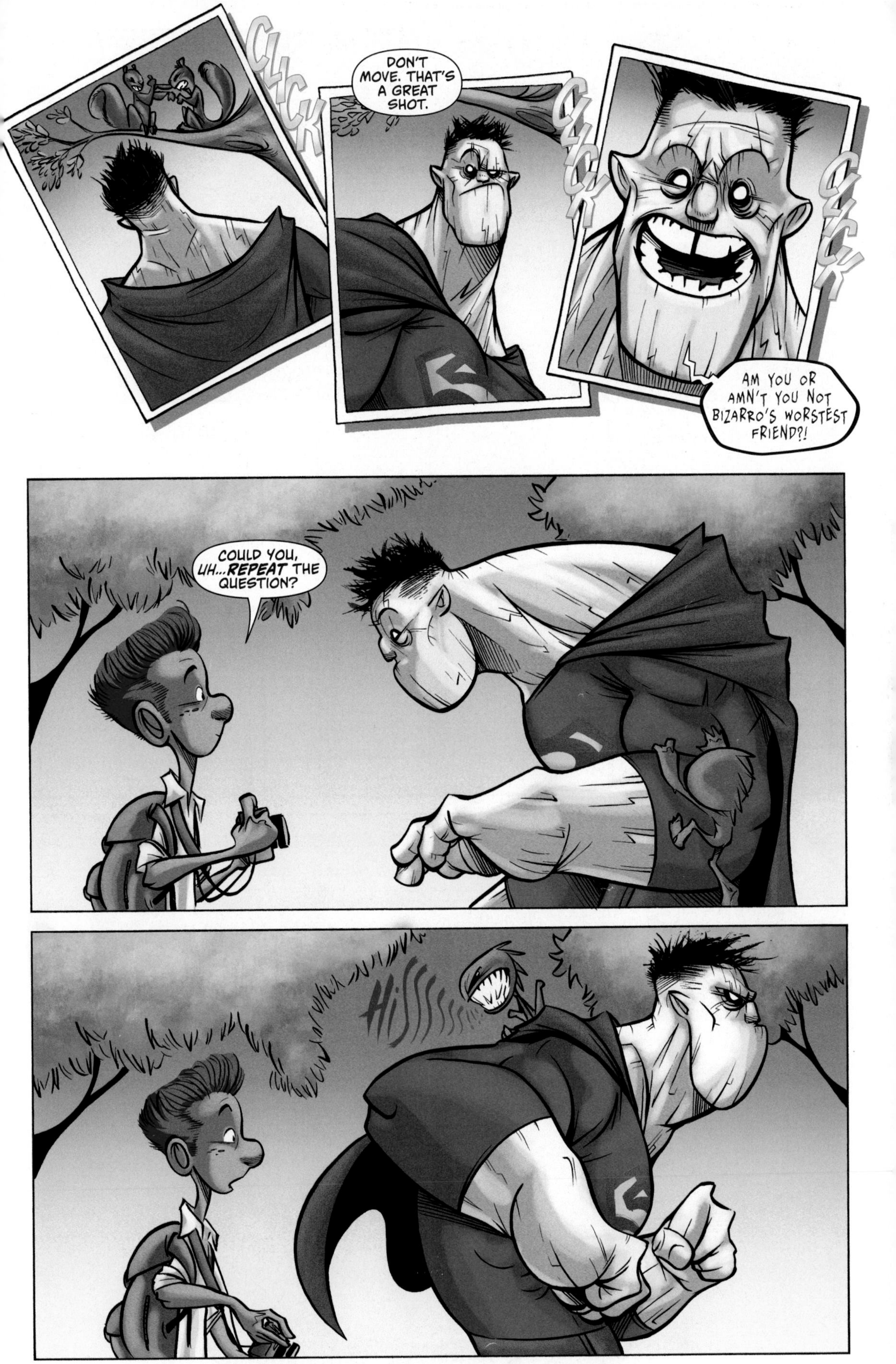
CLICK
DON'T MOVE. THAT'S A GREAT SHOT.
CLICK
CLICK
AM YOU OR AMN'T YOU NOT BIZARRO'S WORSTEST FRIEND?!
COULD YOU, UH...REPEAT THE QUESTION?
HISSSSSSS

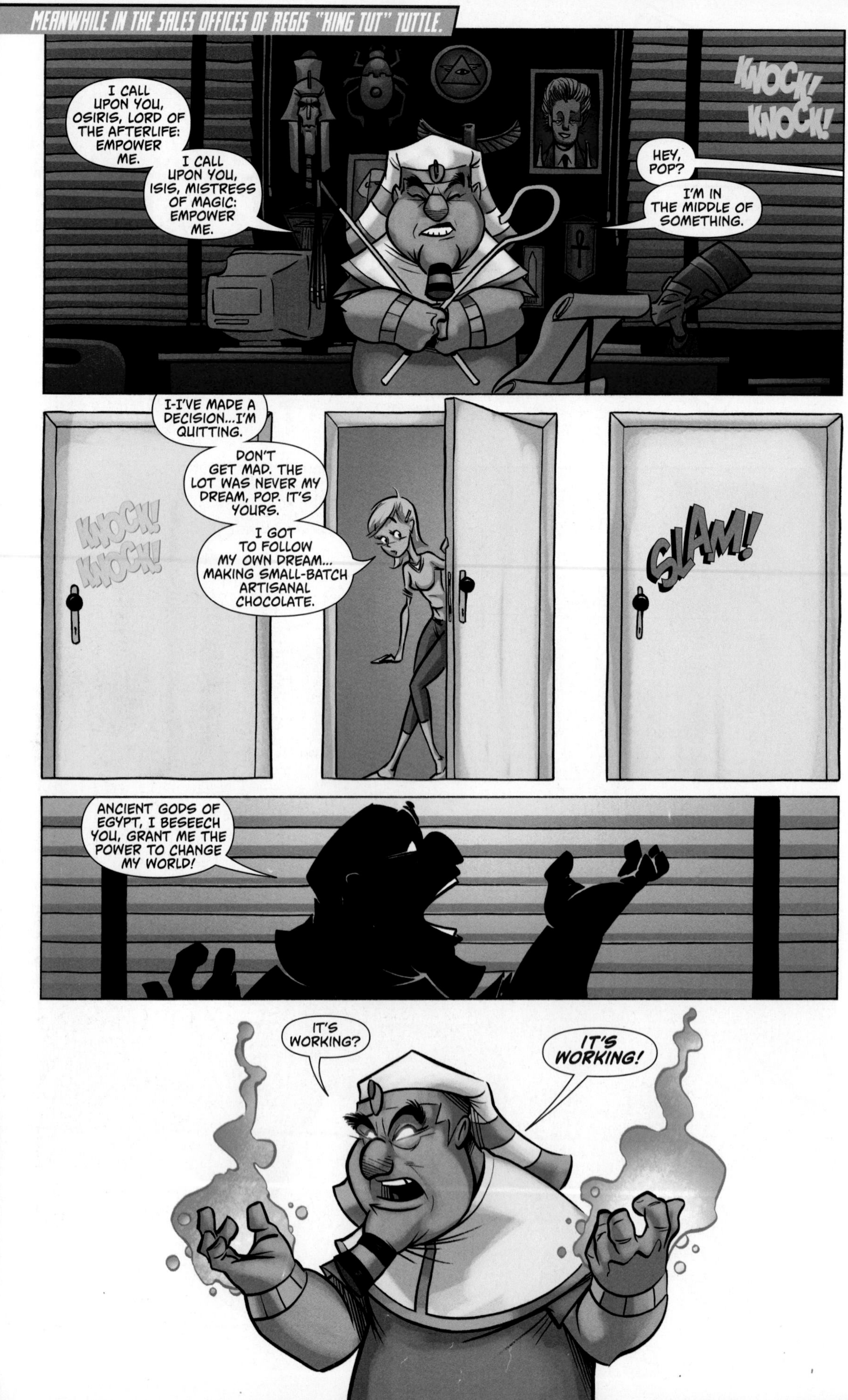
MEANWHILE IN THE SALES OFFICES OF REGIS "KING TUT" TUTTLE.
I CALL UPON YOU, OSIRIS, LORD OF THE AFTERLIFE: EMPOWER ME.
I CALL UPON YOU, ISIS, MISTRESS OF MAGIC: EMPOWER ME.
KNOCK! KNOCK!
HEY, POP?
I'M IN THE MIDDLE OF SOMETHING.
KNOCK! KNOCK!
I-I'VE MADE A DECISION...I'M QUITTING.
DON'T GET MAD. THE LOT WAS NEVER MY DREAM, POP. IT'S YOURS.
I GOT TO FOLLOW MY OWN DREAM... MAKING SMALL-BATCH ARTISANAL CHOCOLATE.
SLAM!
ANCIENT GODS OF EGYPT, I BESEECH YOU, GRANT ME THE POWER TO CHANGE MY WORLD!
IT'S WORKING?
IT'S WORKING!

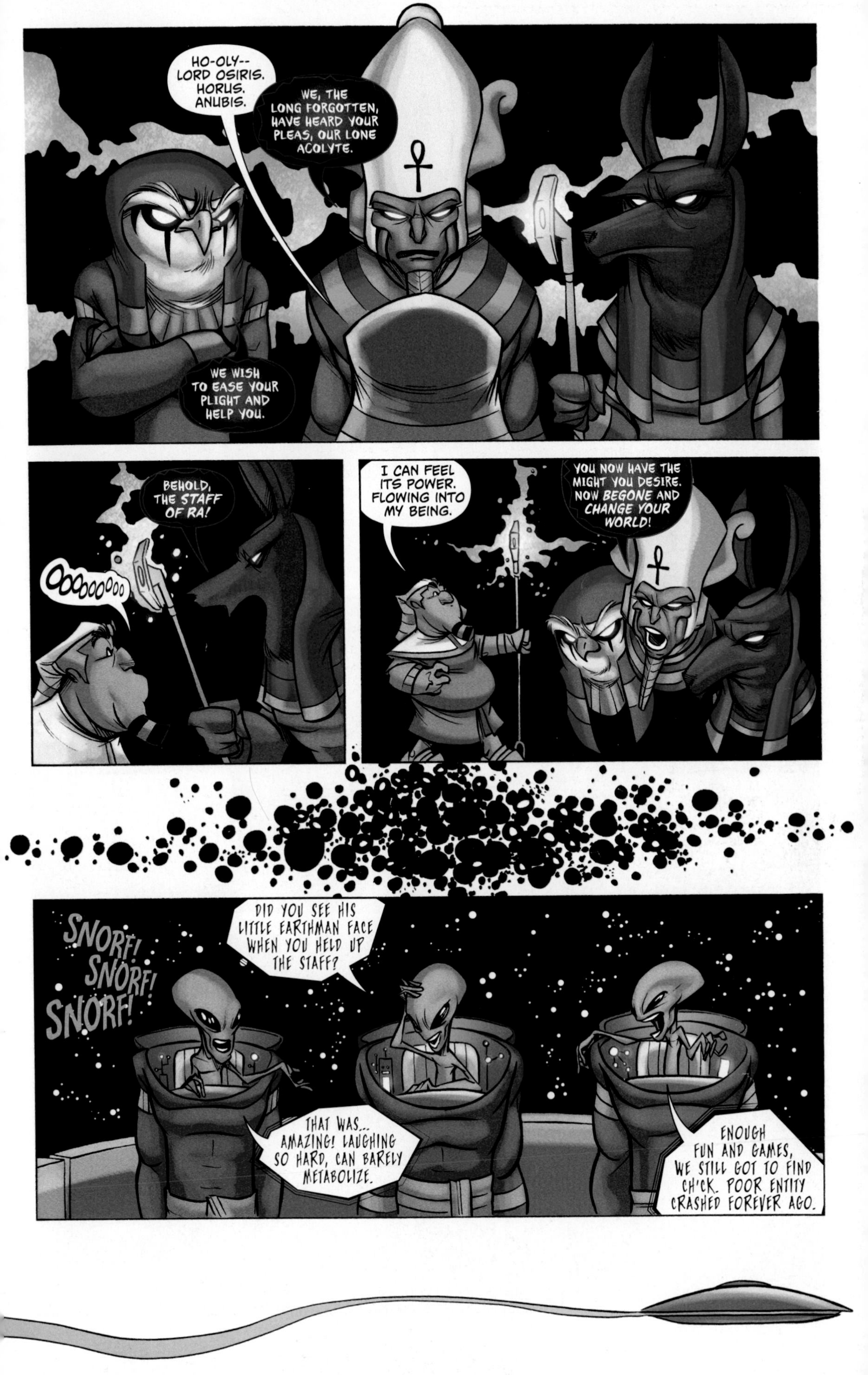
HO-OLY-- LORD OSIRIS. HORUS. ANUBIS.
WE, THE LONG FORGOTTEN, HAVE HEARD YOUR PLEAS, OUR LONE ACOLYTE.
WE WISH TO EASE YOUR PLIGHT AND HELP YOU.
BEHOLD, THE STAFF OF RA!
OOOOOOOOO
I CAN FEEL ITS POWER. FLOWING INTO MY BEING.
YOU NOW HAVE THE MIGHT YOU DESIRE. NOW BEGONE AND CHANGE YOUR WORLD!
SNORF! SNORF! SNORF!
DID YOU SEE HIS LITTLE EARTHMAN FACE WHEN YOU HELD UP THE STAFF?
THAT WAS... AMAZING! LAUGHING SO HARD, CAN BARELY METABOLIZE.
ENOUGH FUN AND GAMES, WE STILL GOT TO FIND CH'CK. POOR ENTITY CRASHED FOREVER AGO.

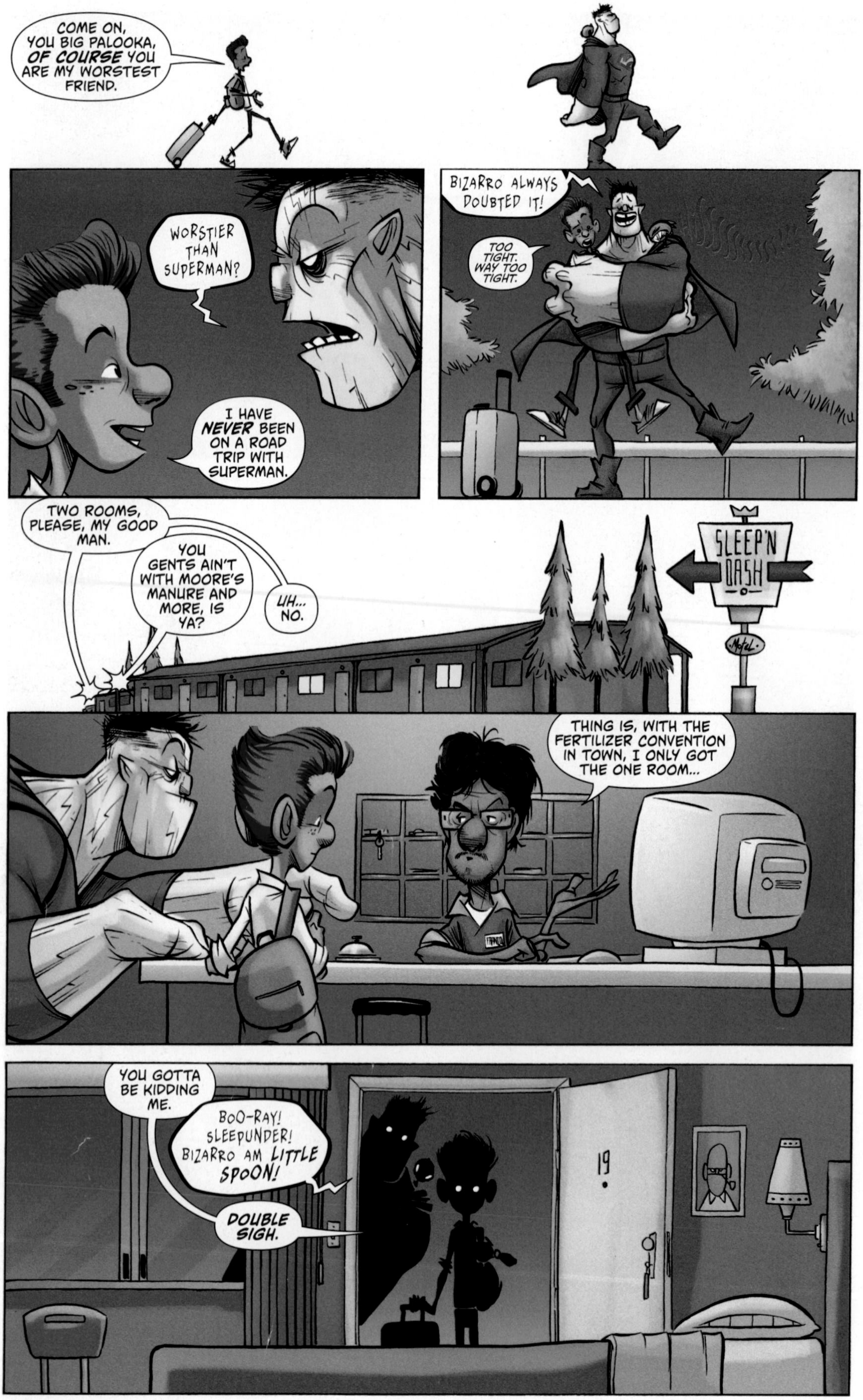
COME ON, YOU BIG PALOOKA, OF COURSE YOU ARE MY WORSTEST FRIEND.
WORSTIER THAN SUPERMAN?
I HAVE NEVER BEEN ON A ROAD TRIP WITH SUPERMAN.
BIZARRO ALWAYS DOUBTED IT!
TOO TIGHT. WAY TOO TIGHT.
TWO ROOMS, PLEASE, MY GOOD MAN.
YOU GENTS AIN'T WITH MOORE'S MANURE AND MORE, IS YA?
UH... NO.
SLEEP'N DASH
Motel
THING IS, WITH THE FERTILIZER CONVENTION IN TOWN, I ONLY GOT THE ONE ROOM...
YOU GOTTA BE KIDDING ME.
BOO-RAY! SLEEPUNDER! BIZARRO AM LITTLE SPOON!
DOUBLE SIGH.
19

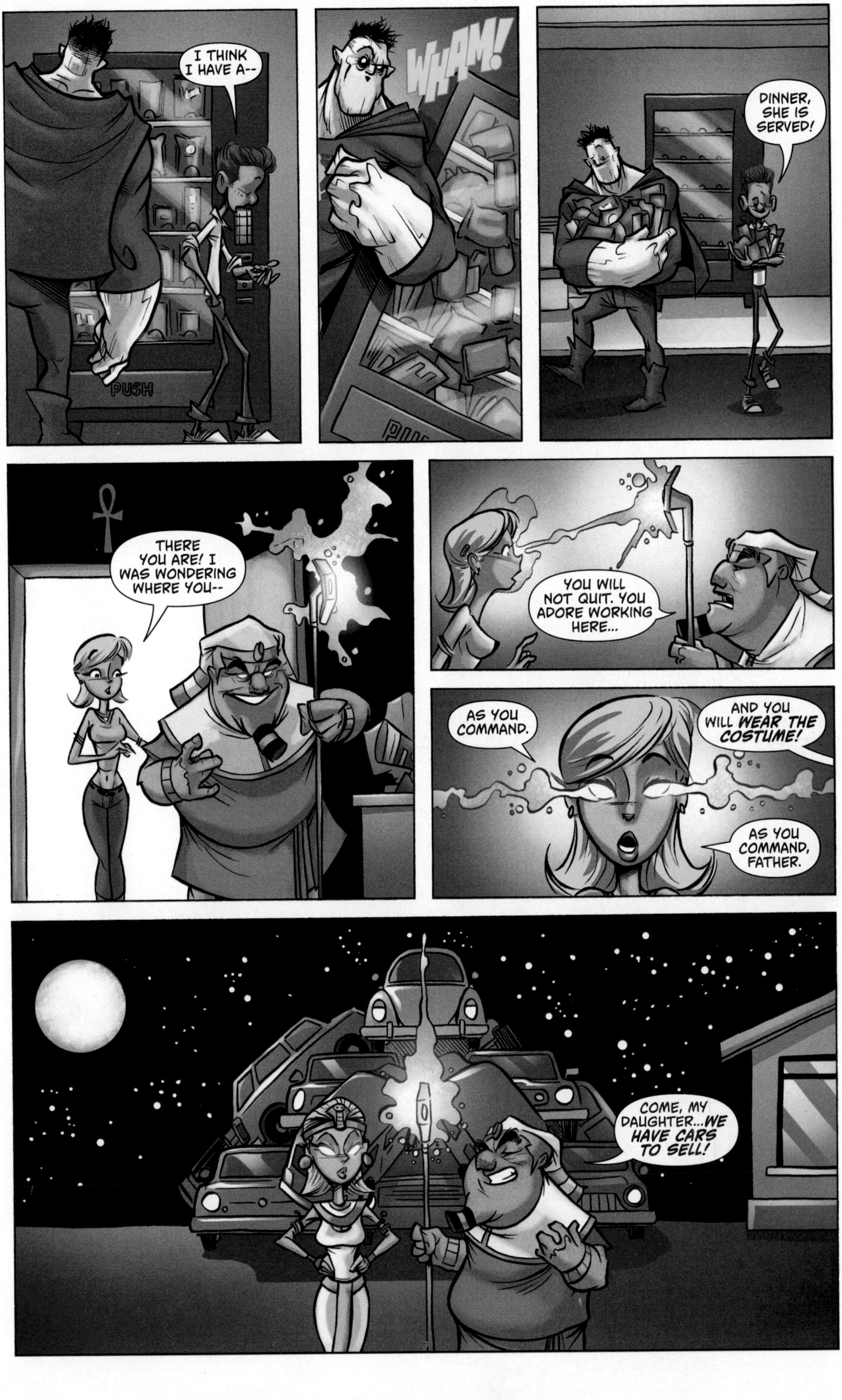
I THINK I HAVE A--
PUSH
WHAM!
DINNER, SHE IS SERVED!
THERE YOU ARE! I WAS WONDERING WHERE YOU--
YOU WILL NOT QUIT. YOU ADORE WORKING HERE...
AS YOU COMMAND.
AND YOU WILL WEAR THE COSTUME!
AS YOU COMMAND, FATHER.
COME, MY DAUGHTER...WE HAVE CARS TO SELL!

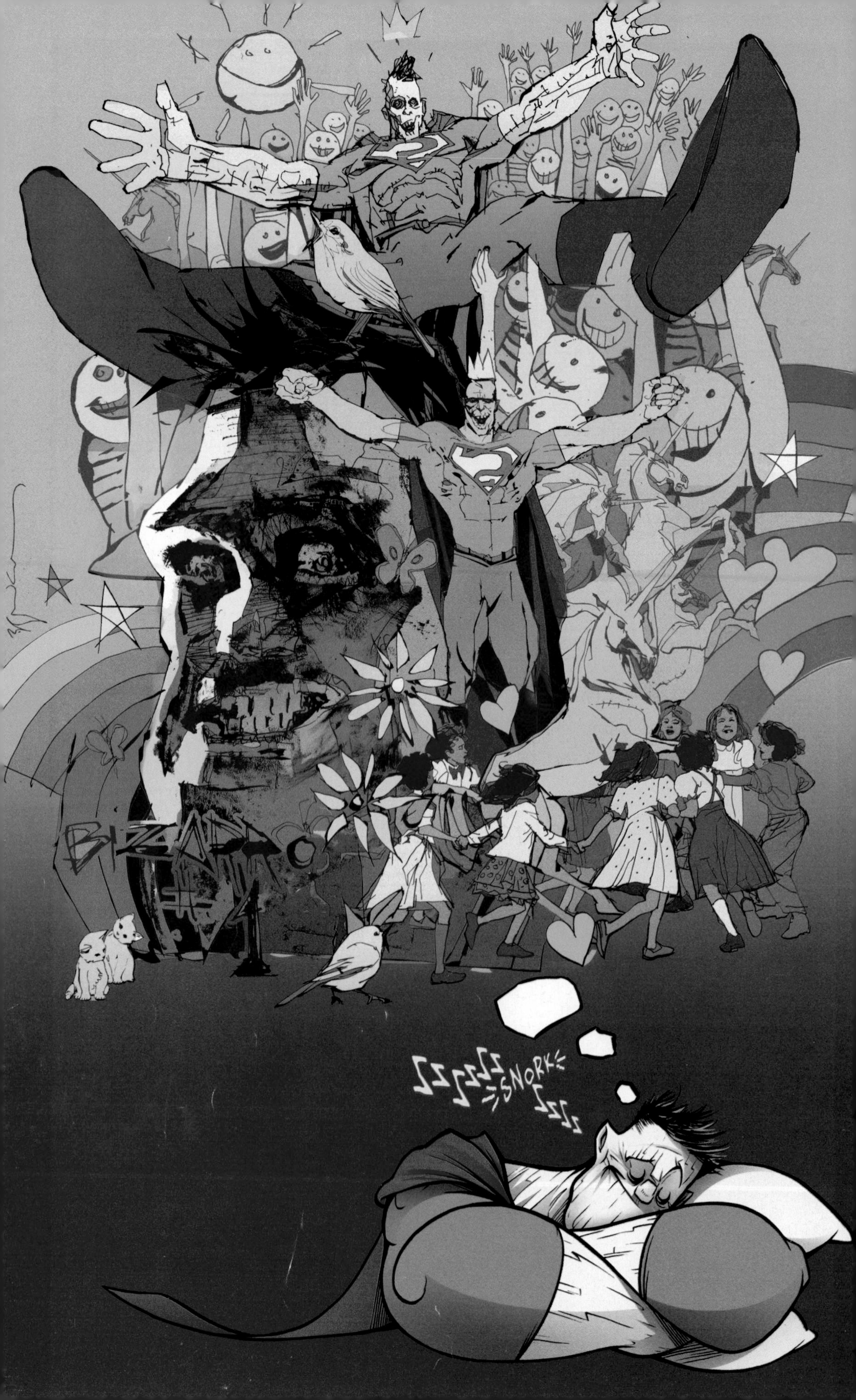
ZZZZZZ SNORK ZZZZ

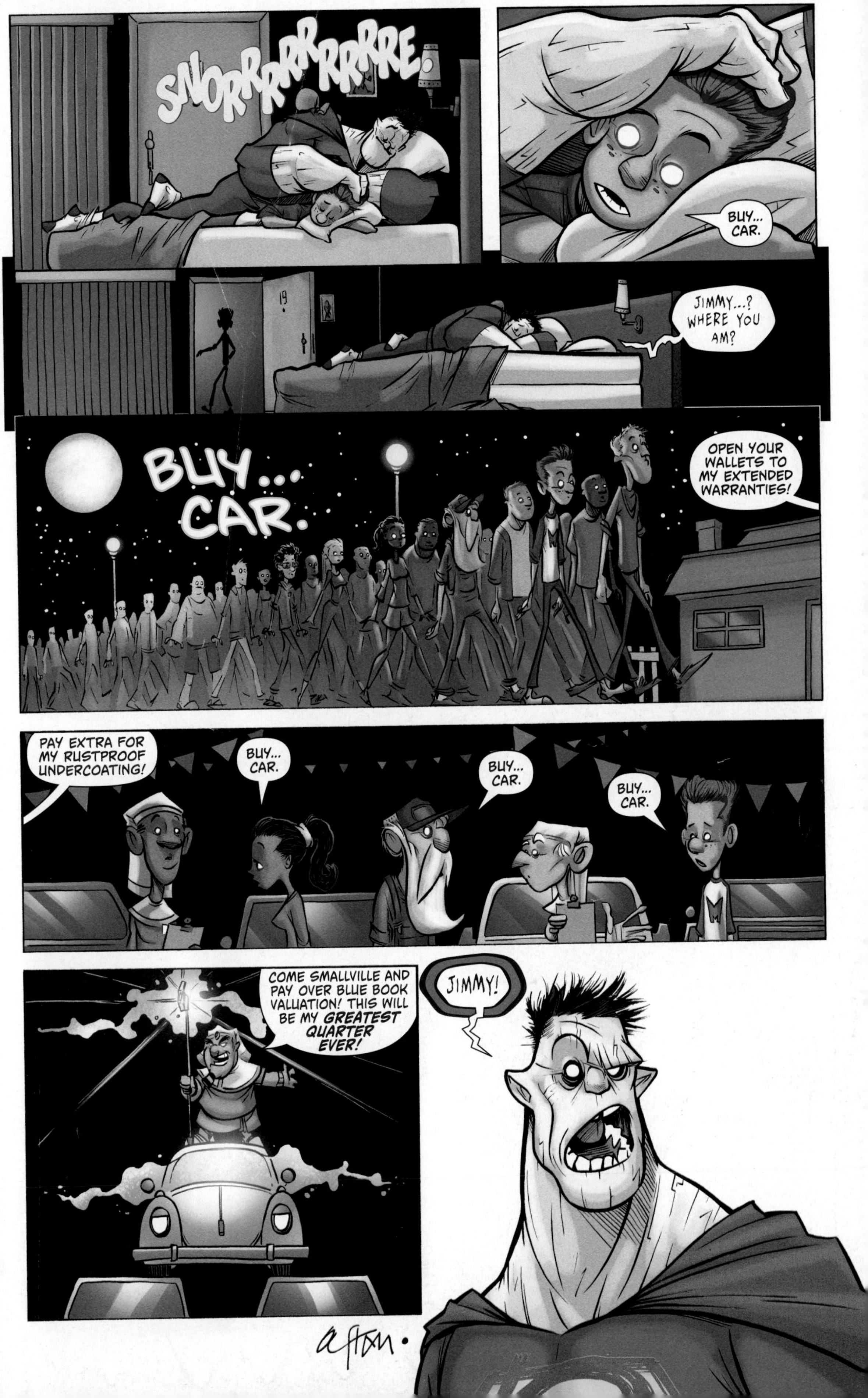
SNORRRRRRRRRE.
BUY... CAR.
JIMMY...? WHERE YOU AM?
BUY... CAR.
OPEN YOUR WALLETS TO MY EXTENDED WARRANTIES!
PAY EXTRA FOR MY RUSTPROOF UNDERCOATING!
BUY... CAR.
BUY... CAR.
BUY... CAR.
COME SMALLVILLE AND PAY OVER BLUE BOOK VALUATION! THIS WILL BE MY GREATEST QUARTER EVER!
JIMMY!

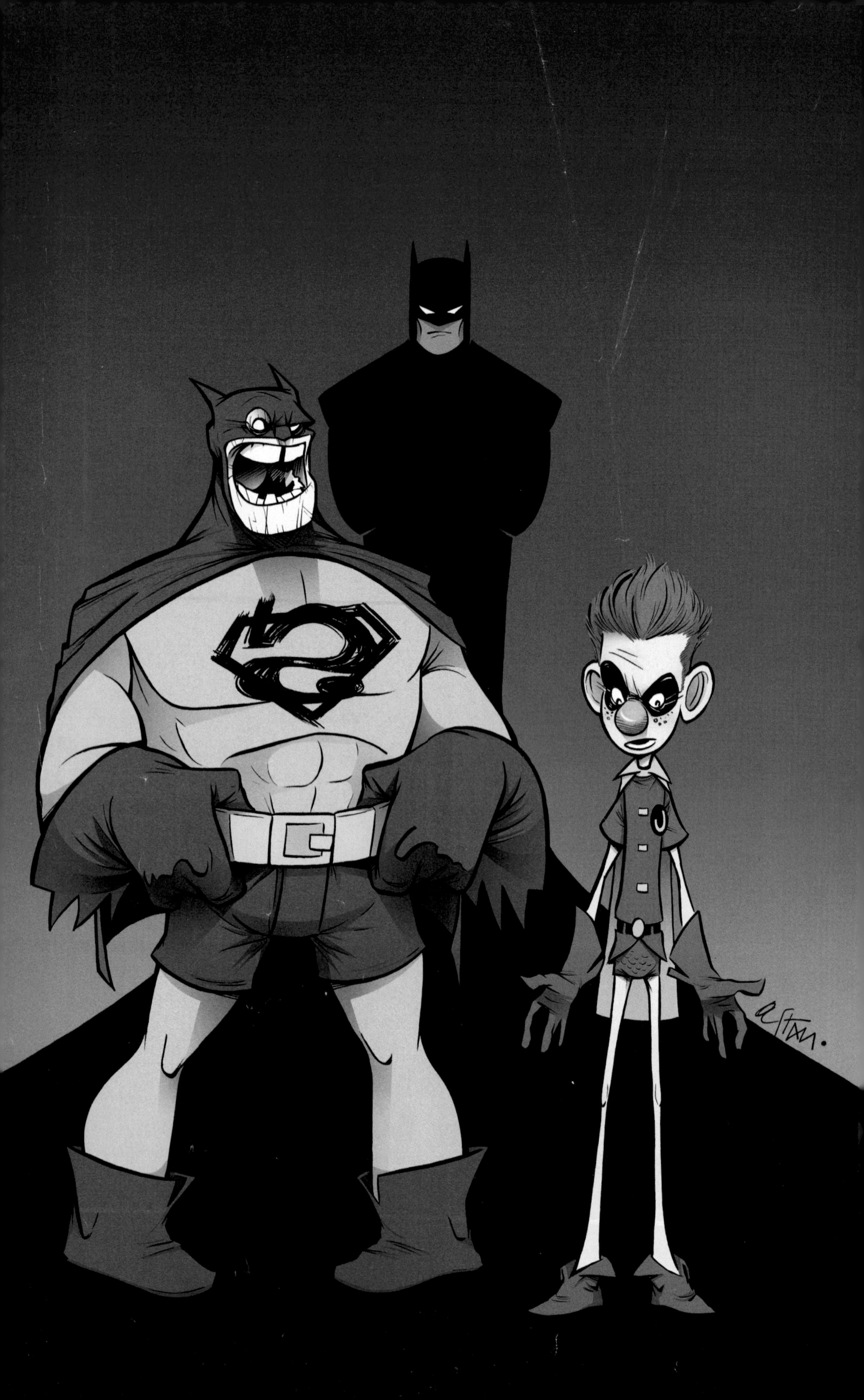

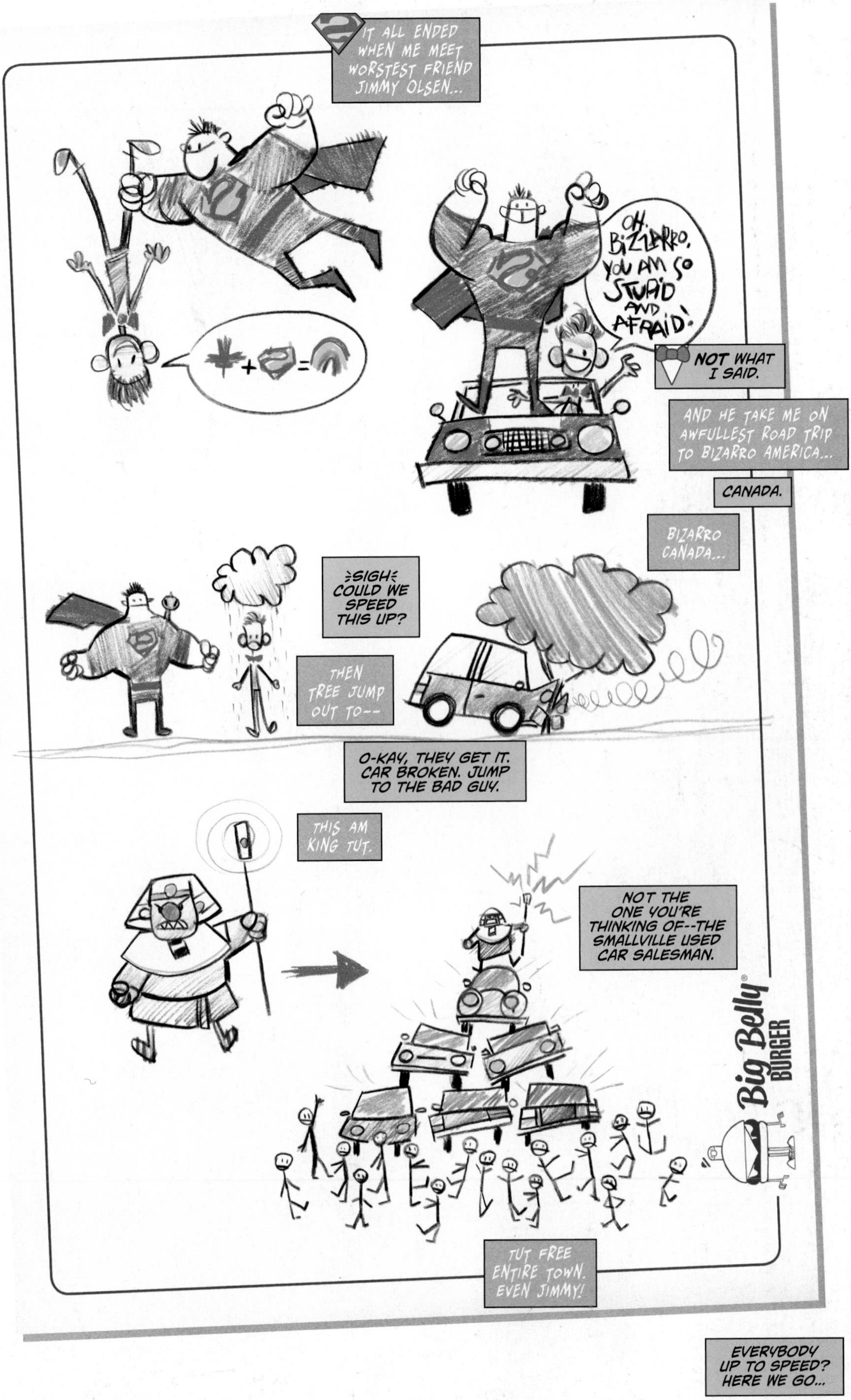
IT ALL ENDED WHEN ME MEET WORSTEST FRIEND JIMMY OLSEN...
OH, BIZZARRO, YOU AM SO STUPID AND AFRAID!
NOT WHAT I SAID.
AND HE TAKE ME ON AWFULLEST ROAD TRIP TO BIZARRO AMERICA...
CANADA.
BIZARRO CANADA...
SIGH COULD WE SPEED THIS UP?
THEN TREE JUMP OUT TO--
O-KAY, THEY GET IT. CAR BROKEN. JUMP TO THE BAD GUY.
THIS AM KING TUT.
NOT THE ONE YOU'RE THINKING OF--THE SMALLVILLE USED CAR SALESMAN.
Big Belly BURGER
TUT FREE ENTIRE TOWN. EVEN JIMMY!
EVERYBODY UP TO SPEED? HERE WE GO...

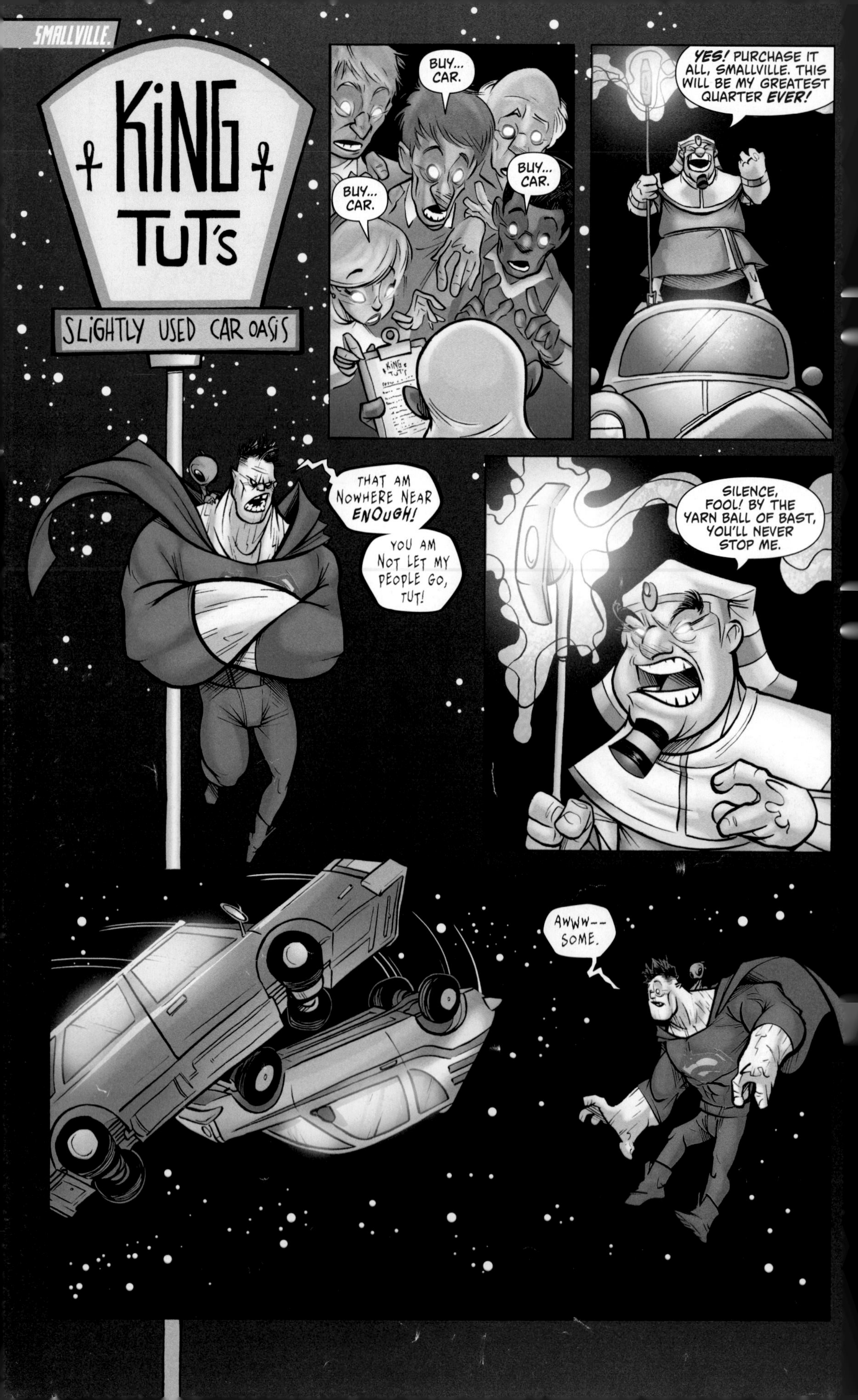
SMALLVILLE.
KING TUT'S
SLIGHTLY USED CAR OASIS
BUY... CAR.
BUY... CAR.
BUY... CAR.
YES! PURCHASE IT ALL, SMALLVILLE. THIS WILL BE MY GREATEST QUARTER EVER!
THAT AM NOWHERE NEAR ENOUGH!
YOU AM NOT LET MY PEOPLE GO, TUT!
SILENCE, FOOL! BY THE YARN BALL OF BAST, YOU'LL NEVER STOP ME.
AWWW--SOME.

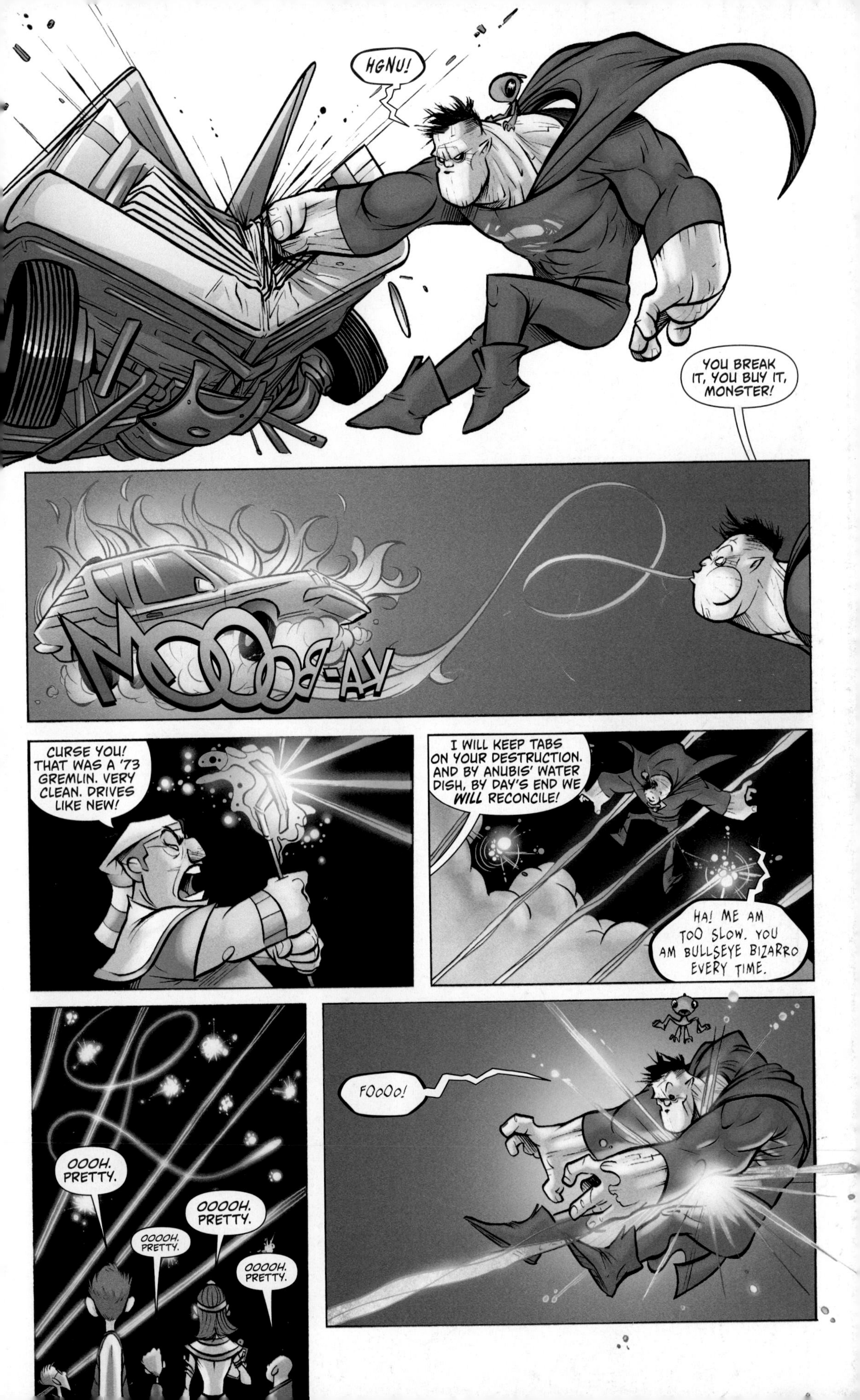
HGNU!
YOU BREAK IT, YOU BUY IT, MONSTER!
KA-BOOOOM
CURSE YOU! THAT WAS A '73 GREMLIN. VERY CLEAN. DRIVES LIKE NEW!
I WILL KEEP TABS ON YOUR DESTRUCTION. AND BY ANUBIS' WATER DISH, BY DAY'S END WE WILL RECONCILE!
HA! ME AM TOO SLOW. YOU AM BULLSEYE BIZARRO EVERY TIME.
OOOH. PRETTY.
OOOOH. PRETTY.
OOOOH. PRETTY.
OOOOH. PRETTY.
FOOOO!

BIZARRO'S UNDERCONFIDENCE HIS OVERDOING.

CRRRASH!

BIZARRO AM OKAY. ME FELL ON BRAIN.

COLIN, GO DE-ENSLAVE JIMMY. HE AM KNOW WHAT TO DO!

HISSSSS.

HISSSSSSSSSS

DOWN, DOWN AND NEA----!

WHA--?!

COME CLOSE!

HOLD TIGHT!

GET HIM!

GRAB HIM!

HOLD HIM!

THAT'S RIGHT, SMALLVILLE, RESTRAIN HIM. NO ONE CAN STOP MY LIQUIDATION SALE!

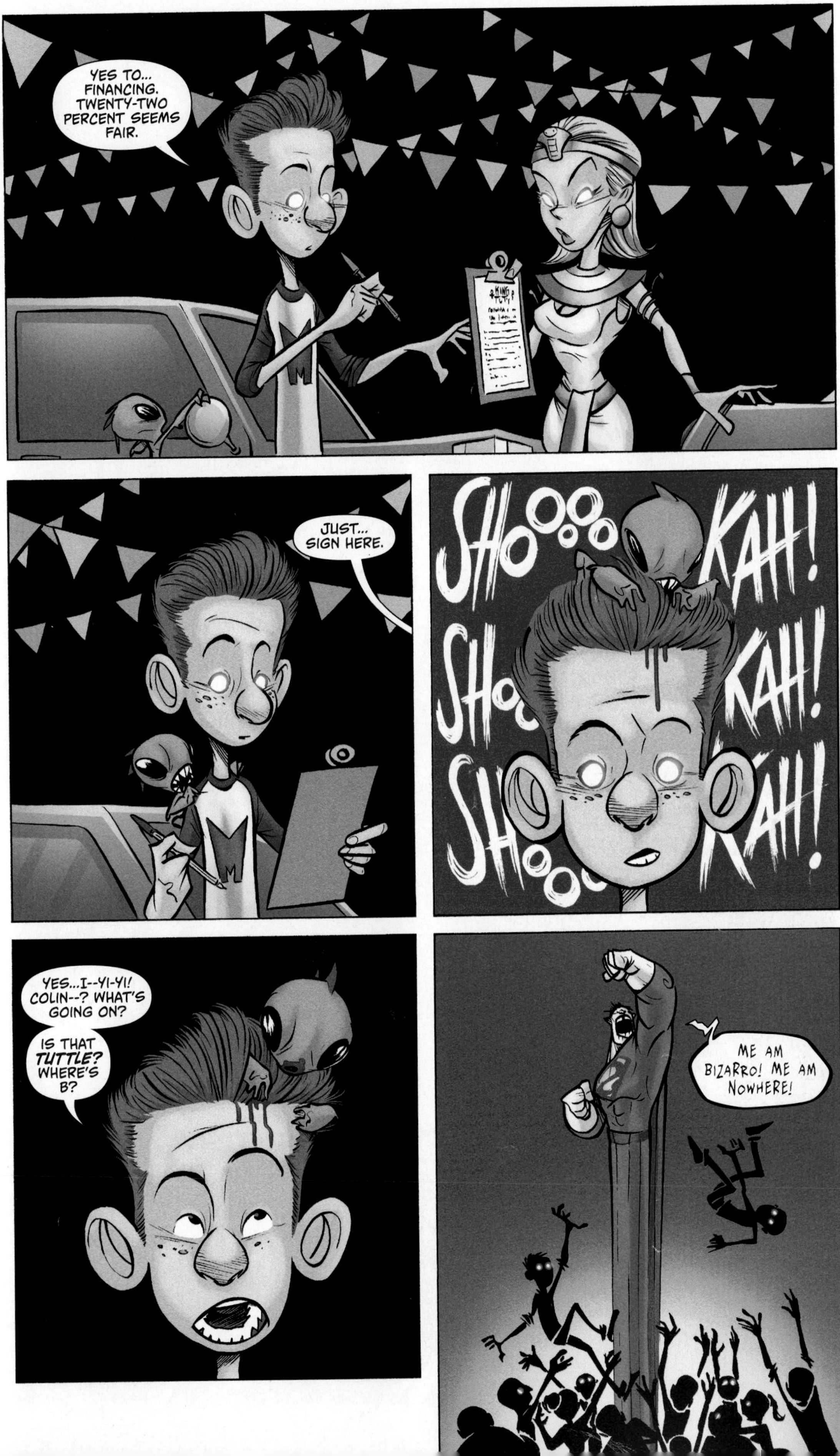

YES TO... FINANCING. TWENTY-TWO PERCENT SEEMS FAIR.
JUST... SIGN HERE.
SHOOOOOKAH!
SHOO KAH!
SHOOO KAH!
YES...I--YI-YI! COLIN--? WHAT'S GOING ON?
IS THAT TUTTLE? WHERE'S B?
ME AM BIZARRO! ME AM NOWHERE!

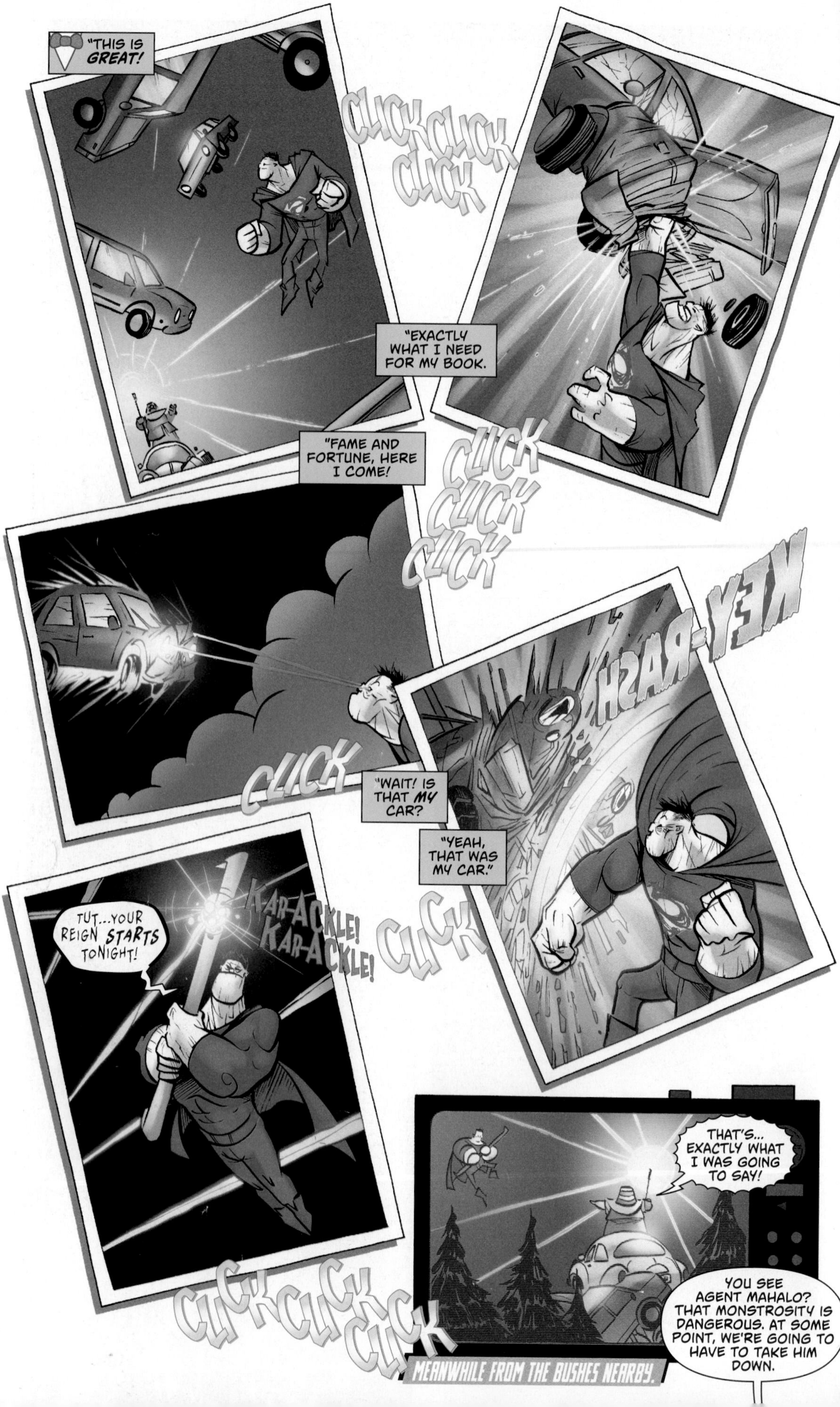
"THIS IS GREAT!
CLICK CLICK CLICK
"EXACTLY WHAT I NEED FOR MY BOOK.
"FAME AND FORTUNE, HERE I COME!
CLICK CLICK CLICK
KEY-RASH
CLICK
"WAIT! IS THAT MY CAR?
"YEAH, THAT WAS MY CAR."
TUT...YOUR REIGN STARTS TONIGHT!
KAR-ACKLE! KAR-ACKLE!
CLICK
THAT'S... EXACTLY WHAT I WAS GOING TO SAY!
CLICK CLICK CLICK
MEANWHILE FROM THE BUSHES NEARBY.
YOU SEE AGENT MAHALO? THAT MONSTROSITY IS DANGEROUS. AT SOME POINT, WE'RE GOING TO HAVE TO TAKE HIM DOWN.

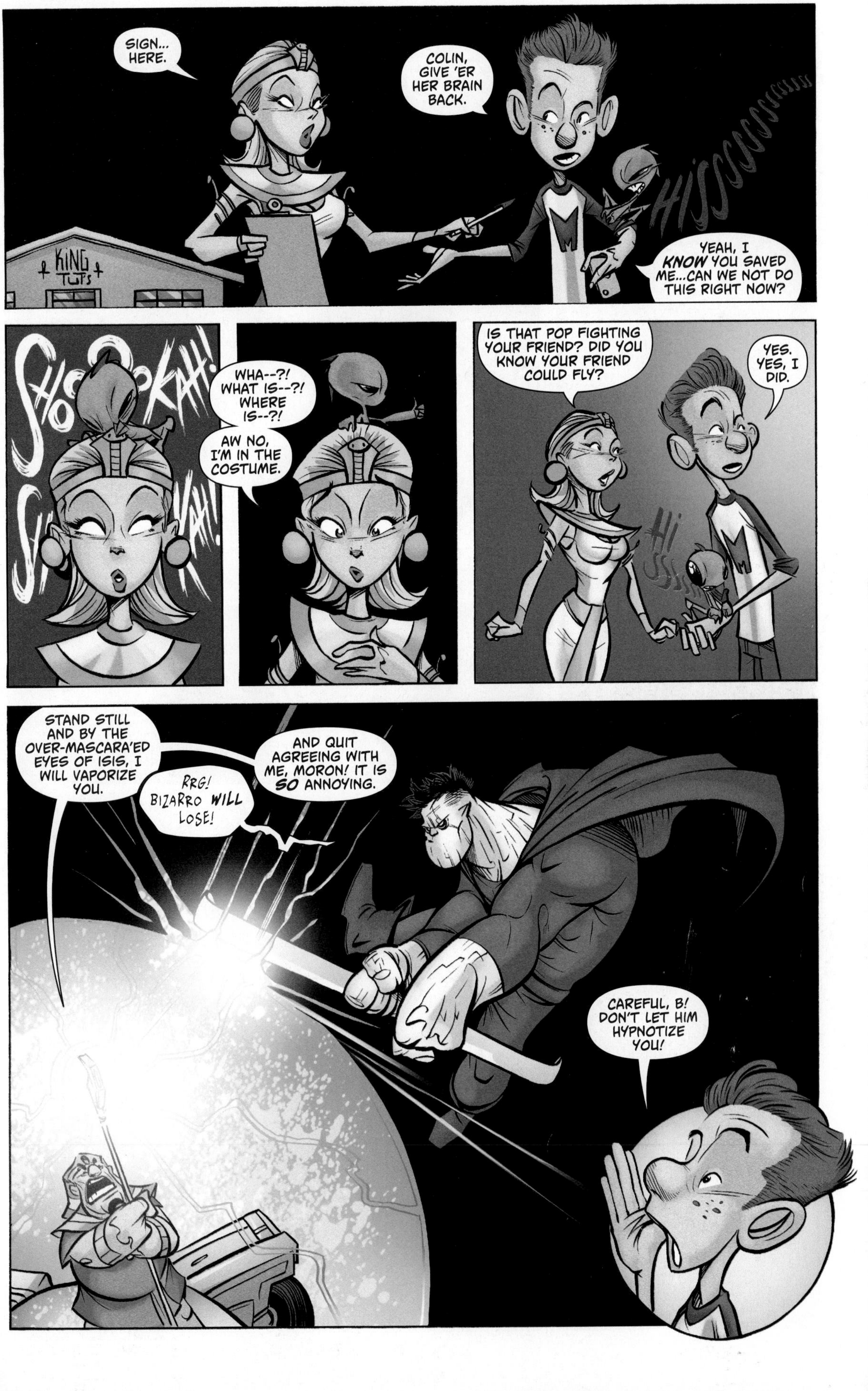
SIGN... HERE.
COLIN, GIVE 'ER HER BRAIN BACK.
YEAH, I KNOW YOU SAVED ME...CAN WE NOT DO THIS RIGHT NOW?
WHA--?! WHAT IS--?! WHERE IS--?!
AW NO, I'M IN THE COSTUME.
IS THAT POP FIGHTING YOUR FRIEND? DID YOU KNOW YOUR FRIEND COULD FLY?
YES. YES, I DID.
STAND STILL AND BY THE OVER-MASCARA'ED EYES OF ISIS, I WILL VAPORIZE YOU.
AND QUIT AGREEING WITH ME, MORON! IT IS SO ANNOYING.
RRG! BIZARRO WILL LOSE!
CAREFUL, B! DON'T LET HIM HYPNOTIZE YOU!

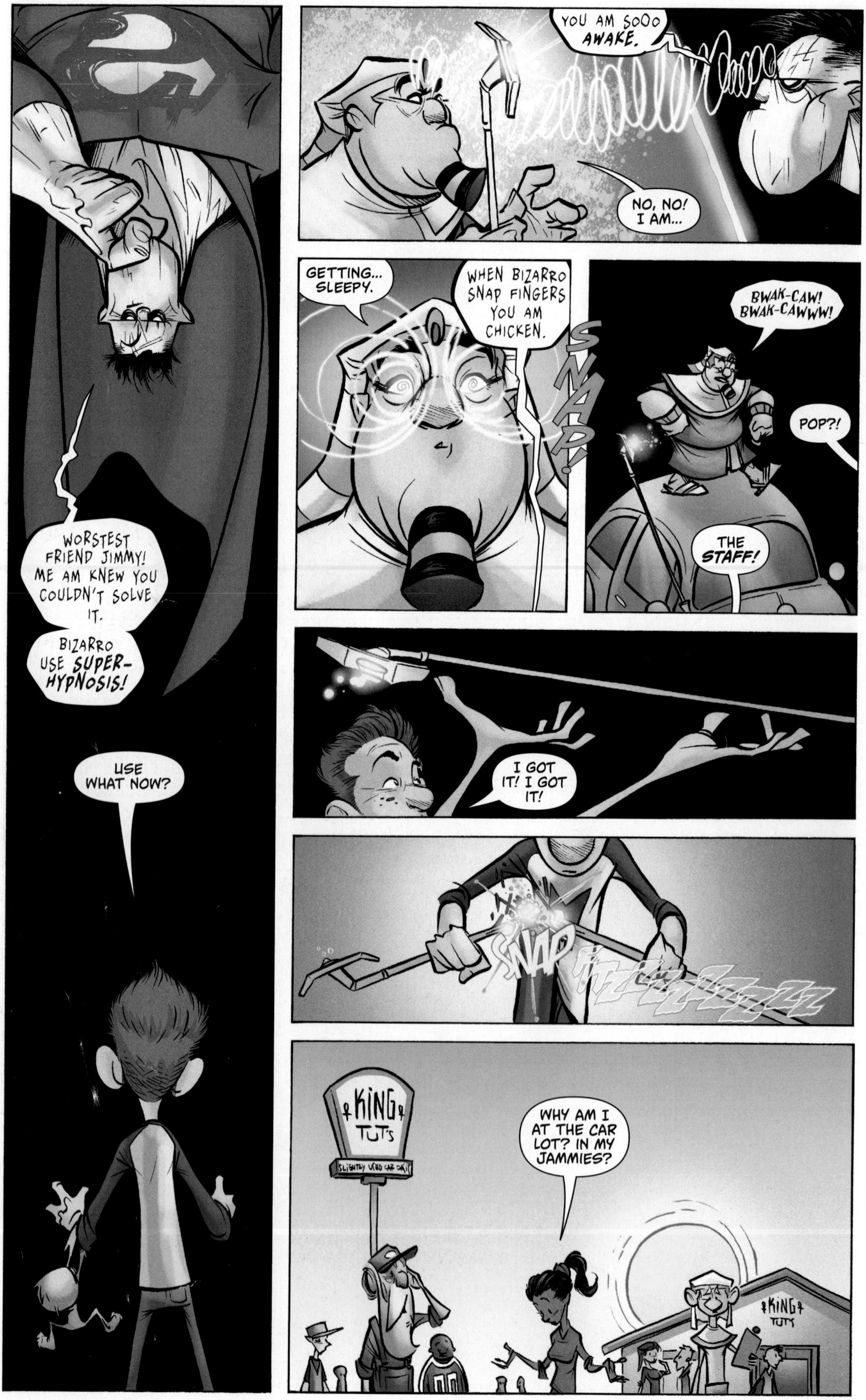
WORSTEST FRIEND JIMMY! ME AM KNEW YOU COULDN'T SOLVE IT.
BIZARRO USE SUPER-HYPNOSIS!
USE WHAT NOW?
YOU AM SOOO AWAKE.
NO, NO! I AM...
GETTING... SLEEPY.
WHEN BIZARRO SNAP FINGERS YOU AM CHICKEN.
SNAP!
BWAK-CAW! BWAK-CAWWW!
POP?!
THE STAFF!
I GOT IT! I GOT IT!
SNAP
FZZZZZZZZZZZZ
KING TUT'S
SLIGHTLY USED CAR DEALS
WHY AM I AT THE CAR LOT? IN MY JAMMIES?
KING TUT'S

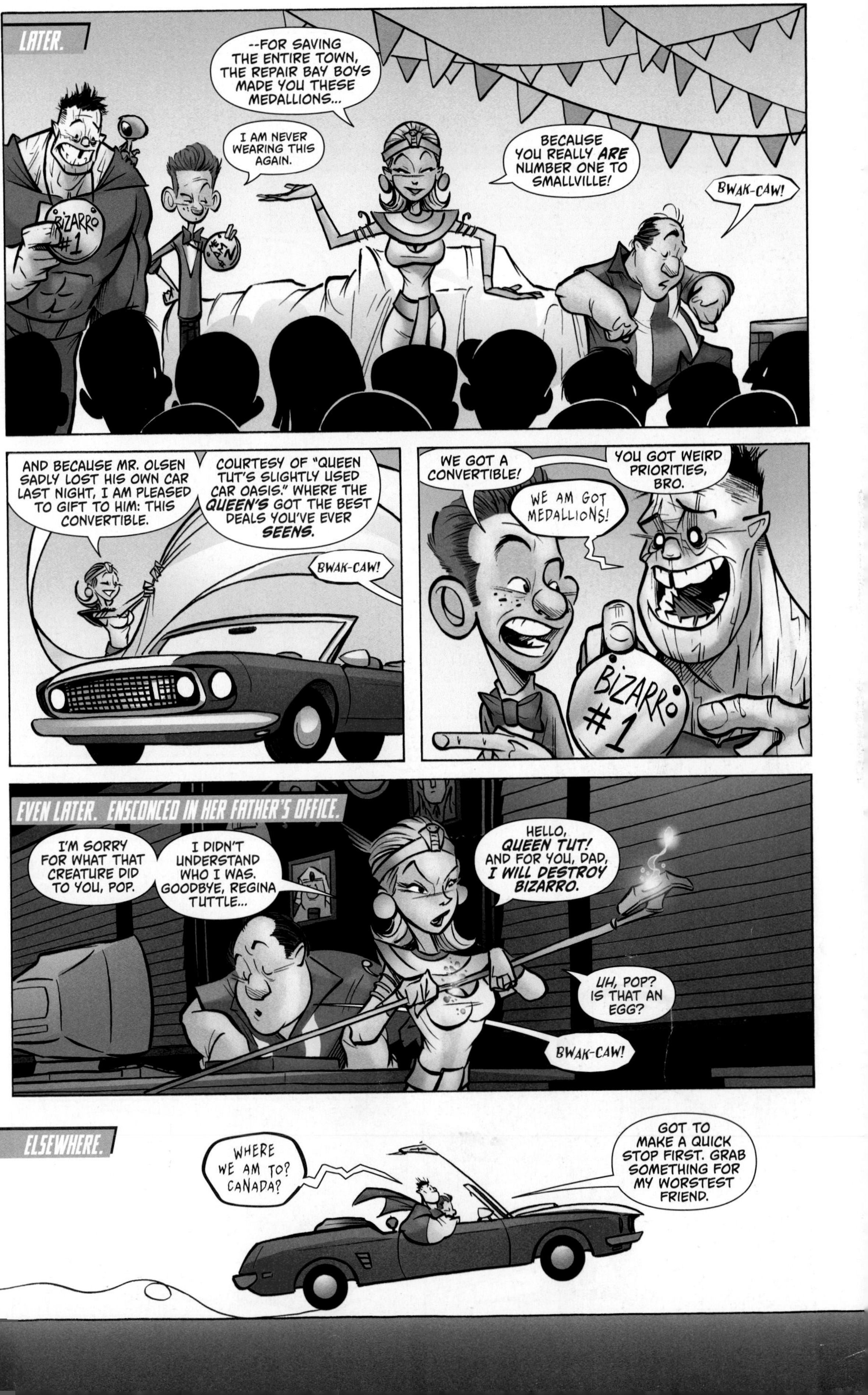
LATER.
--FOR SAVING THE ENTIRE TOWN, THE REPAIR BAY BOYS MADE YOU THESE MEDALLIONS...
I AM NEVER WEARING THIS AGAIN.
BECAUSE YOU REALLY ARE NUMBER ONE TO SMALLVILLE!
BWAK-CAW!
BIZARRO #1
AND BECAUSE MR. OLSEN SADLY LOST HIS OWN CAR LAST NIGHT, I AM PLEASED TO GIFT TO HIM: THIS CONVERTIBLE.
COURTESY OF "QUEEN TUT'S SLIGHTLY USED CAR OASIS." WHERE THE QUEEN'S GOT THE BEST DEALS YOU'VE EVER SEENS.
BWAK-CAW!
WE GOT A CONVERTIBLE!
YOU GOT WEIRD PRIORITIES, BRO.
WE AM GOT MEDALLIONS!
BIZARRO #1
EVEN LATER. ENSCONCED IN HER FATHER'S OFFICE.
I'M SORRY FOR WHAT THAT CREATURE DID TO YOU, POP.
I DIDN'T UNDERSTAND WHO I WAS. GOODBYE, REGINA TUTTLE...
HELLO, QUEEN TUT! AND FOR YOU, DAD, I WILL DESTROY BIZARRO.
UH, POP? IS THAT AN EGG?
BWAK-CAW!
ELSEWHERE.
WHERE WE AM TO? CANADA?
GOT TO MAKE A QUICK STOP FIRST. GRAB SOMETHING FOR MY WORSTEST FRIEND.

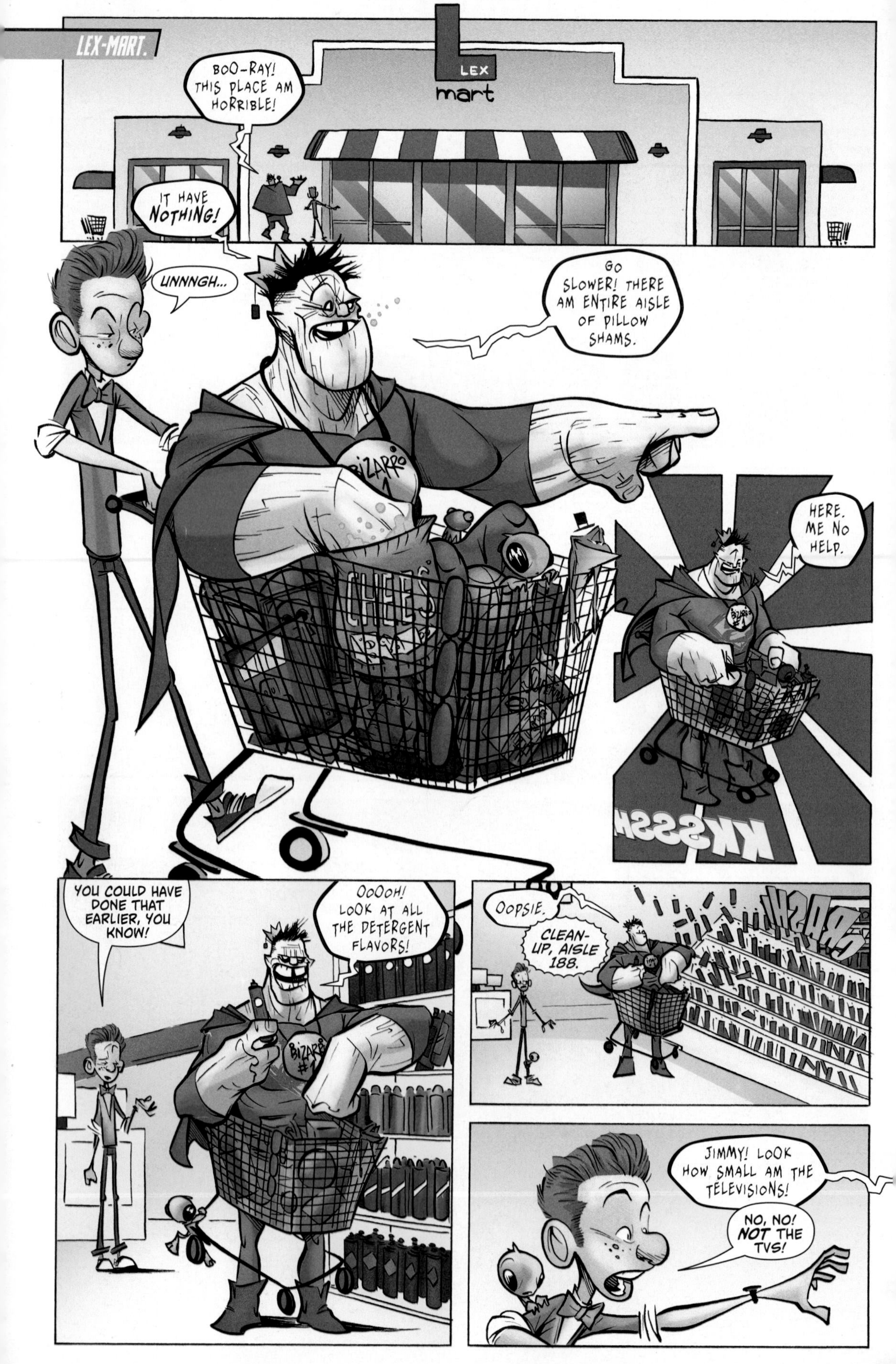
LEX-MART.
LEX mart
BOO-RAY! THIS PLACE AM HORRIBLE!
IT HAVE NOTHING!
UNNNGH...
GO SLOWER! THERE AM ENTIRE AISLE OF PILLOW SHAMS.
HERE. ME NO HELP.
KKSSSH
YOU COULD HAVE DONE THAT EARLIER, YOU KNOW!
OOOOH! LOOK AT ALL THE DETERGENT FLAVORS!
OOPSIE.
CLEAN-UP, AISLE 188.
JIMMY! LOOK HOW SMALL AM THE TELEVISIONS!
NO, NO! NOT THE TVS!

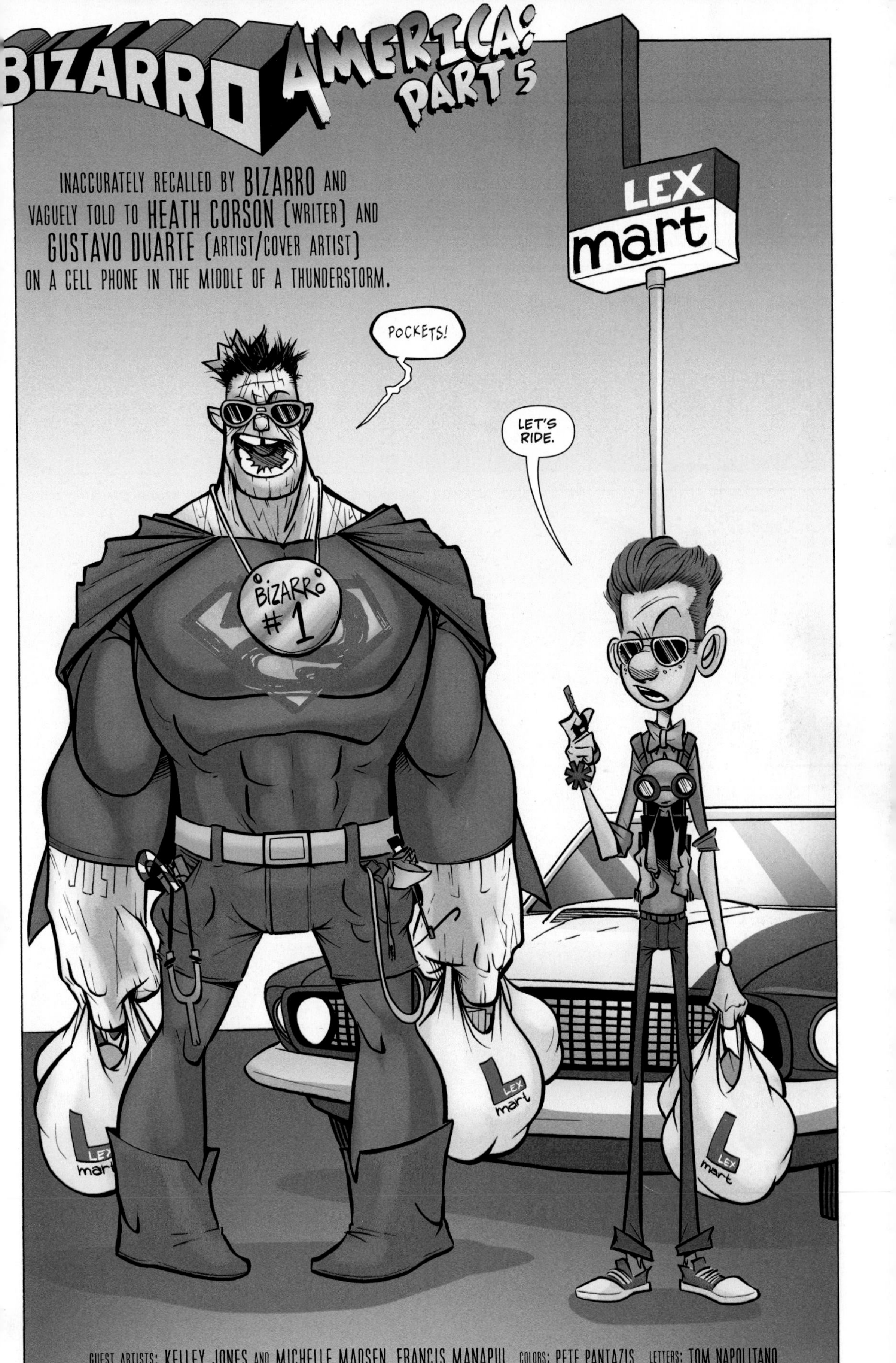

BIZARRO AMERICA: PART 5
INACCURATELY RECALLED BY BIZARRO AND VAGUELY TOLD TO HEATH CORSON (WRITER) AND GUSTAVO DUARTE (ARTIST/COVER ARTIST) ON A CELL PHONE IN THE MIDDLE OF A THUNDERSTORM.
LEX mart
POCKETS!
LET'S RIDE.
BIZARRO #1
GUEST ARTISTS: KELLEY JONES AND MICHELLE MADSEN, FRANCIS MANAPUL COLORS: PETE PANTAZIS LETTERS: TOM NAPOLITANO

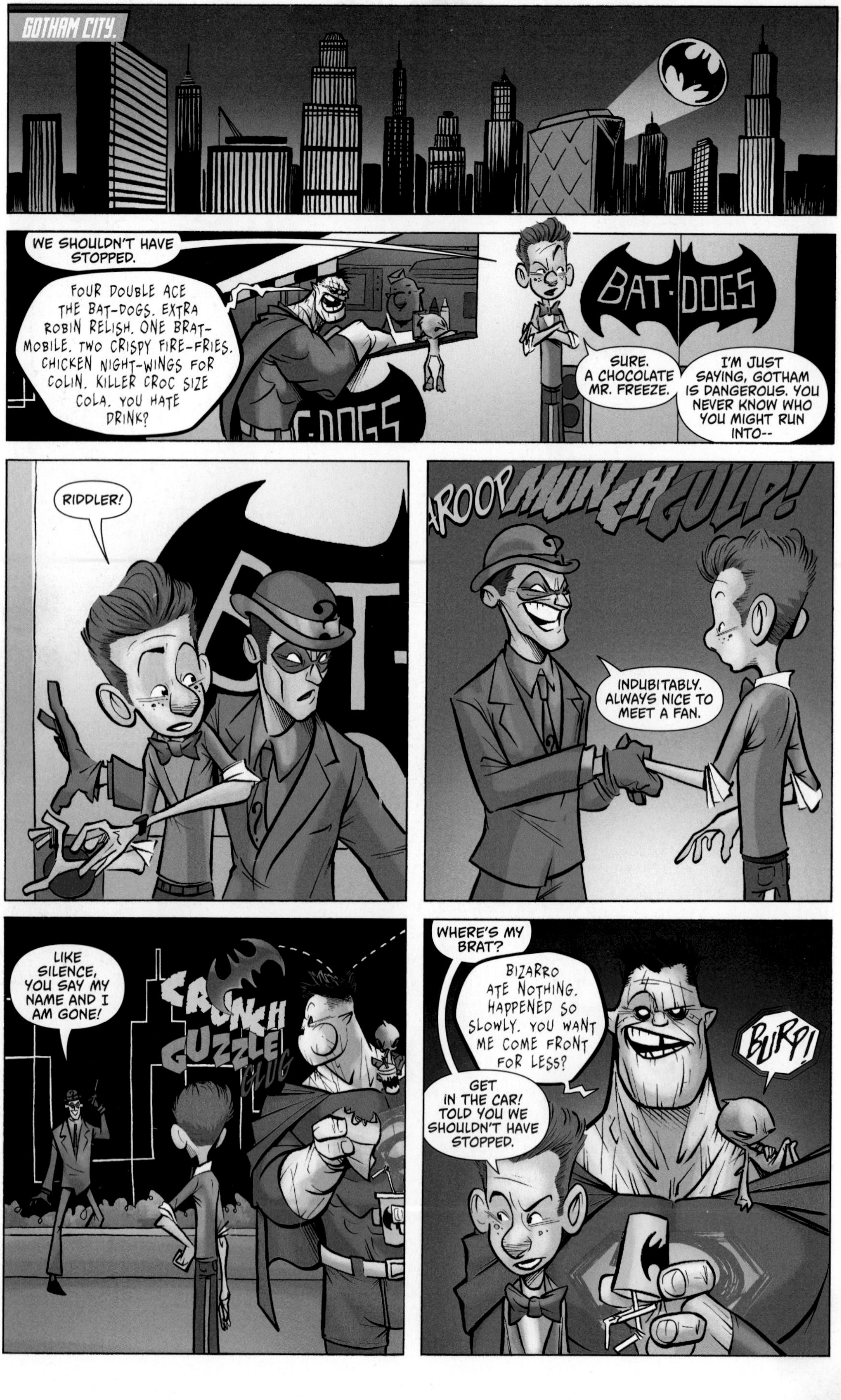

GOTHAM CITY.
WE SHOULDN'T HAVE STOPPED.
FOUR DOUBLE ACE THE BAT-DOGS. EXTRA ROBIN RELISH. ONE BRAT-MOBILE. TWO CRISPY FIRE-FRIES. CHICKEN NIGHT-WINGS FOR COLIN. KILLER CROC SIZE COLA. YOU HATE DRINK?
BAT-DOGS
SURE. A CHOCOLATE MR. FREEZE.
I'M JUST SAYING, GOTHAM IS DANGEROUS. YOU NEVER KNOW WHO YOU MIGHT RUN INTO--
RIDDLER!
AROOP MUNCH GULP!
INDUBITABLY. ALWAYS NICE TO MEET A FAN.
LIKE SILENCE, YOU SAY MY NAME AND I AM GONE!
CRUNCH GUZZLE GLUG
WHERE'S MY BRAT?
BIZARRO ATE NOTHING. HAPPENED SO SLOWLY. YOU WANT ME COME FRONT FOR LESS?
BURP!
GET IN THE CAR! TOLD YOU WE SHOULDN'T HAVE STOPPED.

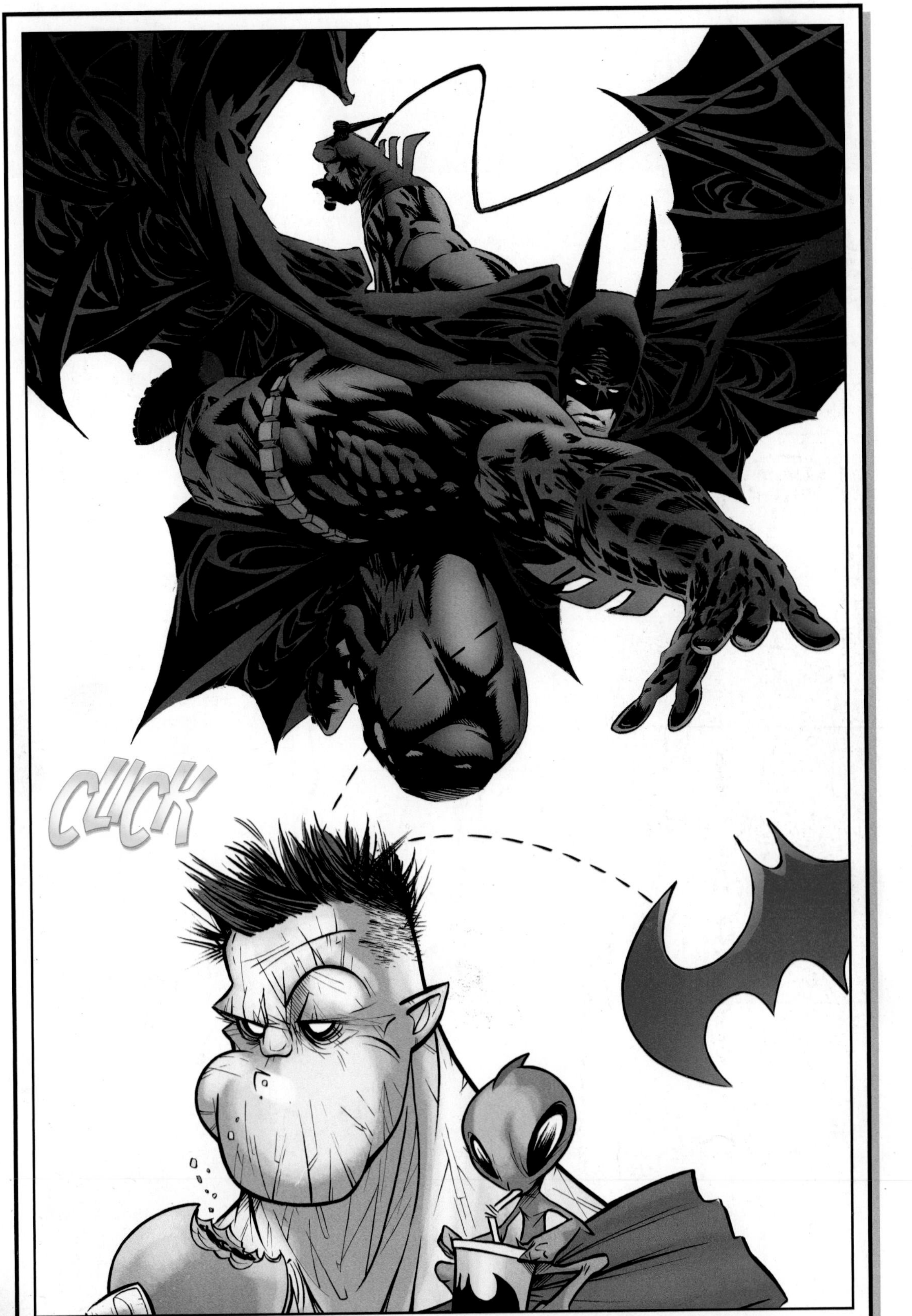
CLICK

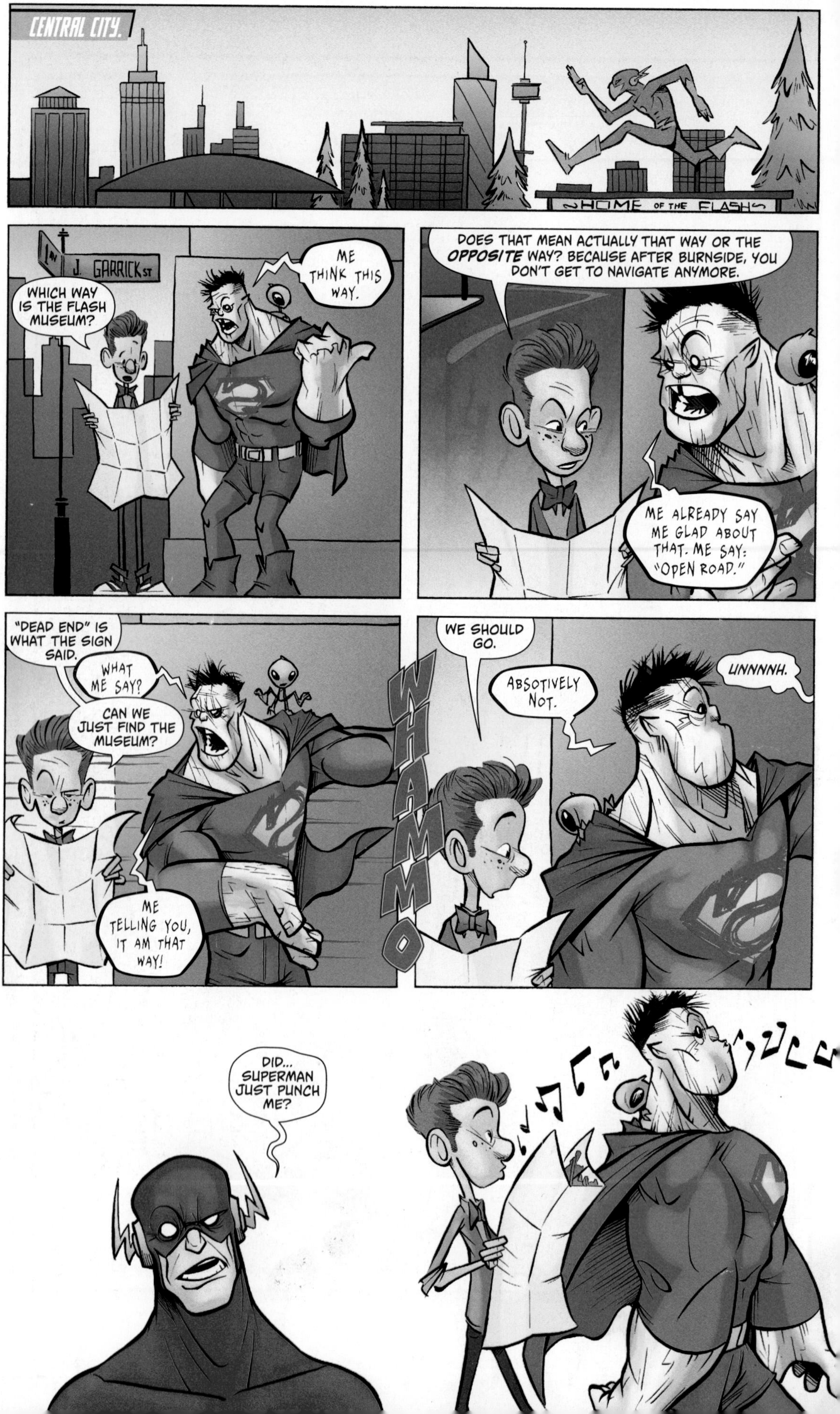
CENTRAL CITY.
HOME OF THE FLASH
1st AV
J. GARRICK ST
WHICH WAY IS THE FLASH MUSEUM?
ME THINK THIS WAY.
DOES THAT MEAN ACTUALLY THAT WAY OR THE OPPOSITE WAY? BECAUSE AFTER BURNSIDE, YOU DON'T GET TO NAVIGATE ANYMORE.
ME ALREADY SAY ME GLAD ABOUT THAT. ME SAY: "OPEN ROAD."
"DEAD END" IS WHAT THE SIGN SAID.
WHAT ME SAY?
CAN WE JUST FIND THE MUSEUM?
ME TELLING YOU, IT AM THAT WAY!
WHAMMO
WE SHOULD GO.
ABSOTIVELY NOT.
UNNNNH.
DID... SUPERMAN JUST PUNCH ME?

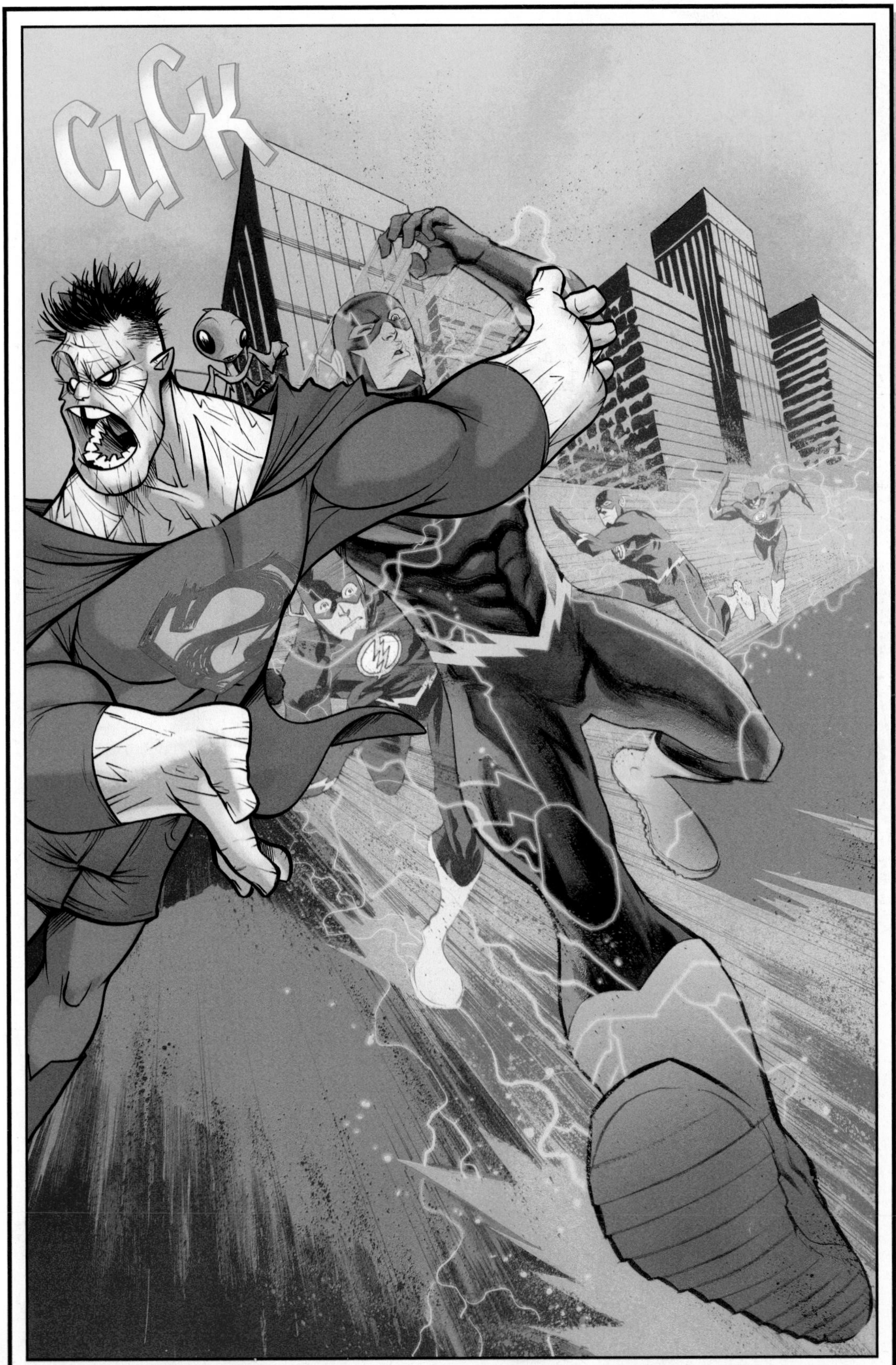
CLICK

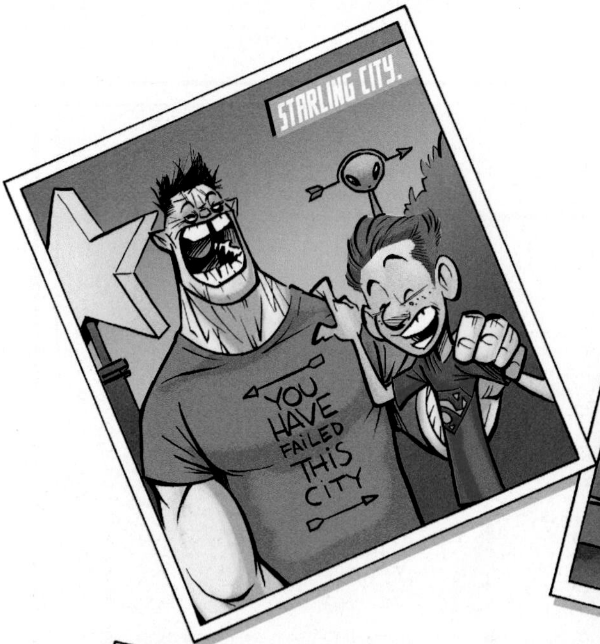
STARLING CITY.
YOU HAVE FAILED THIS CITY

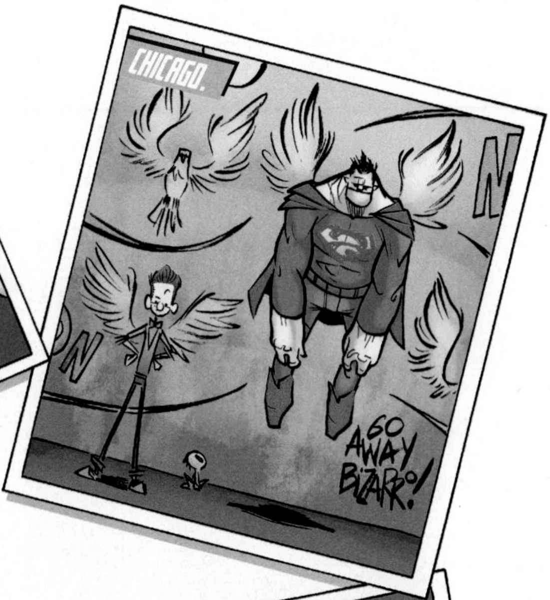
CHICAGO.
GO AWAY BIZARRO!

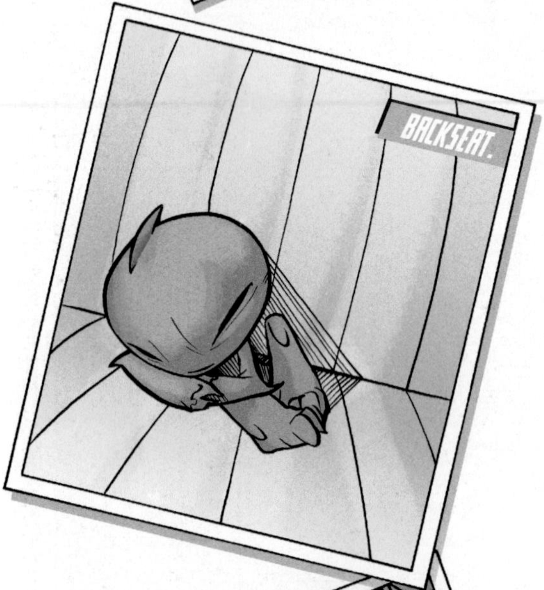
BACKSEAT.

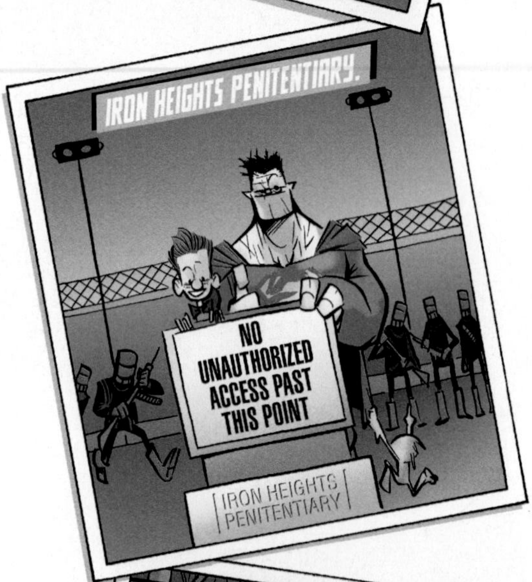
IRON HEIGHTS PENITENTIARY.
NO UNAUTHORIZED ACCESS PAST THIS POINT
IRON HEIGHTS PENITENTIARY

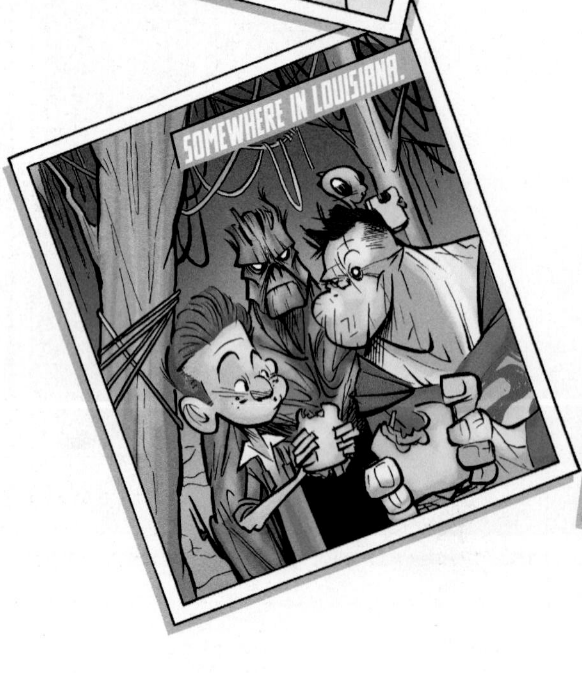
SOMEWHERE IN LOUISIANA.

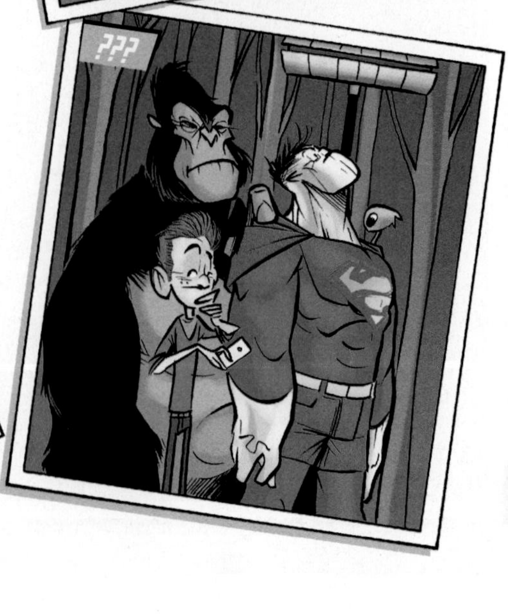
???

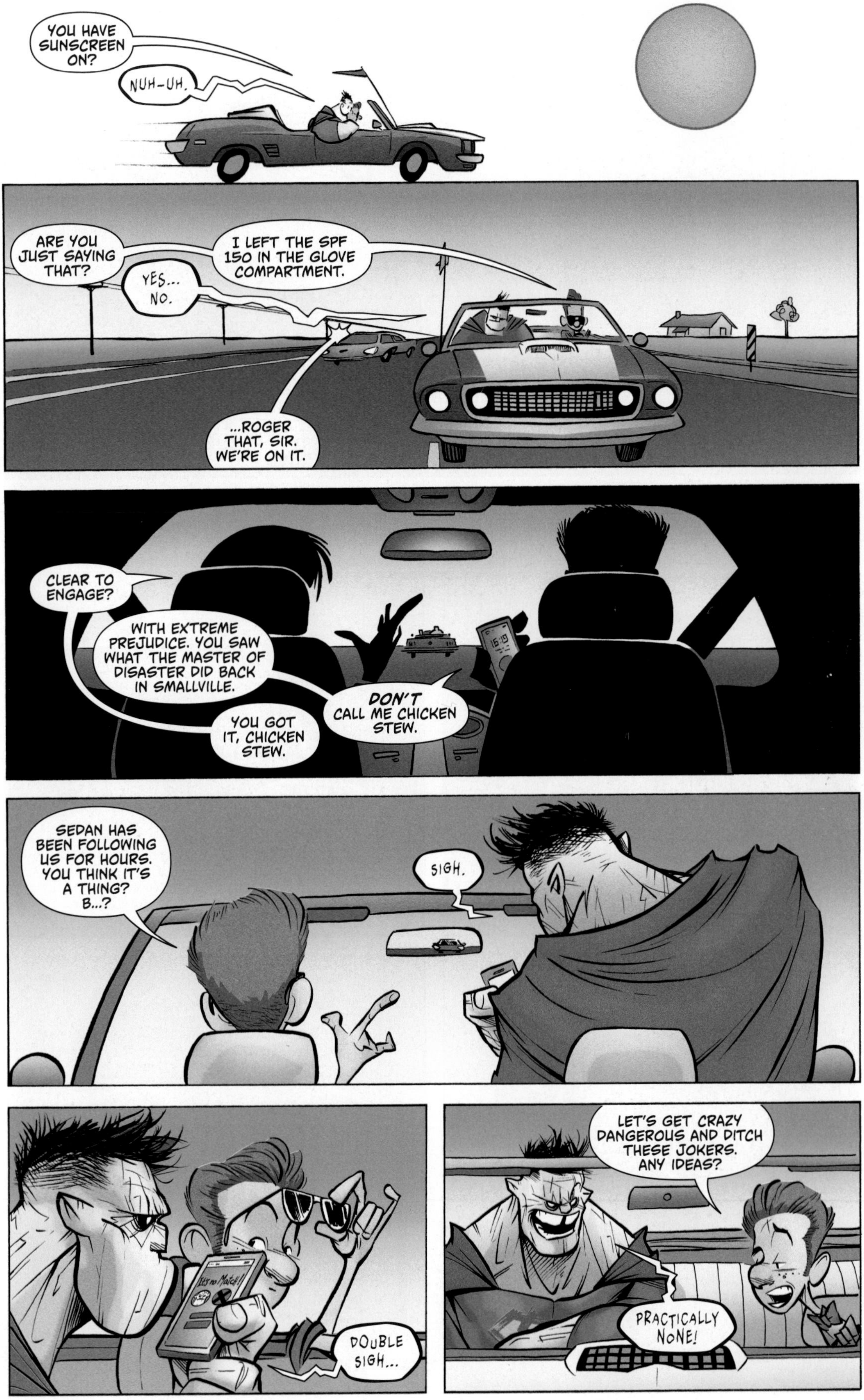
YOU HAVE SUNSCREEN ON?
NUH-UH.
ARE YOU JUST SAYING THAT?
YES... NO.
I LEFT THE SPF 150 IN THE GLOVE COMPARTMENT.
...ROGER THAT, SIR. WE'RE ON IT.
CLEAR TO ENGAGE?
WITH EXTREME PREJUDICE. YOU SAW WHAT THE MASTER OF DISASTER DID BACK IN SMALLVILLE.
YOU GOT IT, CHICKEN STEW.
DON'T CALL ME CHICKEN STEW.
SEDAN HAS BEEN FOLLOWING US FOR HOURS. YOU THINK IT'S A THING? B...?
SIGH.
DOUBLE SIGH...
LET'S GET CRAZY DANGEROUS AND DITCH THESE JOKERS. ANY IDEAS?
PRACTICALLY NONE!

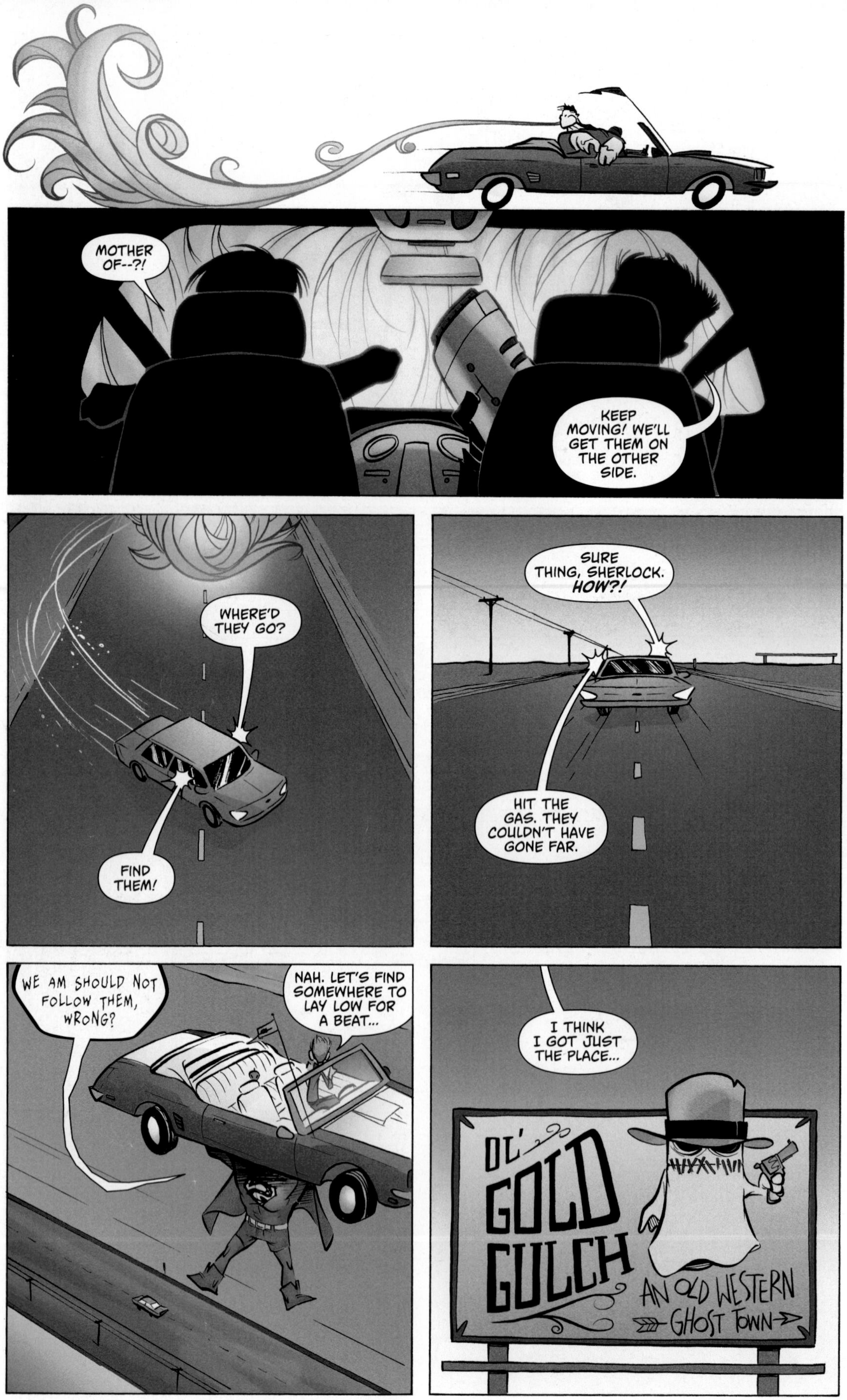
MOTHER OF--?!
KEEP MOVING! WE'LL GET THEM ON THE OTHER SIDE.
WHERE'D THEY GO?
FIND THEM!
SURE THING, SHERLOCK. HOW?!
HIT THE GAS. THEY COULDN'T HAVE GONE FAR.
WE AM SHOULD NOT FOLLOW THEM, WRONG?
NAH. LET'S FIND SOMEWHERE TO LAY LOW FOR A BEAT...
I THINK I GOT JUST THE PLACE...
OL' GOLD GULCH
AN OLD WESTERN GHOST TOWN

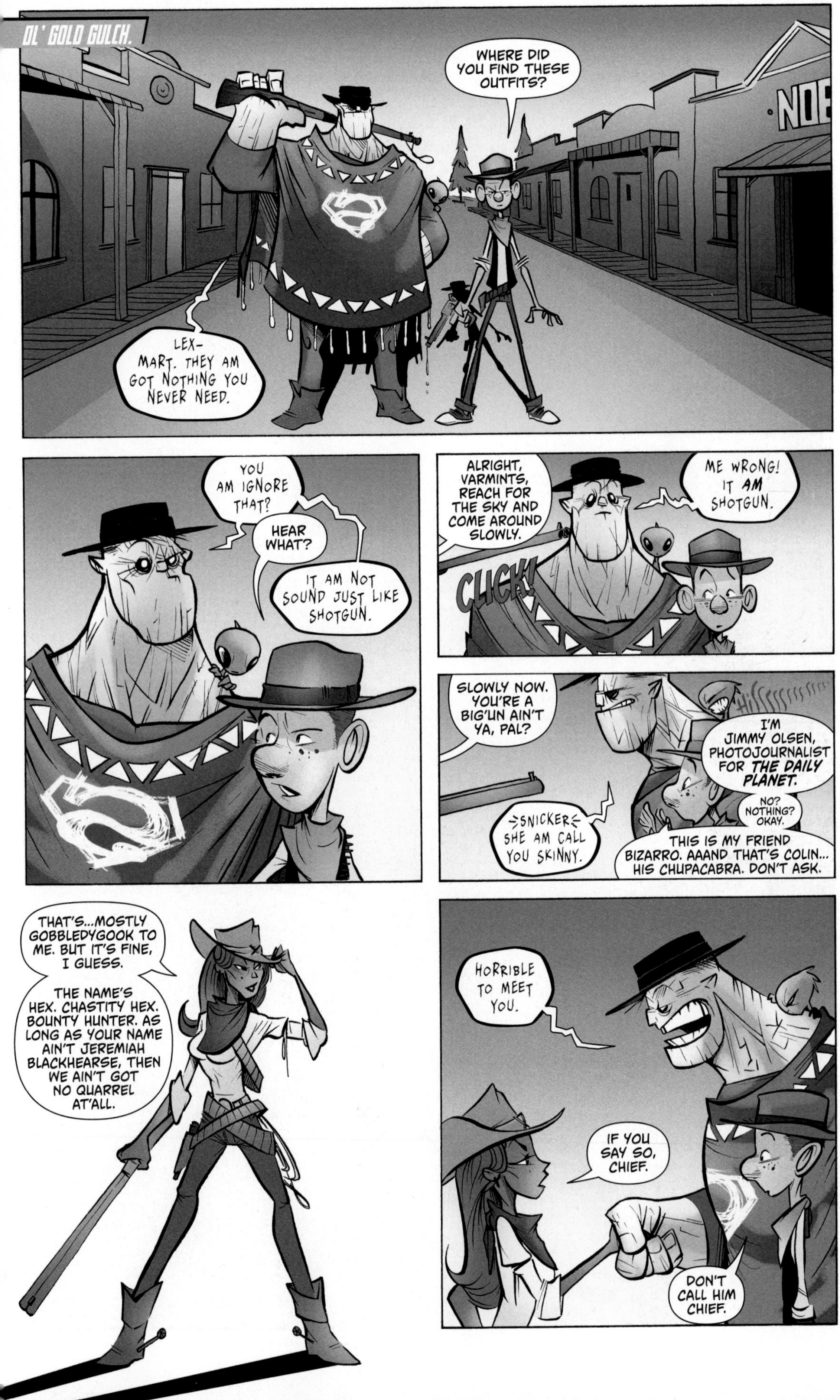

OL' GOLD GULCH.
WHERE DID YOU FIND THESE OUTFITS?
NOE
LEX-MART. THEY AM GOT NOTHING YOU NEVER NEED.
YOU AM IGNORE THAT?
HEAR WHAT?
IT AM NOT SOUND JUST LIKE SHOTGUN.
ALRIGHT, VARMINTS, REACH FOR THE SKY AND COME AROUND SLOWLY.
ME WRONG! IT AM SHOTGUN.
CLICK!
SLOWLY NOW. YOU'RE A BIG'UN AIN'T YA, PAL?
HISSSSSS
I'M JIMMY OLSEN, PHOTOJOURNALIST FOR THE DAILY PLANET.
NO? NOTHING? OKAY.
SNICKER SHE AM CALL YOU SKINNY.
THIS IS MY FRIEND BIZARRO. AAAND THAT'S COLIN... HIS CHUPACABRA. DON'T ASK.
THAT'S...MOSTLY GOBBLEDYGOOK TO ME. BUT IT'S FINE, I GUESS.
THE NAME'S HEX. CHASTITY HEX. BOUNTY HUNTER. AS LONG AS YOUR NAME AIN'T JEREMIAH BLACKHEARSE, THEN WE AIN'T GOT NO QUARREL AT'ALL.
HORRIBLE TO MEET YOU.
IF YOU SAY SO, CHIEF.
DON'T CALL HIM CHIEF.

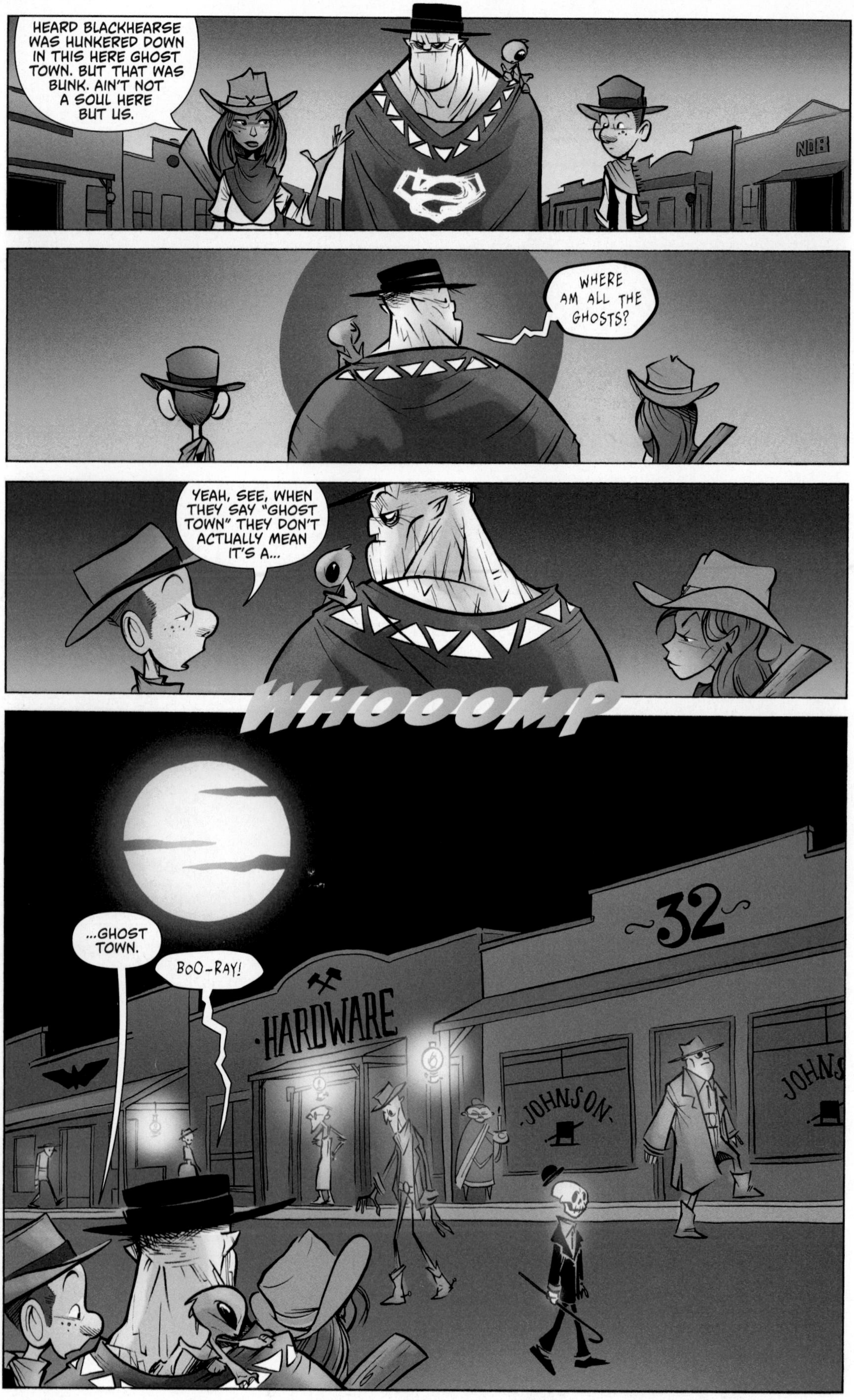
HEARD BLACKHEARSE WAS HUNKERED DOWN IN THIS HERE GHOST TOWN. BUT THAT WAS BUNK. AIN'T NOT A SOUL HERE BUT US.
NDB
WHERE AM ALL THE GHOSTS?
YEAH, SEE, WHEN THEY SAY "GHOST TOWN" THEY DON'T ACTUALLY MEAN IT'S A...
WHOOOOMP
32
HARDWARE
JOHNSON
...GHOST TOWN.
BOO-RAY!

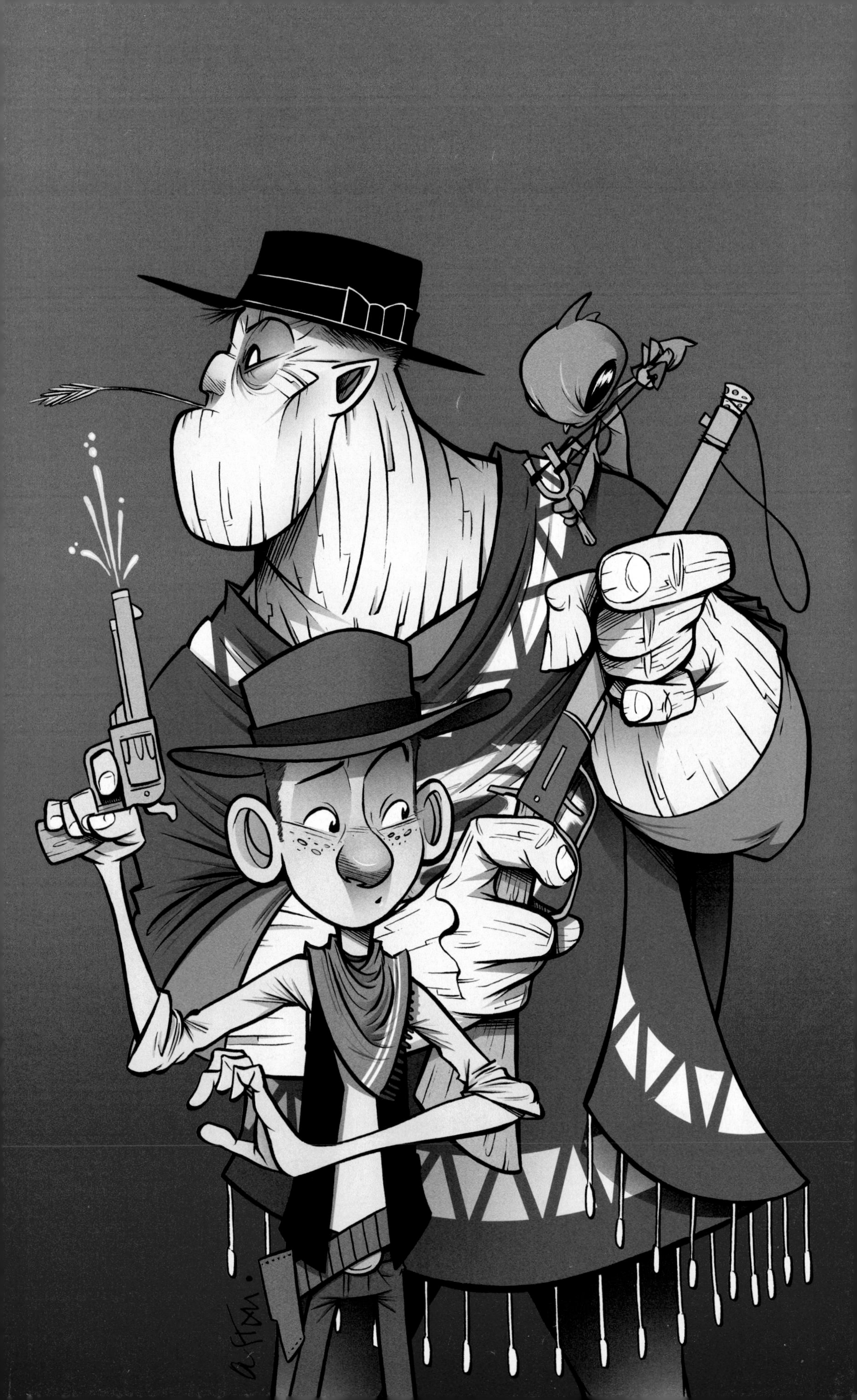

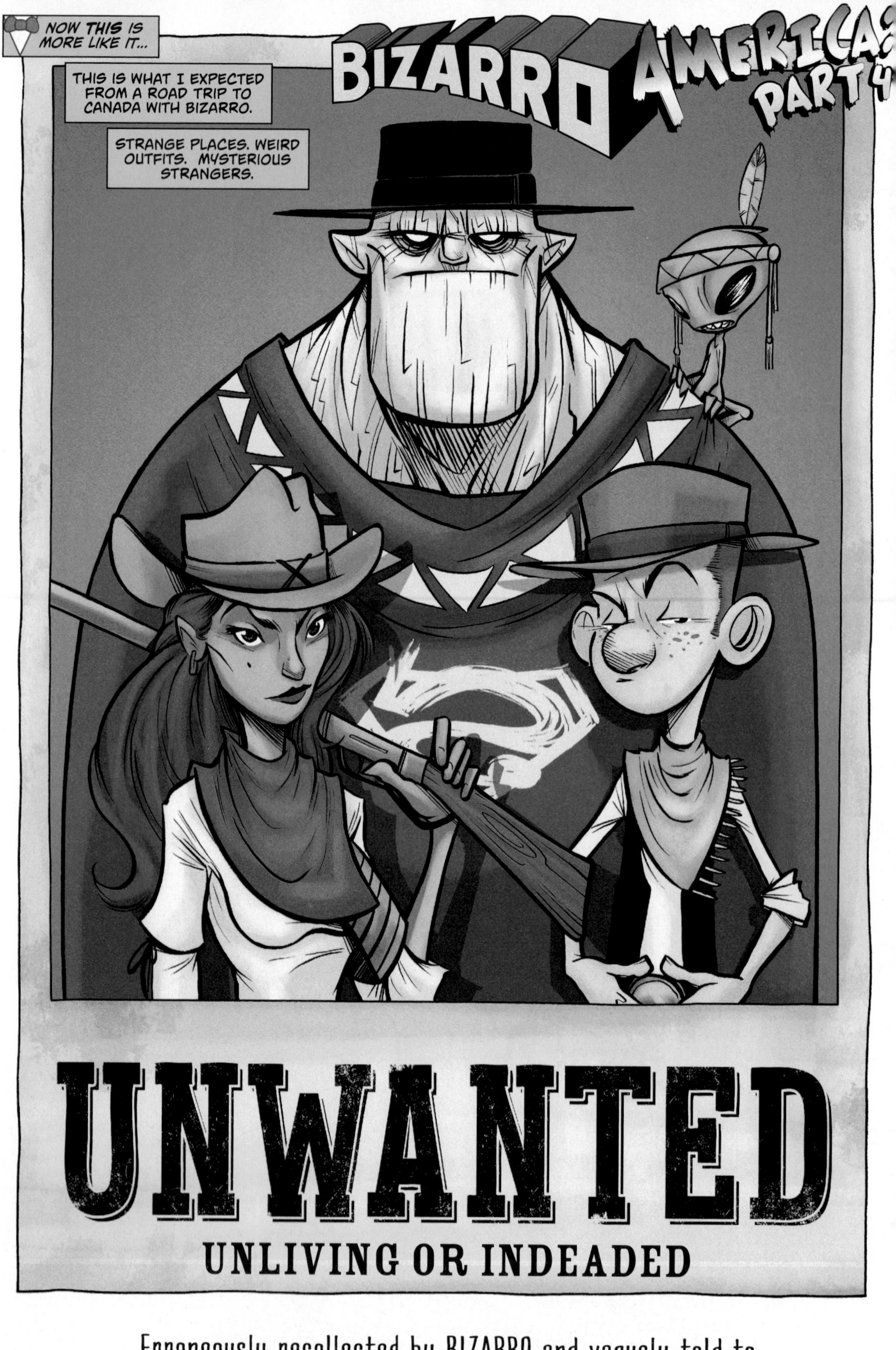
NOW THIS IS MORE LIKE IT...
THIS IS WHAT I EXPECTED FROM A ROAD TRIP TO CANADA WITH BIZARRO.
STRANGE PLACES. WEIRD OUTFITS. MYSTERIOUS STRANGERS.
BIZARRO AMERICA: PART 4
UNWANTED
UNLIVING OR INDEADED

Erroneously recollected by BIZARRO and vaguely told to
HEATH CORSON (WRITER) and GUSTAVO DUARTE (ARTIST/COVER ARTIST)
at the bottom of a coal mine over two cans and a length of string.
GUEST ARTISTS-FÁBIO MOON & GABRIEL BÁ LETTERIST-TOM NAPOLITANO COLORIST-PETE PANTAZIS

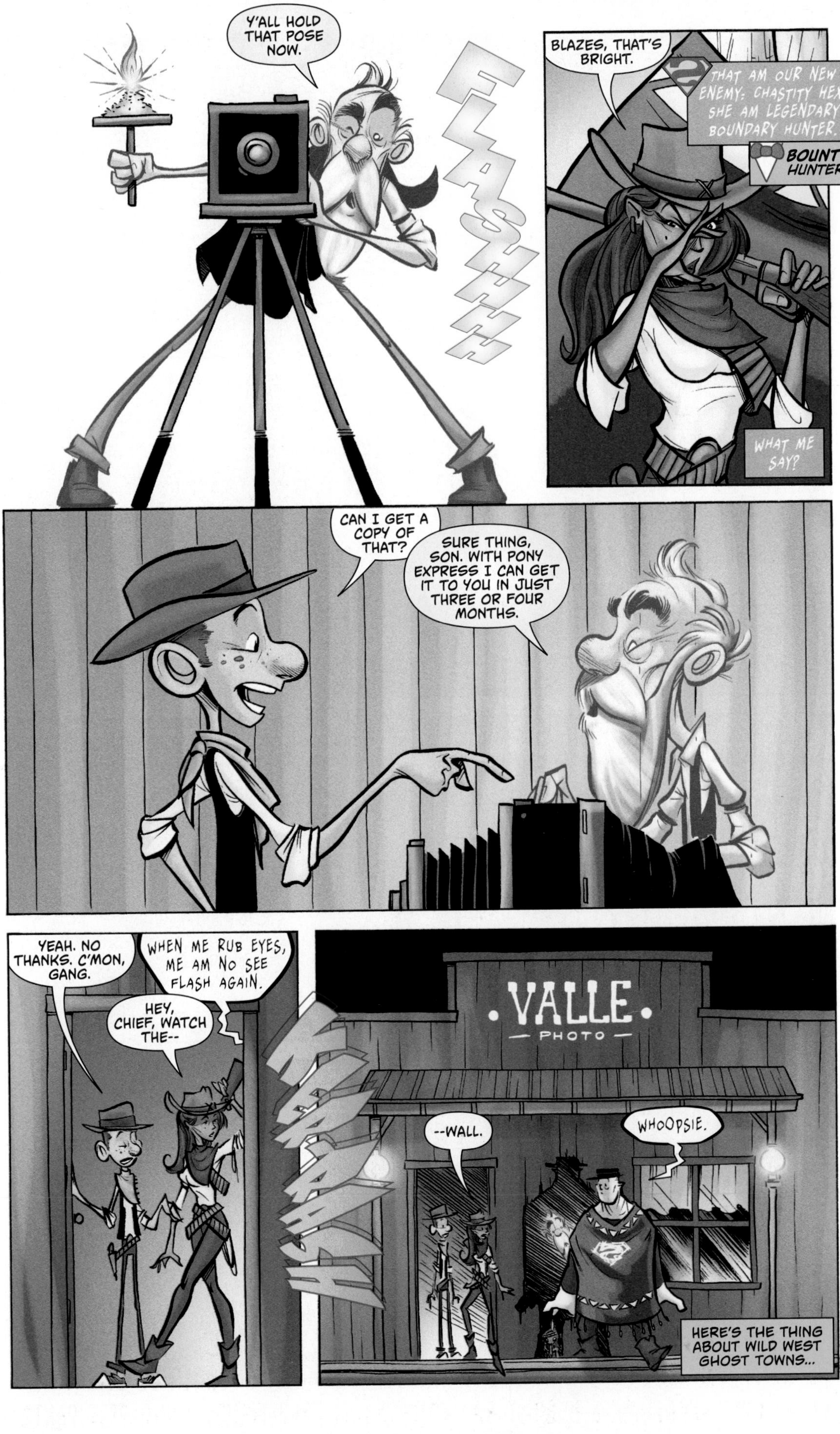
Y'ALL HOLD THAT POSE NOW.
FLASHHHHH
BLAZES, THAT'S BRIGHT.
THAT AM OUR NEW ENEMY: CHASTITY HEX. SHE AM LEGENDARY BOUNDARY HUNTER.
BOUNTY HUNTER.
WHAT ME SAY?
CAN I GET A COPY OF THAT?
SURE THING, SON. WITH PONY EXPRESS I CAN GET IT TO YOU IN JUST THREE OR FOUR MONTHS.
YEAH. NO THANKS. C'MON, GANG.
WHEN ME RUB EYES, ME AM NO SEE FLASH AGAIN.
HEY, CHIEF, WATCH THE--
VALLE
PHOTO
--WALL.
WHOOPSIE.
HERE'S THE THING ABOUT WILD WEST GHOST TOWNS...

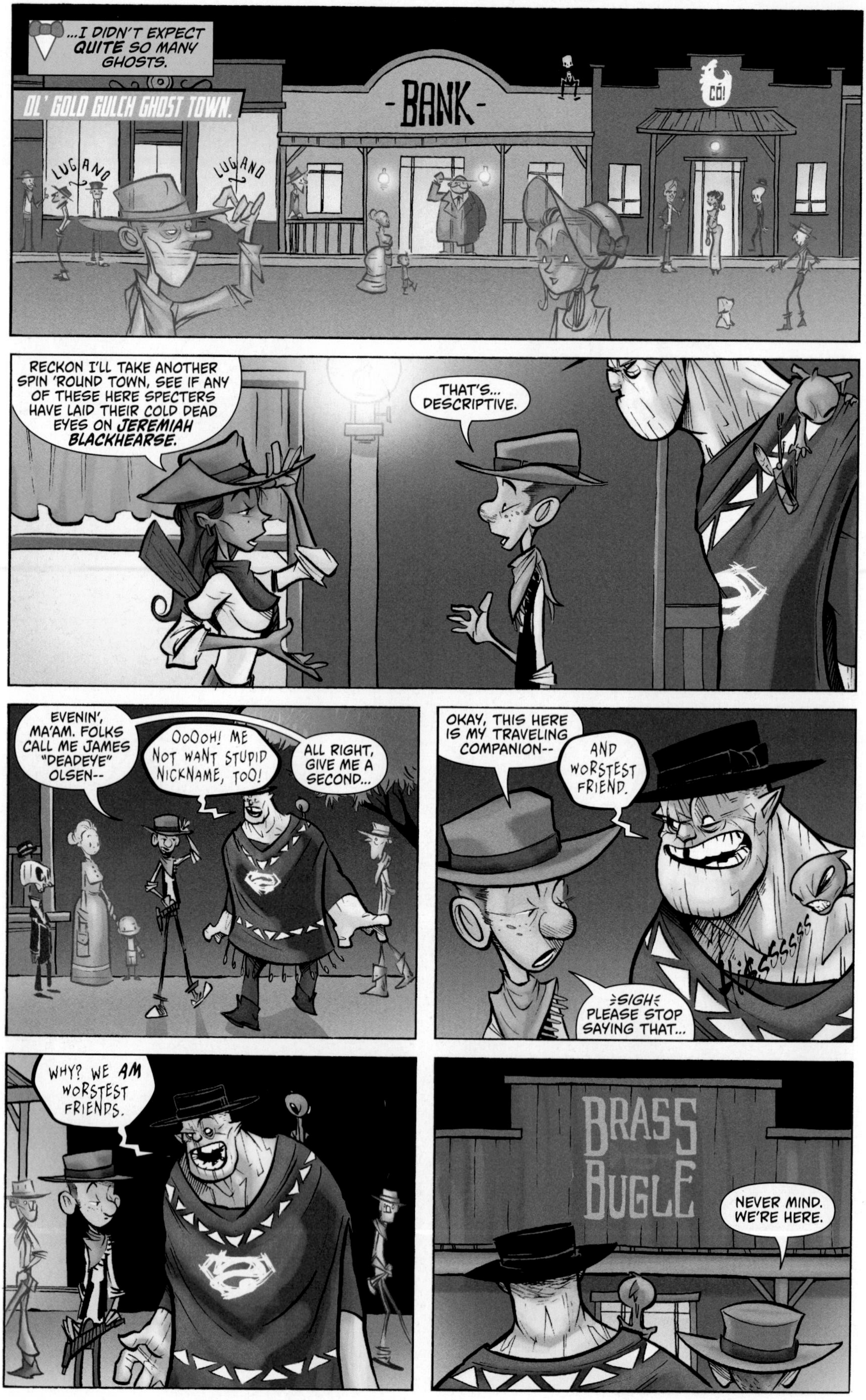
...I DIDN'T EXPECT QUITE SO MANY GHOSTS.
OL' GOLD GULCH GHOST TOWN.
BANK
LUGANO
LUGANO
RECKON I'LL TAKE ANOTHER SPIN 'ROUND TOWN, SEE IF ANY OF THESE HERE SPECTERS HAVE LAID THEIR COLD DEAD EYES ON JEREMIAH BLACKHEARSE.
THAT'S... DESCRIPTIVE.
EVENIN', MA'AM. FOLKS CALL ME JAMES "DEADEYE" OLSEN--
OOOOH! ME NOT WANT STUPID NICKNAME, TOO!
ALL RIGHT, GIVE ME A SECOND...
OKAY, THIS HERE IS MY TRAVELING COMPANION--
AND WORSTEST FRIEND.
HISSSSSS
SIGH PLEASE STOP SAYING THAT...
WHY? WE AM WORSTEST FRIENDS.
BRASS BUGLE
NEVER MIND. WE'RE HERE.

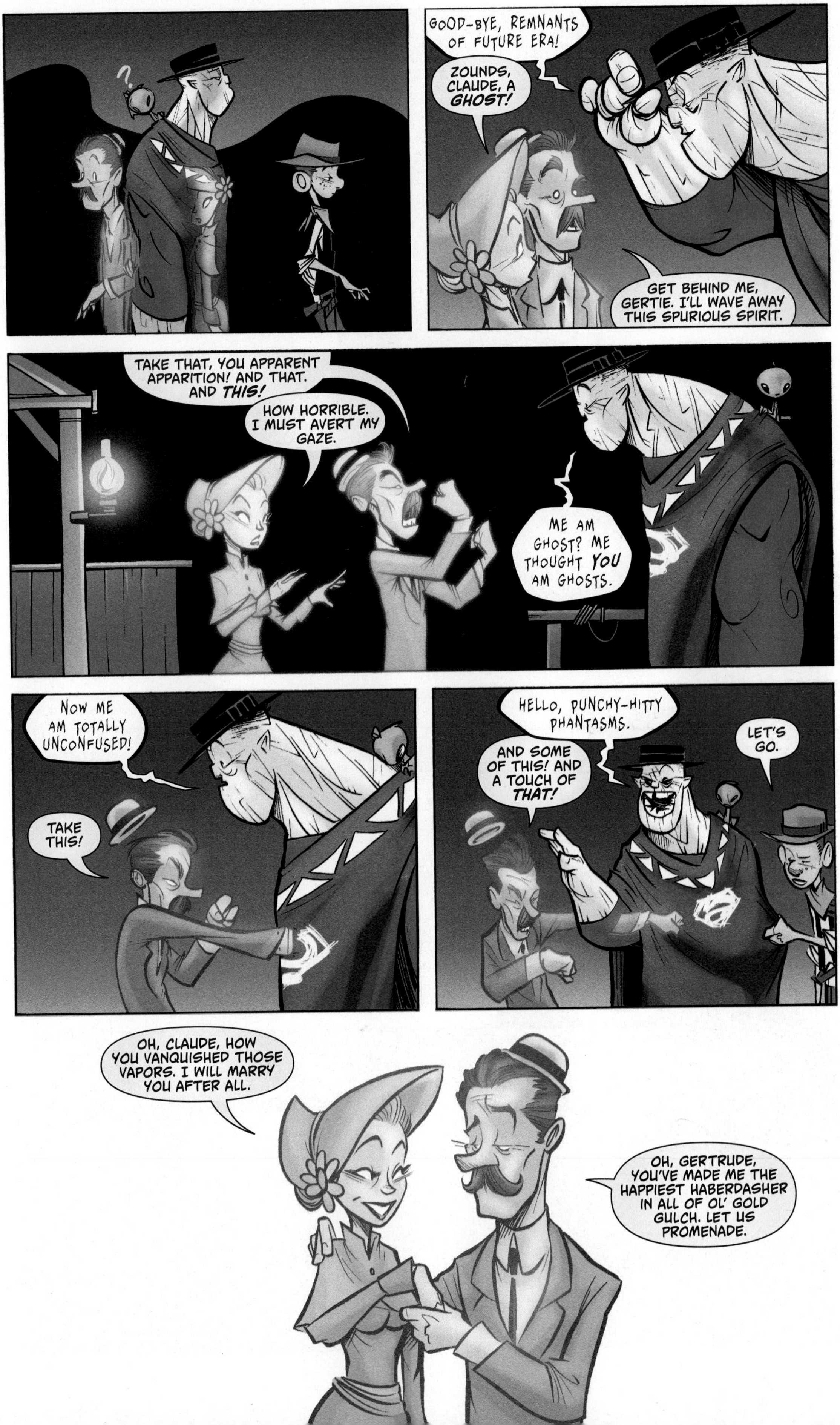
?
GOOD-BYE, REMNANTS OF FUTURE ERA!
ZOUNDS, CLAUDE, A GHOST!
GET BEHIND ME, GERTIE. I'LL WAVE AWAY THIS SPURIOUS SPIRIT.
TAKE THAT, YOU APPARENT APPARITION! AND THAT. AND THIS!
HOW HORRIBLE. I MUST AVERT MY GAZE.
ME AM GHOST? ME THOUGHT YOU AM GHOSTS.
NOW ME AM TOTALLY UNCONFUSED!
TAKE THIS!
HELLO, PUNCHY-HITTY PHANTASMS.
AND SOME OF THIS! AND A TOUCH OF THAT!
LET'S GO.
OH, CLAUDE, HOW YOU VANQUISHED THOSE VAPORS. I WILL MARRY YOU AFTER ALL.
OH, GERTRUDE, YOU'VE MADE ME THE HAPPIEST HABERDASHER IN ALL OF OL' GOLD GULCH. LET US PROMENADE.

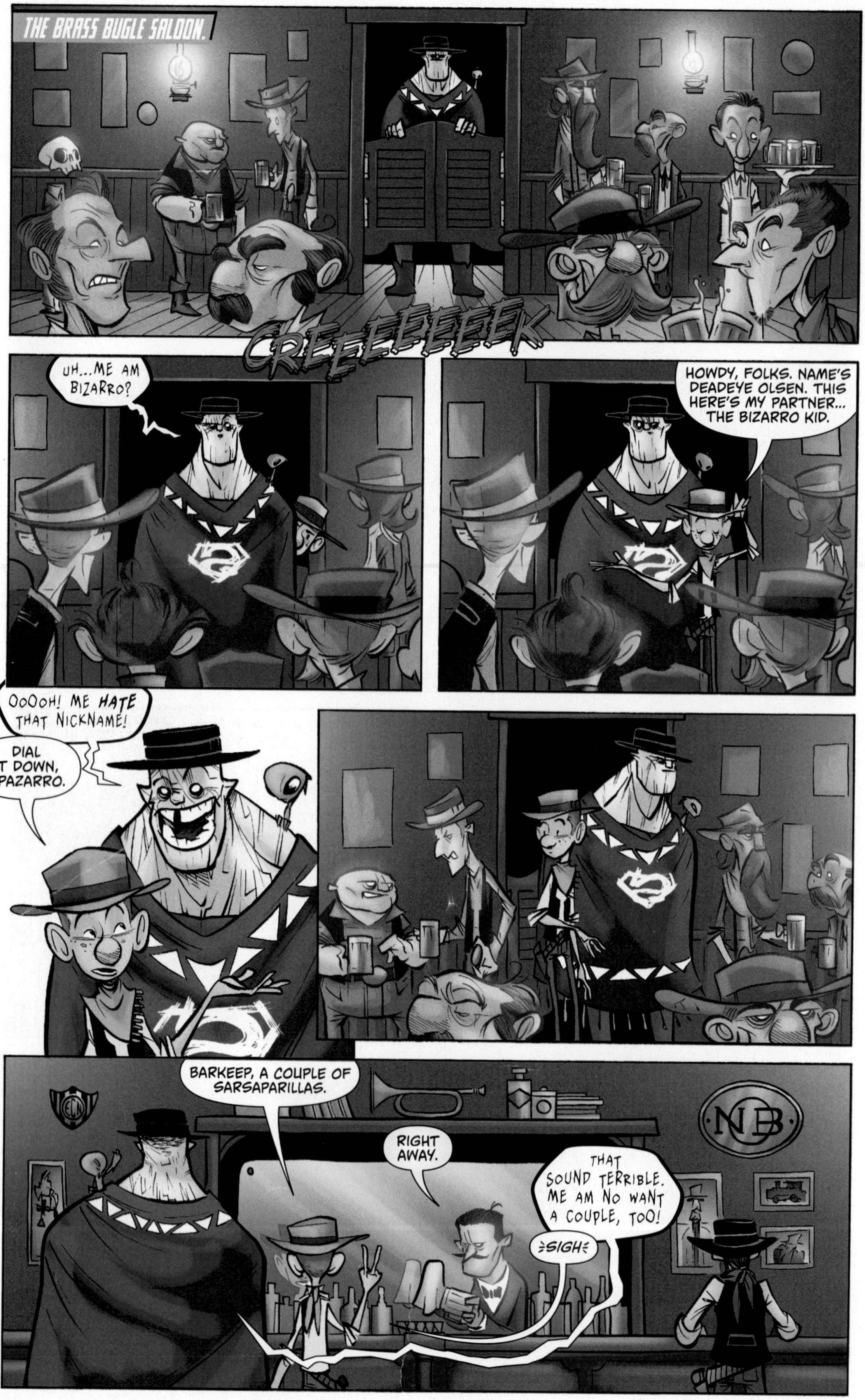
THE BRASS BUGLE SALOON.
CREEEEEEEEK
UH...ME AM BIZARRO?
HOWDY, FOLKS. NAME'S DEADEYE OLSEN. THIS HERE'S MY PARTNER... THE BIZARRO KID.
OOOOH! ME HATE THAT NICKNAME!
DIAL IT DOWN, SPAZARRO.
BARKEEP, A COUPLE OF SARSAPARILLAS.
RIGHT AWAY.
THAT SOUND TERRIBLE. ME AM NO WANT A COUPLE, TOO!
SIGH

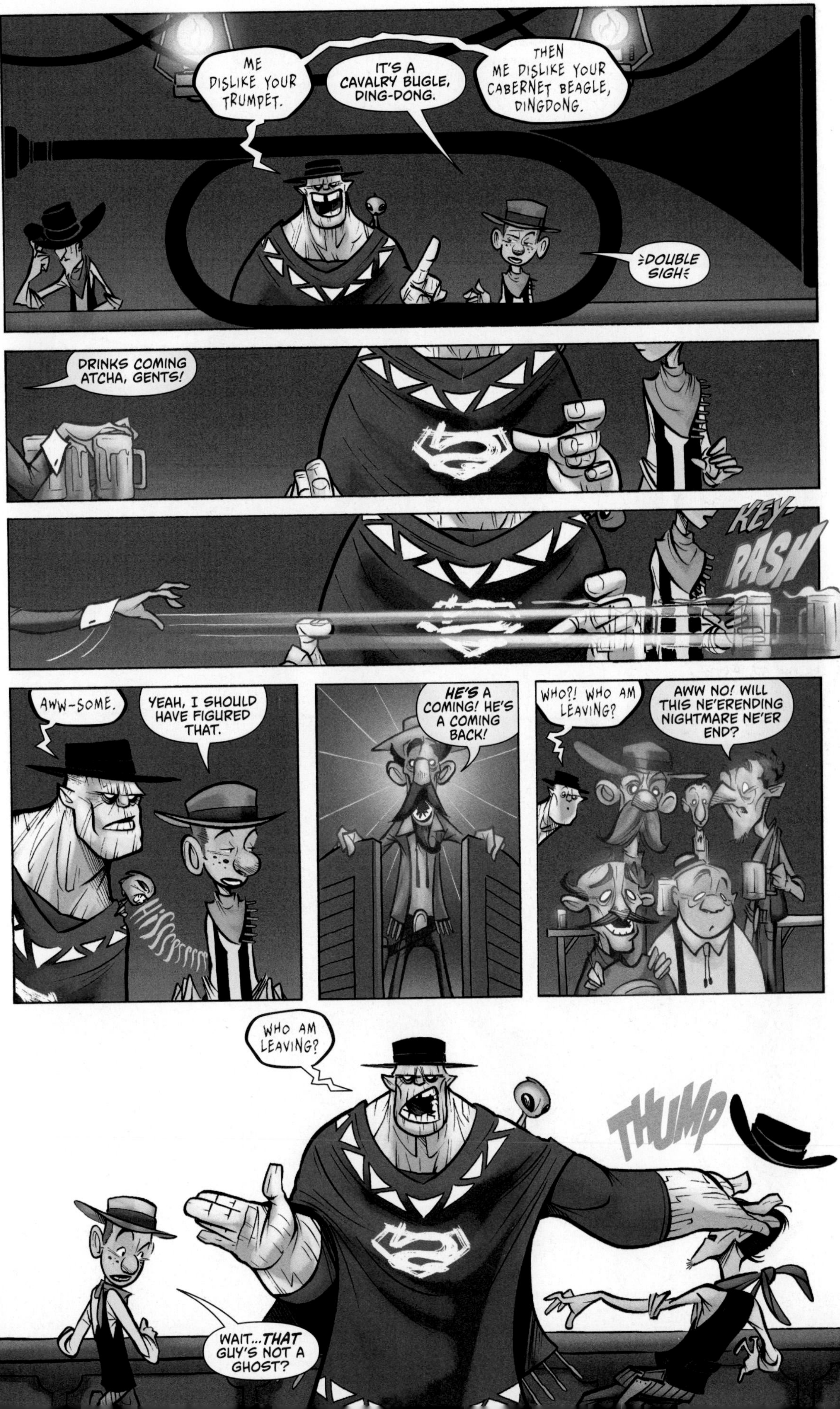
ME DISLIKE YOUR TRUMPET.
IT'S A CAVALRY BUGLE, DING-DONG.
THEN ME DISLIKE YOUR CABERNET BEAGLE, DINGDONG.
DOUBLE SIGH
DRINKS COMING ATCHA, GENTS!
KEY-RASH
AWW-SOME.
YEAH, I SHOULD HAVE FIGURED THAT.
HISSSSSSSS
HE'S A COMING! HE'S A COMING BACK!
WHO?! WHO AM LEAVING?
AWW NO! WILL THIS NE'ERENDING NIGHTMARE NE'ER END?
WHO AM LEAVING?
THUMP
WAIT... THAT GUY'S NOT A GHOST?

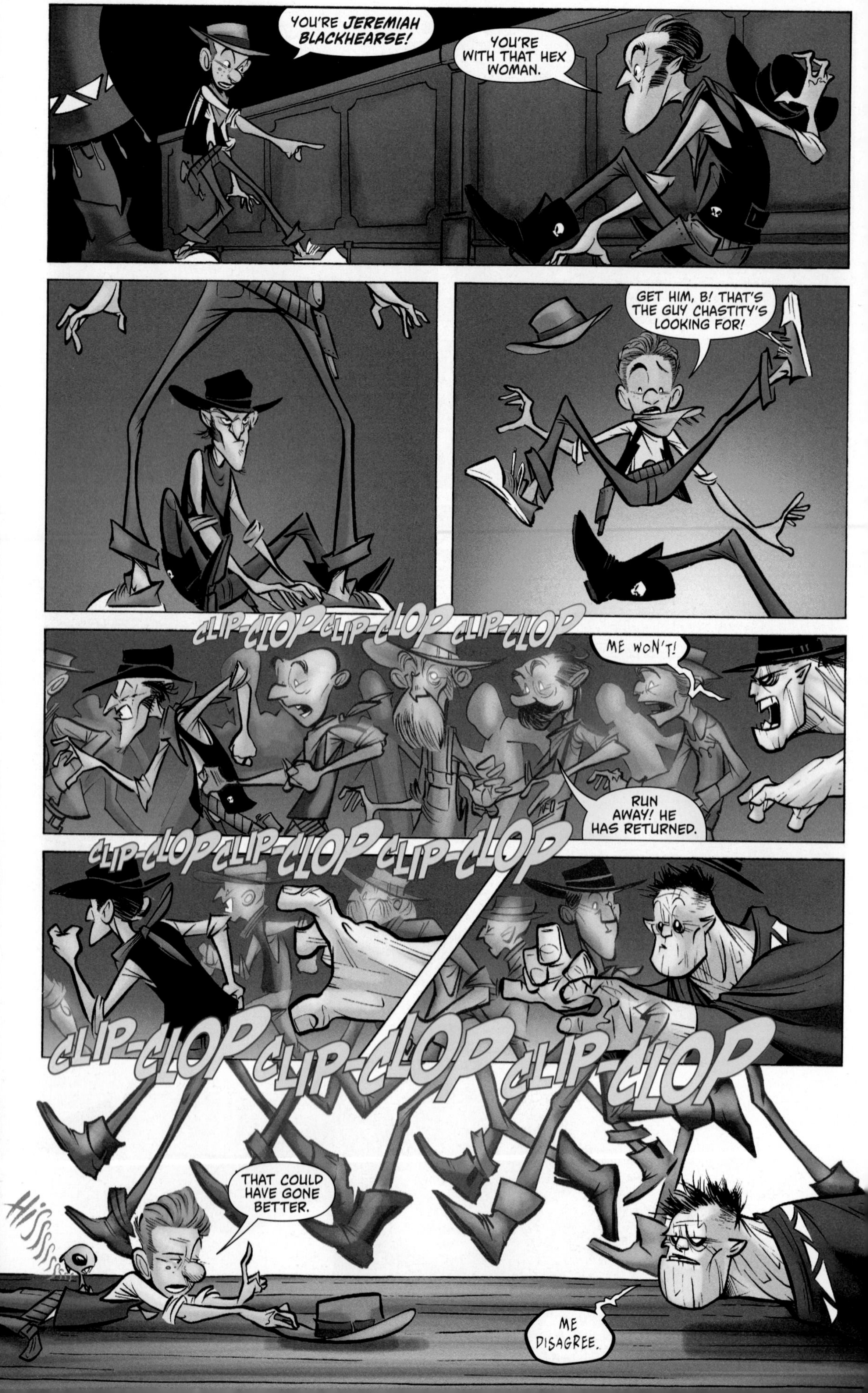
YOU'RE JEREMIAH BLACKHEARSE!
YOU'RE WITH THAT HEX WOMAN.
GET HIM, B! THAT'S THE GUY CHASTITY'S LOOKING FOR!
CLIP-CLOP CLIP-CLOP CLIP-CLOP
ME WON'T!
RUN AWAY! HE HAS RETURNED.
CLIP-CLOP CLIP-CLOP CLIP-CLOP
CLIP-CLOP CLIP-CLOP CLIP-CLOP
HISSSSSSS
THAT COULD HAVE GONE BETTER.
ME DISAGREE.

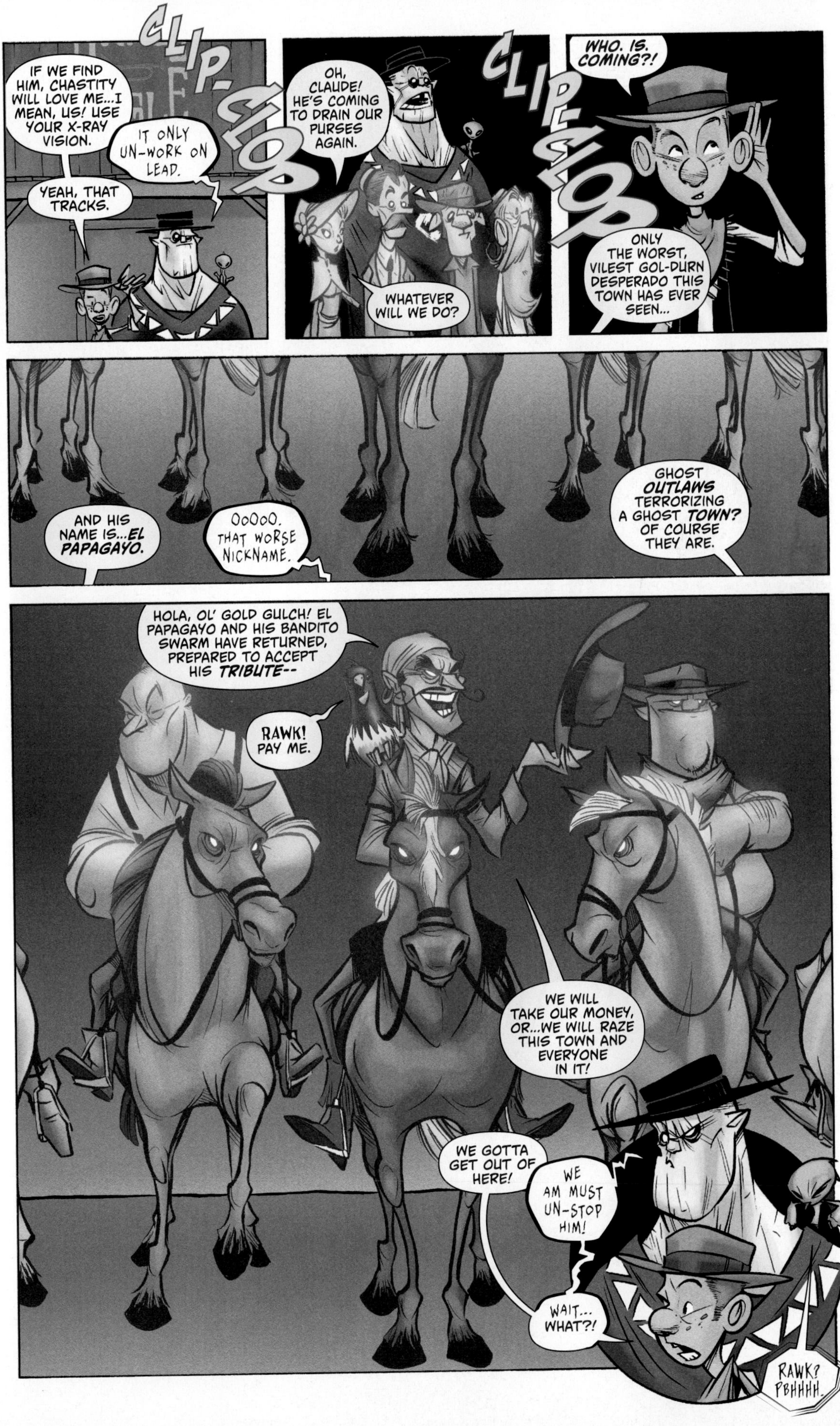
CLIP-CLOP
IF WE FIND HIM, CHASTITY WILL LOVE ME...I MEAN, US! USE YOUR X-RAY VISION.
IT ONLY UN-WORK ON LEAD.
YEAH, THAT TRACKS.
OH, CLAUDE! HE'S COMING TO DRAIN OUR PURSES AGAIN.
WHATEVER WILL WE DO?
CLIP-CLOP
WHO. IS. COMING?!
ONLY THE WORST, VILEST GOL-DURN DESPERADO THIS TOWN HAS EVER SEEN...
AND HIS NAME IS...EL PAPAGAYO.
OOOOO. THAT WORSE NICKNAME.
GHOST OUTLAWS TERRORIZING A GHOST TOWN? OF COURSE THEY ARE.
HOLA, OL' GOLD GULCH! EL PAPAGAYO AND HIS BANDITO SWARM HAVE RETURNED, PREPARED TO ACCEPT HIS TRIBUTE--
RAWK! PAY ME.
WE WILL TAKE OUR MONEY, OR...WE WILL RAZE THIS TOWN AND EVERYONE IN IT!
WE GOTTA GET OUT OF HERE!
WE AM MUST UN-STOP HIM!
WAIT... WHAT?!
RAWK? PBHHHH.

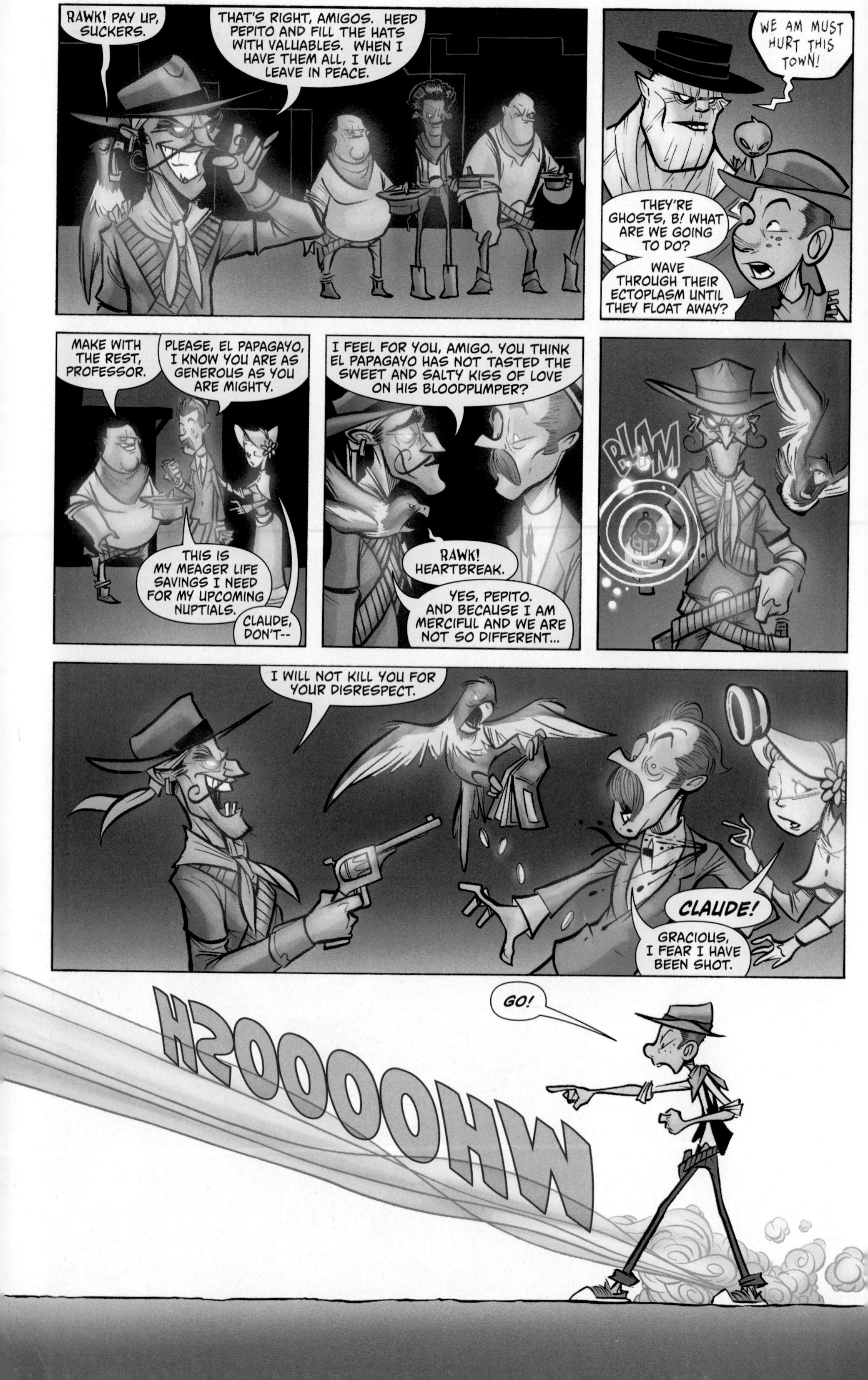
RAWK! PAY UP, SUCKERS.
THAT'S RIGHT, AMIGOS. HEED PEPITO AND FILL THE HATS WITH VALUABLES. WHEN I HAVE THEM ALL, I WILL LEAVE IN PEACE.
WE AM MUST HURT THIS TOWN!
THEY'RE GHOSTS, B! WHAT ARE WE GOING TO DO?
WAVE THROUGH THEIR ECTOPLASM UNTIL THEY FLOAT AWAY?
MAKE WITH THE REST, PROFESSOR.
PLEASE, EL PAPAGAYO, I KNOW YOU ARE AS GENEROUS AS YOU ARE MIGHTY.
THIS IS MY MEAGER LIFE SAVINGS I NEED FOR MY UPCOMING NUPTIALS.
CLAUDE, DON'T--
I FEEL FOR YOU, AMIGO. YOU THINK EL PAPAGAYO HAS NOT TASTED THE SWEET AND SALTY KISS OF LOVE ON HIS BLOODPUMPER?
RAWK! HEARTBREAK.
YES, PEPITO. AND BECAUSE I AM MERCIFUL AND WE ARE NOT SO DIFFERENT...
BLAM
I WILL NOT KILL YOU FOR YOUR DISRESPECT.
CLAUDE!
GRACIOUS, I FEAR I HAVE BEEN SHOT.
GO!
WHOOOOOSH

YOU AM CONTINUING THIS RIGHT NOW, EL PAPAGUANO!
WHAT DID THE GRINGO CALL ME?
RAWK! BAT POOP.
THEN I HEARD WHAT I THOUGHT I HEARD. SHOOT HIM DOWN.
HISSSSSS
RAWK! NICE TRY.
YOU AVOID DEADEYE OLSEN AND THE BIZARRO KID.
NOW WE AM HAVE SHOWUP, EL PAMPLEMOUSSE.

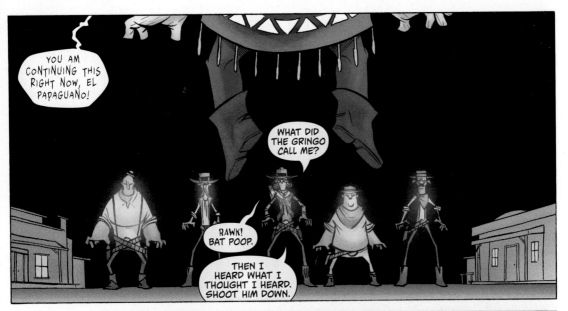

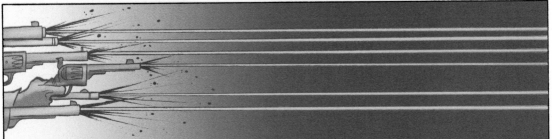

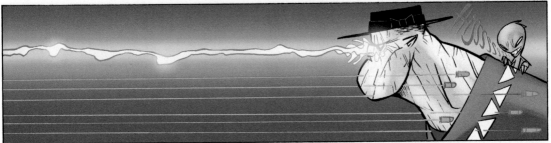

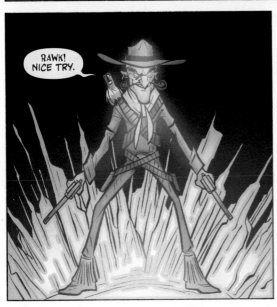

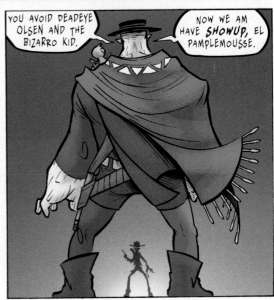

IT IS *PAPAGAYO*, MONSTRUO. I WILL CARVE IT ON YOUR TOMBSTONE FOR YOU!

RAWK! DEAD MEAT WALKIN'.

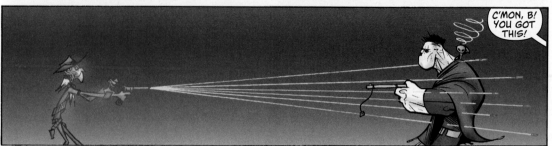

C'MON, B! YOU GOT THIS!

CLICK!

ME CAN'T KEEP THIS UP ALL NIGHT.

YOU'D HAVE TO, GIGANTE. IT SEEMS WE ARE EVENLY MATCHED.

RAWK! CHECKMATE.

BUT THERE IS ONE THING I HAVE NOT YET TRIED...

HISS?

ERK!

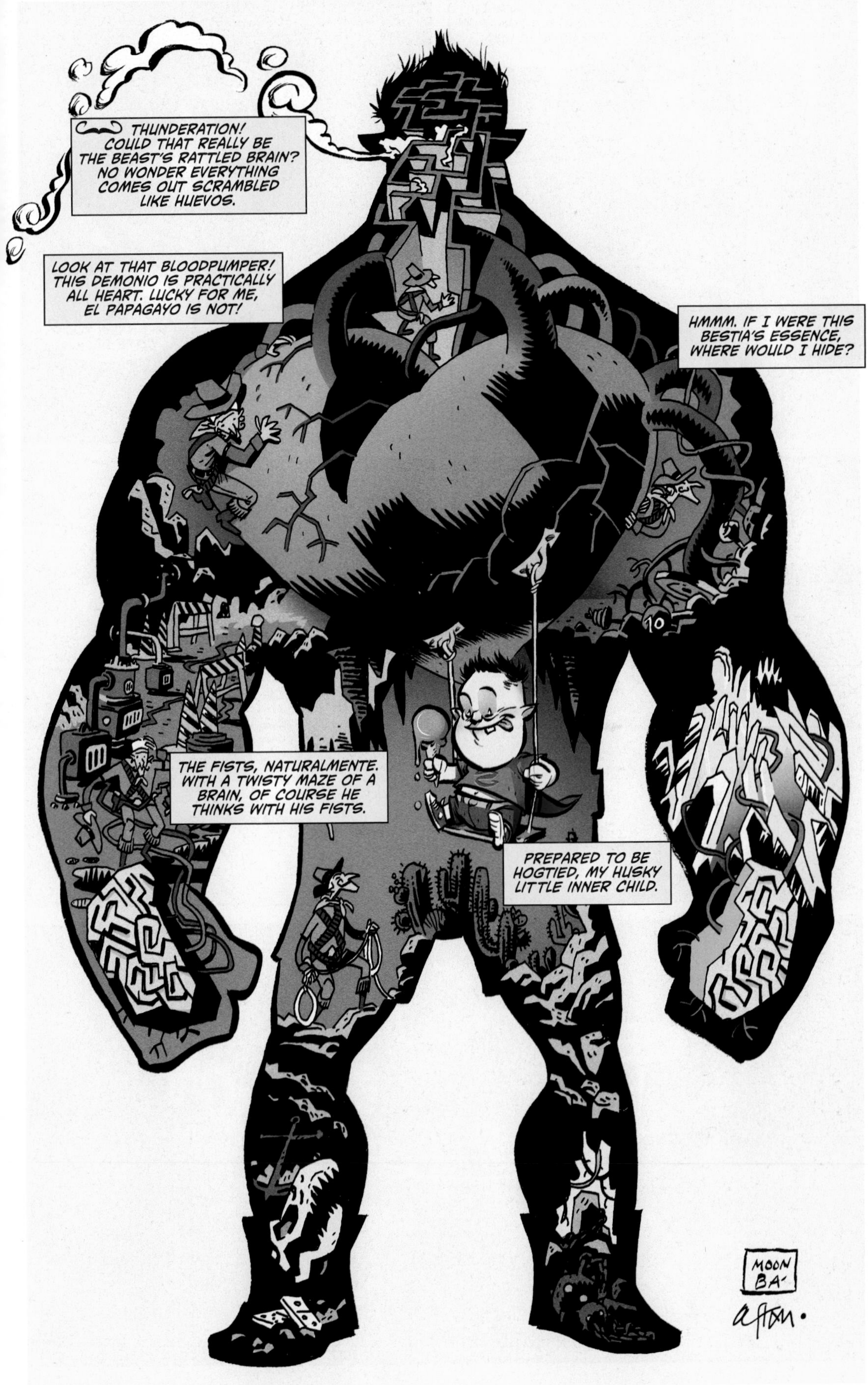
THUNDERATION! COULD THAT REALLY BE THE BEAST'S RATTLED BRAIN? NO WONDER EVERYTHING COMES OUT SCRAMBLED LIKE HUEVOS.
LOOK AT THAT BLOODPUMPER! THIS DEMONIO IS PRACTICALLY ALL HEART. LUCKY FOR ME, EL PAPAGAYO IS NOT!
HMMM. IF I WERE THIS BESTIA'S ESSENCE, WHERE WOULD I HIDE?
THE FISTS, NATURALMENTE. WITH A TWISTY MAZE OF A BRAIN, OF COURSE HE THINKS WITH HIS FISTS.
PREPARED TO BE HOGTIED, MY HUSKY LITTLE INNER CHILD.
10
MOON BA´

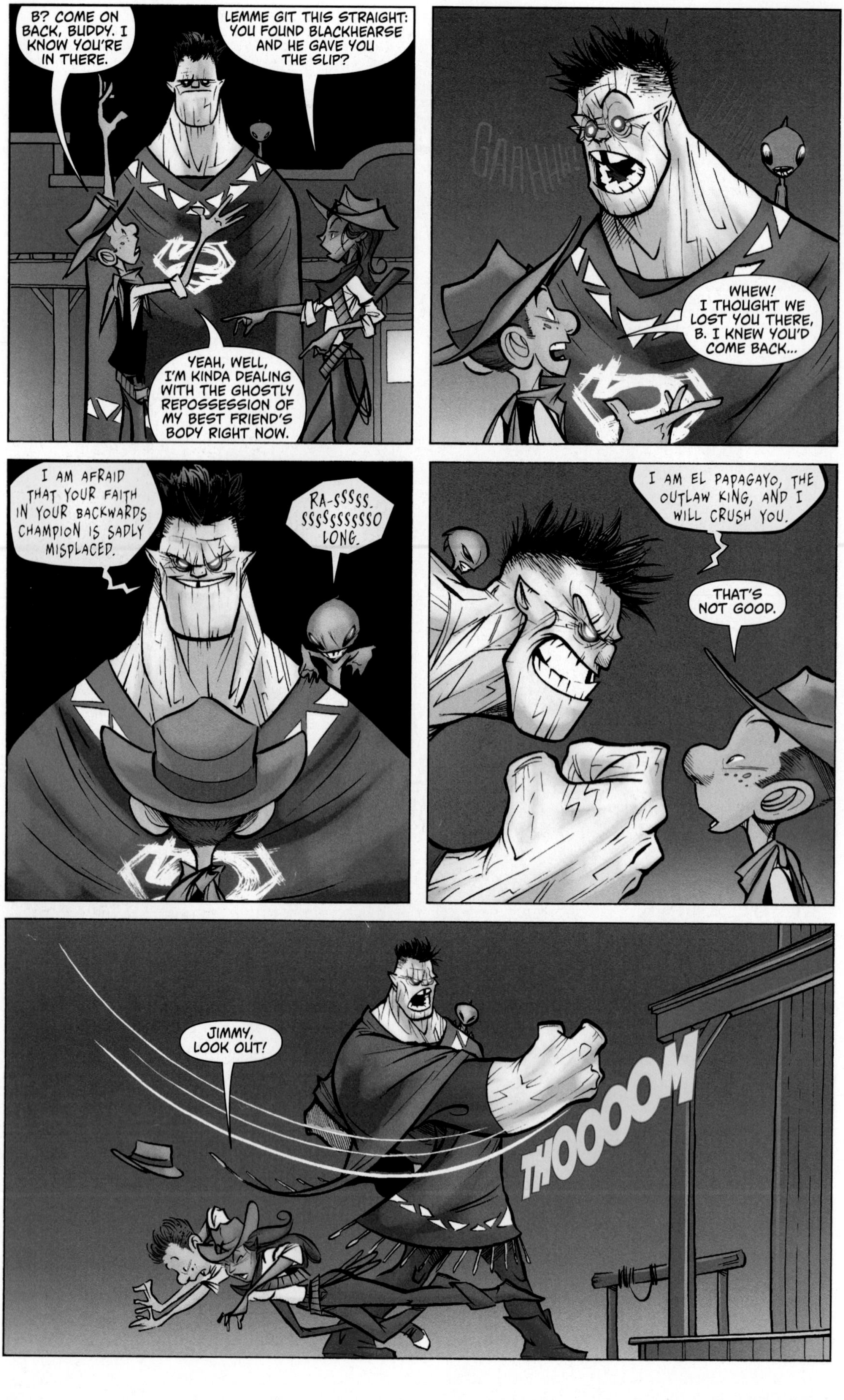
B? COME ON BACK, BUDDY. I KNOW YOU'RE IN THERE.
LEMME GIT THIS STRAIGHT: YOU FOUND BLACKHEARSE AND HE GAVE YOU THE SLIP?
YEAH, WELL, I'M KINDA DEALING WITH THE GHOSTLY REPOSSESSION OF MY BEST FRIEND'S BODY RIGHT NOW.
GAAHHH!
WHEW! I THOUGHT WE LOST YOU THERE, B. I KNEW YOU'D COME BACK...
I AM AFRAID THAT YOUR FAITH IN YOUR BACKWARDS CHAMPION IS SADLY MISPLACED.
RA-SSSSS. SSSSSSSSSSO LONG.
I AM EL PAPAGAYO, THE OUTLAW KING, AND I WILL CRUSH YOU.
THAT'S NOT GOOD.
JIMMY, LOOK OUT!
THOOOOM

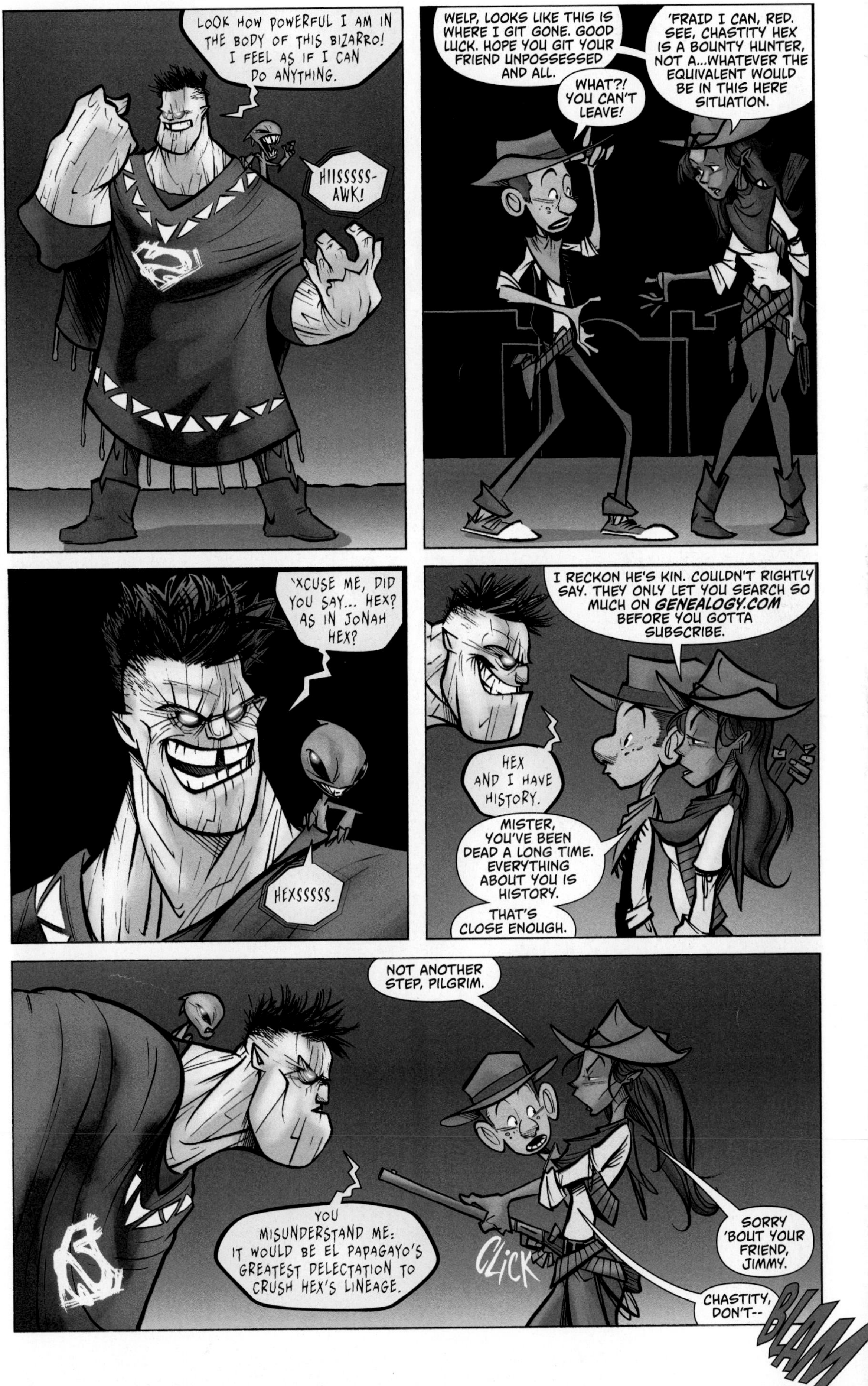
LOOK HOW POWERFUL I AM IN THE BODY OF THIS BIZARRO! I FEEL AS IF I CAN DO ANYTHING.
HIISSSSS-AWK!
WELP, LOOKS LIKE THIS IS WHERE I GIT GONE. GOOD LUCK. HOPE YOU GIT YOUR FRIEND UNPOSSESSED AND ALL.
WHAT?! YOU CAN'T LEAVE!
'FRAID I CAN, RED. SEE, CHASTITY HEX IS A BOUNTY HUNTER, NOT A...WHATEVER THE EQUIVALENT WOULD BE IN THIS HERE SITUATION.
'XCUSE ME, DID YOU SAY... HEX? AS IN JONAH HEX?
HEXSSSSS.
I RECKON HE'S KIN. COULDN'T RIGHTLY SAY. THEY ONLY LET YOU SEARCH SO MUCH ON GENEALOGY.COM BEFORE YOU GOTTA SUBSCRIBE.
HEX AND I HAVE HISTORY.
MISTER, YOU'VE BEEN DEAD A LONG TIME. EVERYTHING ABOUT YOU IS HISTORY.
THAT'S CLOSE ENOUGH.
NOT ANOTHER STEP, PILGRIM.
YOU MISUNDERSTAND ME: IT WOULD BE EL PAPAGAYO'S GREATEST DELECTATION TO CRUSH HEX'S LINEAGE.
CLICK
SORRY 'BOUT YOUR FRIEND, JIMMY.
CHASTITY, DON'T--
BLAM

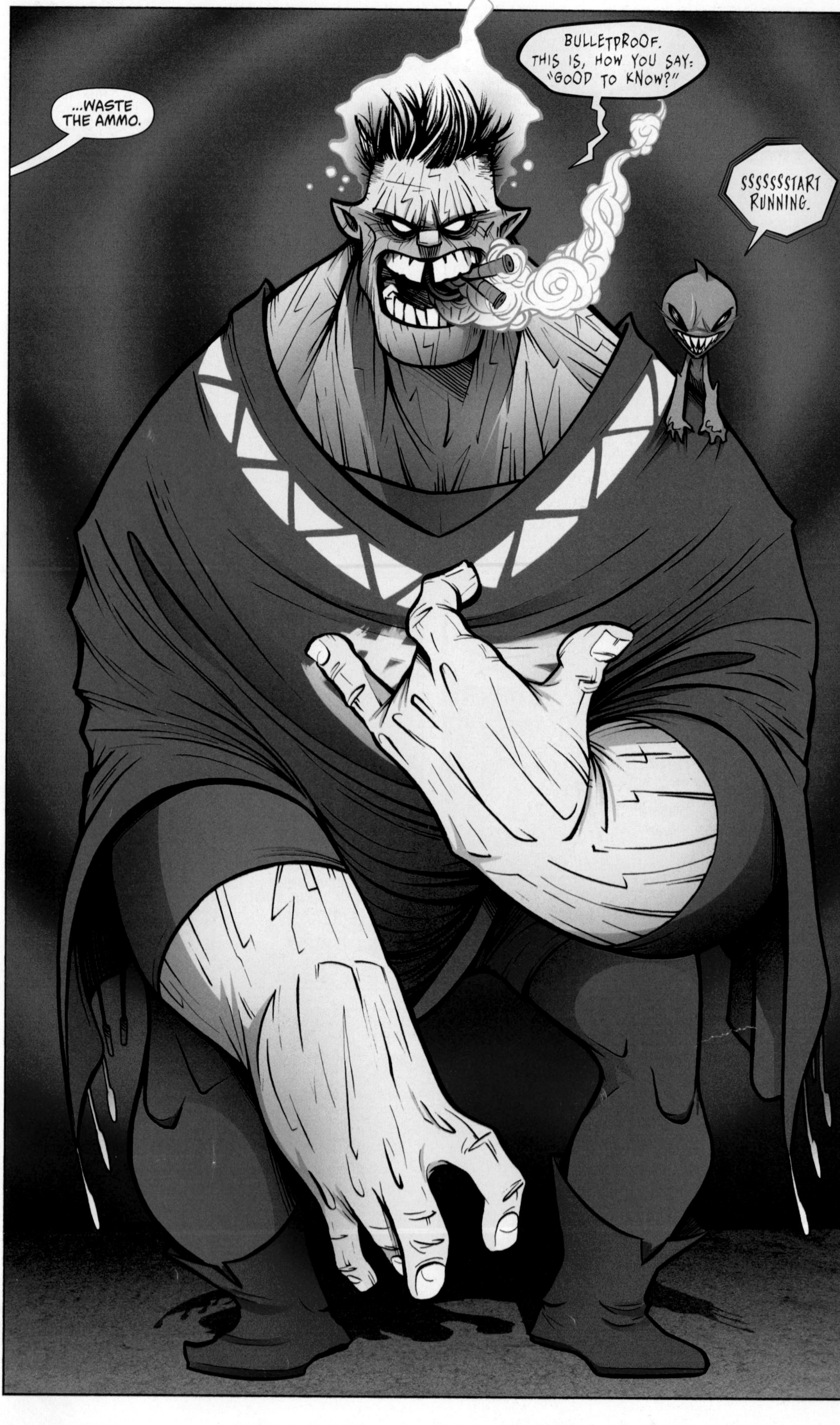
...WASTE THE AMMO.
BULLETPROOF. THIS IS, HOW YOU SAY: "GOOD TO KNOW?"
SSSSSSSTART RUNNING.

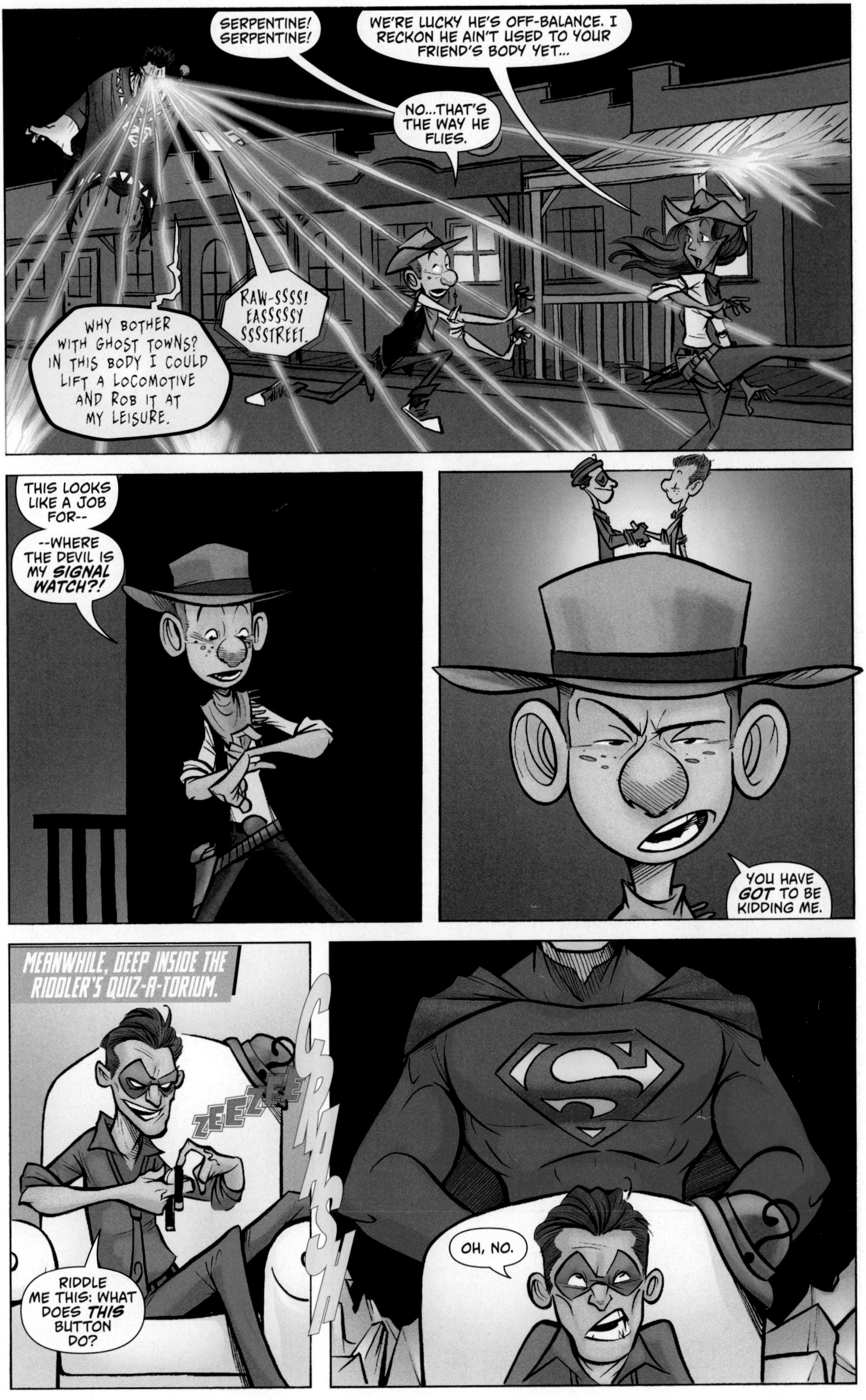
SERPENTINE! SERPENTINE!
WE'RE LUCKY HE'S OFF-BALANCE. I RECKON HE AIN'T USED TO YOUR FRIEND'S BODY YET...
NO...THAT'S THE WAY HE FLIES.
RAW-SSSS! EASSSSSY SSSSTREET.
WHY BOTHER WITH GHOST TOWNS? IN THIS BODY I COULD LIFT A LOCOMOTIVE AND ROB IT AT MY LEISURE.
THIS LOOKS LIKE A JOB FOR--
--WHERE THE DEVIL IS MY SIGNAL WATCH?!
YOU HAVE GOT TO BE KIDDING ME.
MEANWHILE, DEEP INSIDE THE RIDDLER'S QUIZ-A-TORIUM.
ZEEZEEE
RIDDLE ME THIS: WHAT DOES THIS BUTTON DO?
CRASH
OH, NO.

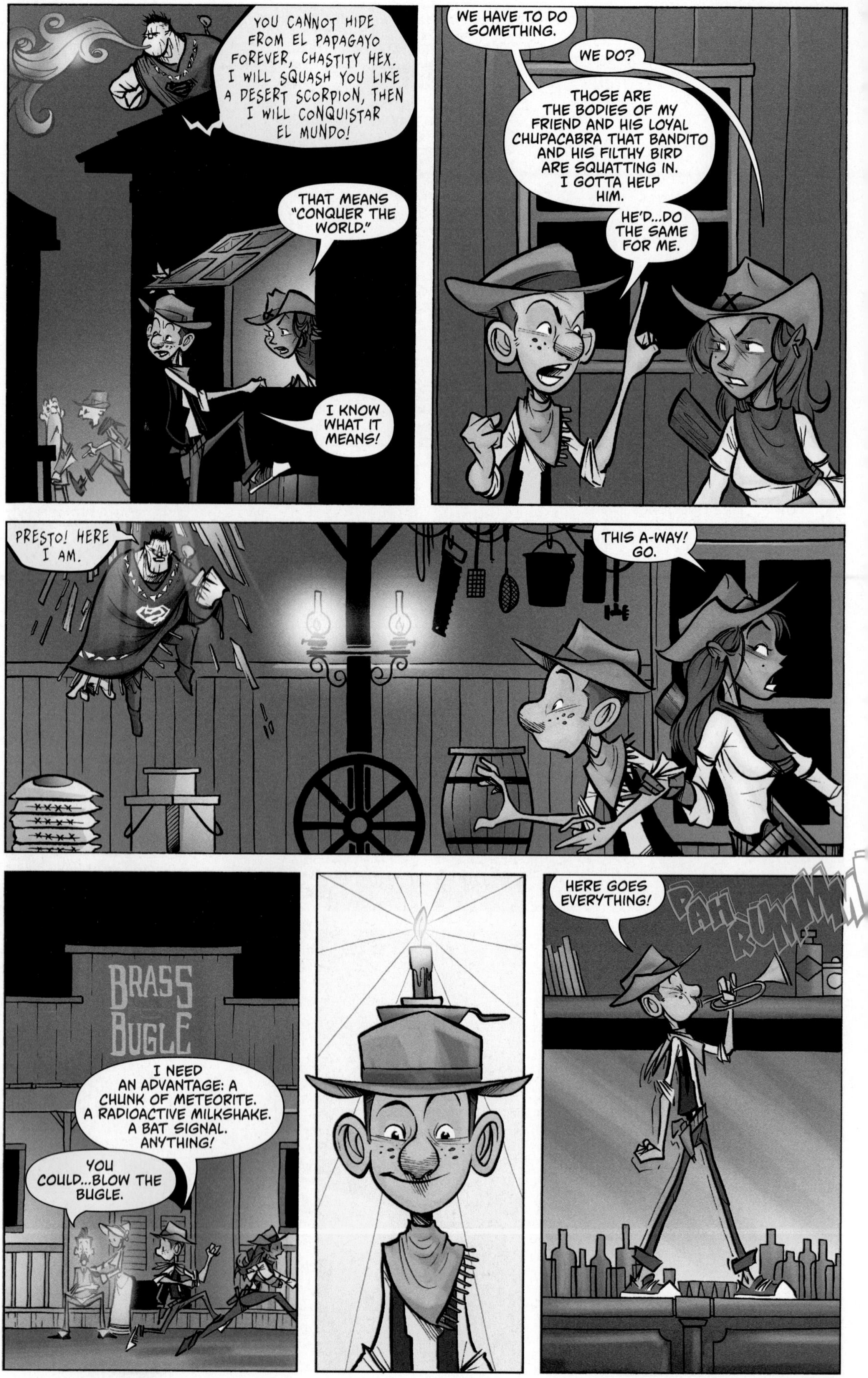
YOU CANNOT HIDE FROM EL PAPAGAYO FOREVER, CHASTITY HEX. I WILL SQUASH YOU LIKE A DESERT SCORPION, THEN I WILL CONQUISTAR EL MUNDO!
THAT MEANS "CONQUER THE WORLD."
I KNOW WHAT IT MEANS!
WE HAVE TO DO SOMETHING.
WE DO?
THOSE ARE THE BODIES OF MY FRIEND AND HIS LOYAL CHUPACABRA THAT BANDITO AND HIS FILTHY BIRD ARE SQUATTING IN. I GOTTA HELP HIM.
HE'D...DO THE SAME FOR ME.
PRESTO! HERE I AM.
THIS A-WAY! GO.
BRASS BUGLE
I NEED AN ADVANTAGE: A CHUNK OF METEORITE. A RADIOACTIVE MILKSHAKE. A BAT SIGNAL. ANYTHING!
YOU COULD...BLOW THE BUGLE.
HERE GOES EVERYTHING!
PAH RUMMM

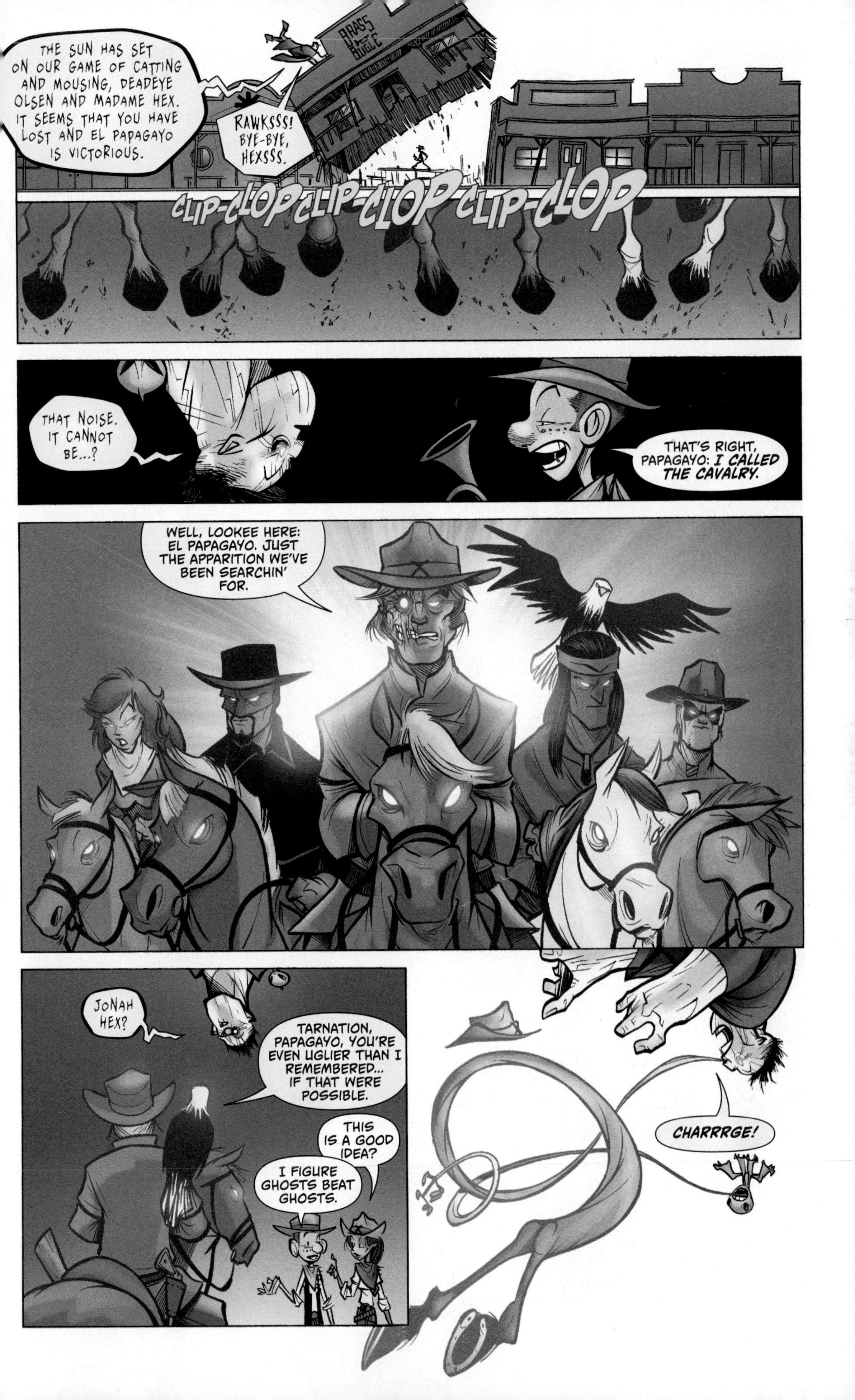
THE SUN HAS SET ON OUR GAME OF CATTING AND MOUSING, DEADEYE OLSEN AND MADAME HEX. IT SEEMS THAT YOU HAVE LOST AND EL PAPAGAYO IS VICTORIOUS.
RAWKSSS! BYE-BYE, HEXSSS.
BRASS BUGLE
CLIP-CLOP CLIP-CLOP CLIP-CLOP
THAT NOISE. IT CANNOT BE...?
THAT'S RIGHT, PAPAGAYO: I CALLED THE CAVALRY.
WELL, LOOKEE HERE: EL PAPAGAYO. JUST THE APPARITION WE'VE BEEN SEARCHIN' FOR.
JONAH HEX?
TARNATION, PAPAGAYO, YOU'RE EVEN UGLIER THAN I REMEMBERED... IF THAT WERE POSSIBLE.
THIS IS A GOOD IDEA?
I FIGURE GHOSTS BEAT GHOSTS.
CHARRRGE!

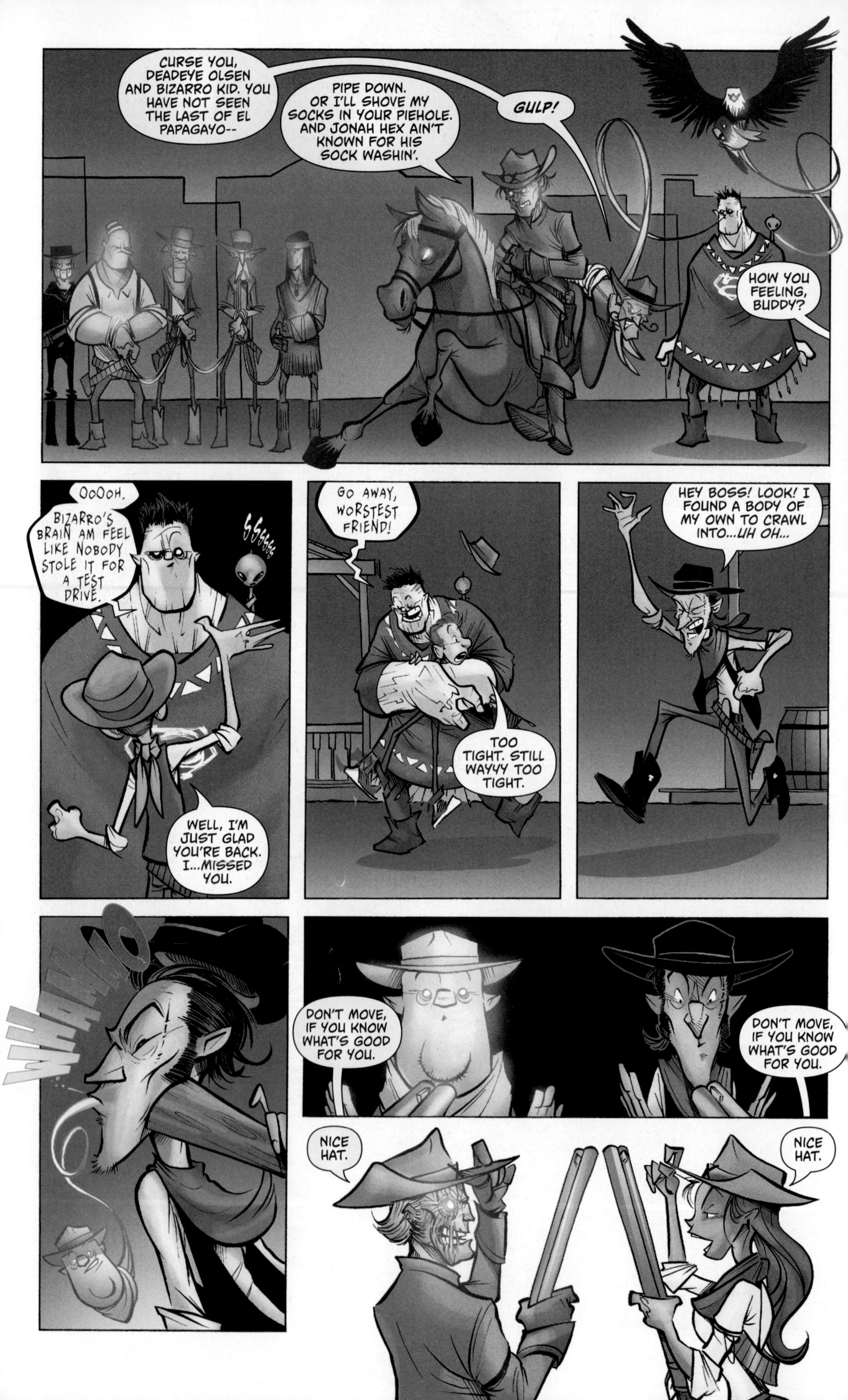
CURSE YOU, DEADEYE OLSEN AND BIZARRO KID. YOU HAVE NOT SEEN THE LAST OF EL PAPAGAYO--
PIPE DOWN. OR I'LL SHOVE MY SOCKS IN YOUR PIEHOLE. AND JONAH HEX AIN'T KNOWN FOR HIS SOCK WASHIN'.
GULP!
HOW YOU FEELING, BUDDY?
OOOOH.
BIZARRO'S BRAIN AM FEEL LIKE NOBODY STOLE IT FOR A TEST DRIVE.
SSSSSSS
WELL, I'M JUST GLAD YOU'RE BACK. I...MISSED YOU.
GO AWAY, WORSTEST FRIEND!
TOO TIGHT. STILL WAYYY TOO TIGHT.
HEY BOSS! LOOK! I FOUND A BODY OF MY OWN TO CRAWL INTO...UH OH...
WHAMO
DON'T MOVE, IF YOU KNOW WHAT'S GOOD FOR YOU.
DON'T MOVE, IF YOU KNOW WHAT'S GOOD FOR YOU.
NICE HAT.
NICE HAT.

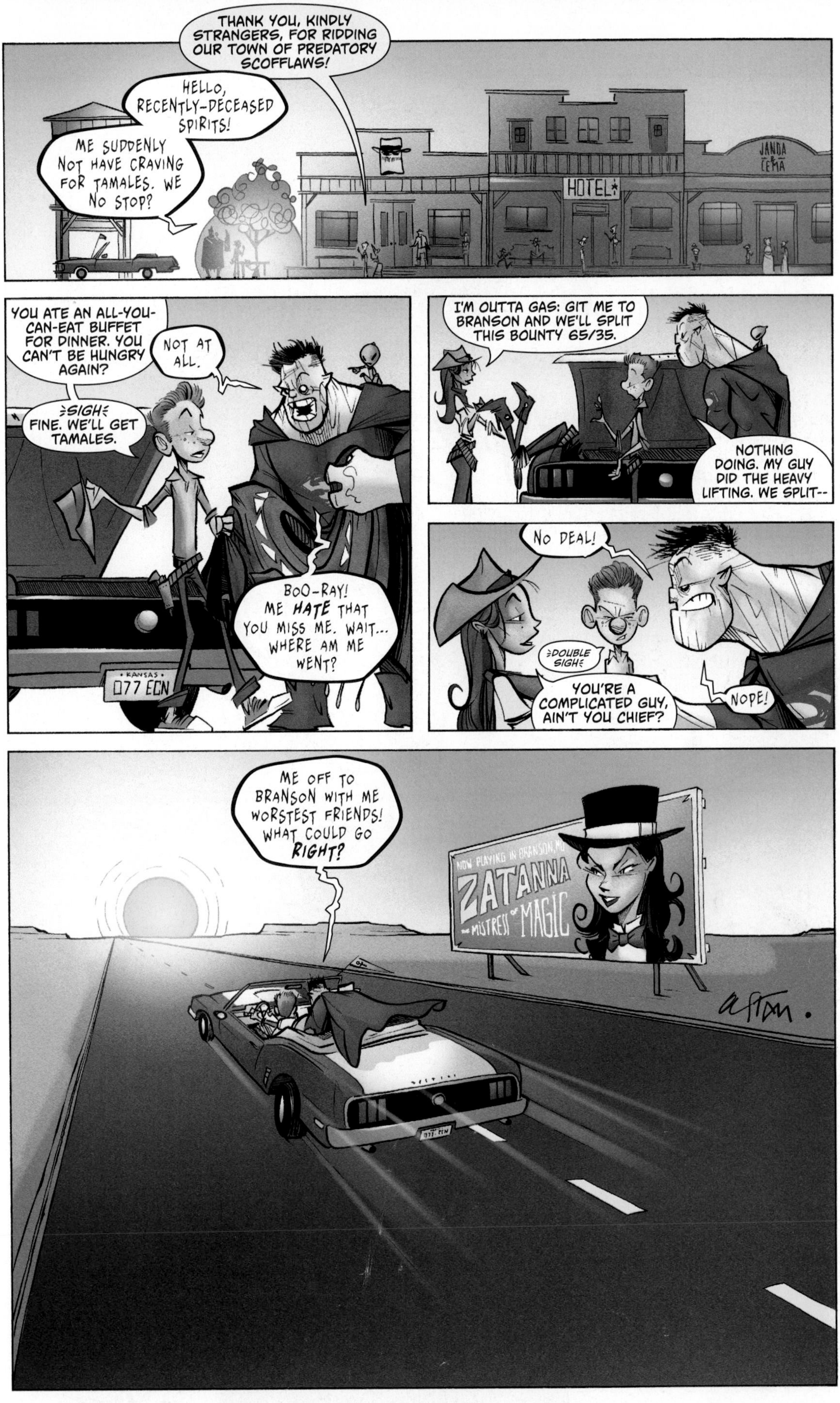
THANK YOU, KINDLY STRANGERS, FOR RIDDING OUR TOWN OF PREDATORY SCOFFLAWS!
HELLO, RECENTLY-DECEASED SPIRITS!
ME SUDDENLY NOT HAVE CRAVING FOR TAMALES. WE NO STOP?
HOTEL
YOU ATE AN ALL-YOU-CAN-EAT BUFFET FOR DINNER. YOU CAN'T BE HUNGRY AGAIN?
NOT AT ALL.
SIGH FINE. WE'LL GET TAMALES.
KANSAS
077 ECN
BOO-RAY! ME HATE THAT YOU MISS ME. WAIT... WHERE AM ME WENT?
I'M OUTTA GAS: GIT ME TO BRANSON AND WE'LL SPLIT THIS BOUNTY 65/35.
NOTHING DOING. MY GUY DID THE HEAVY LIFTING. WE SPLIT--
NO DEAL!
DOUBLE SIGH
YOU'RE A COMPLICATED GUY, AIN'T YOU CHIEF?
NOPE!
ME OFF TO BRANSON WITH ME WORSTEST FRIENDS! WHAT COULD GO RIGHT?
NOW PLAYING IN BRANSON, MO
ZATANNA
THE MISTRESS OF MAGIC

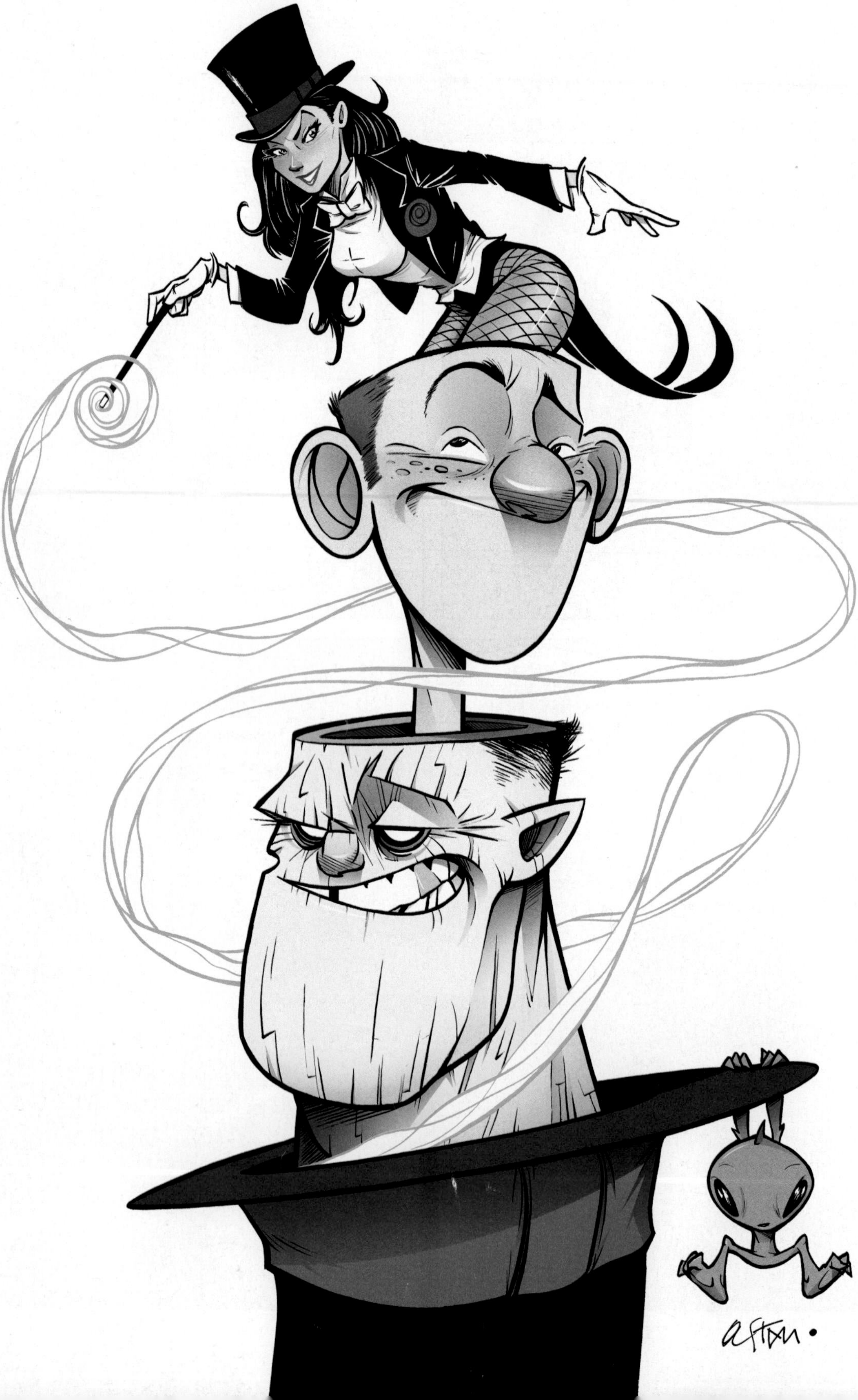

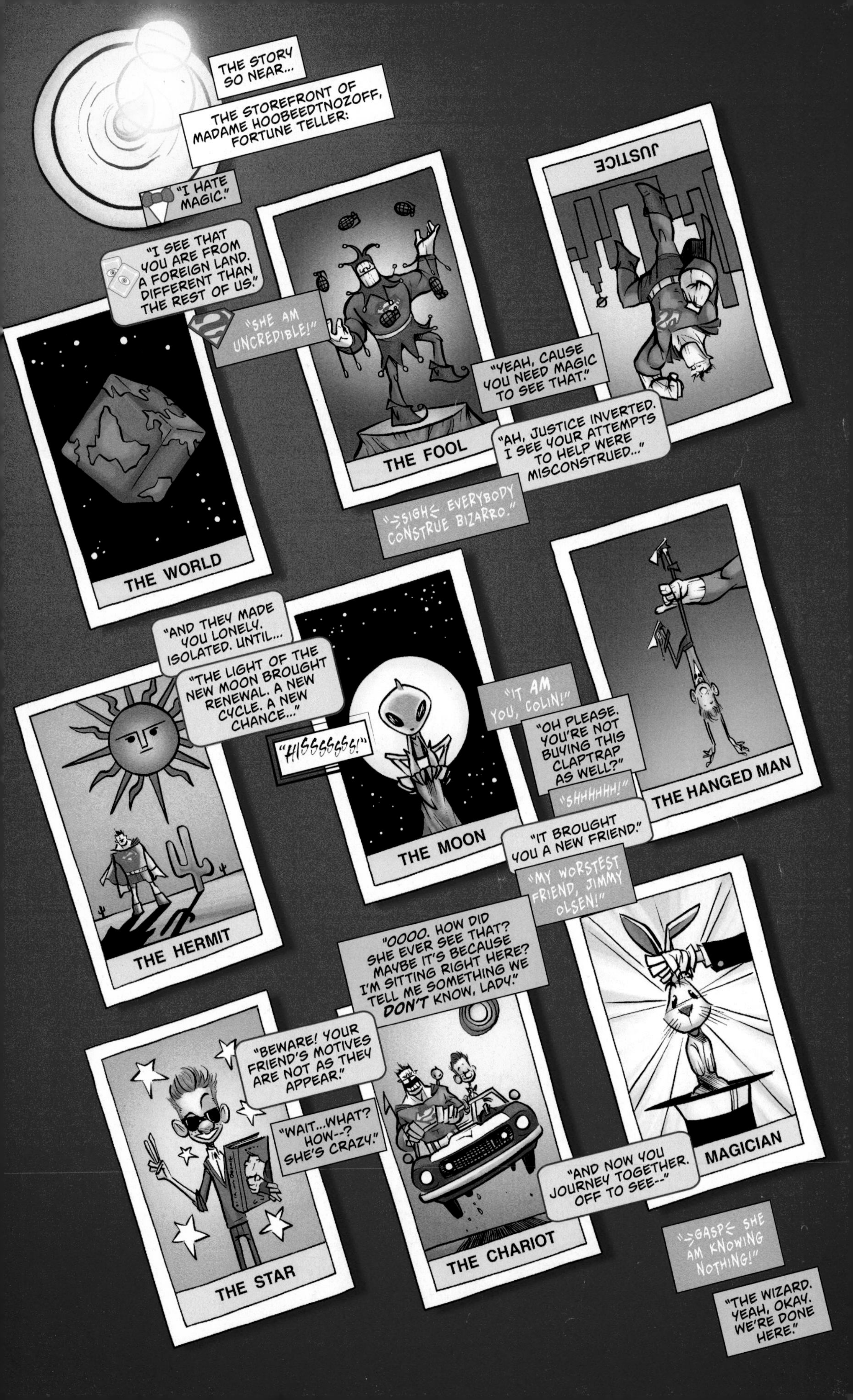

THE STORY SO NEAR...
THE STOREFRONT OF MADAME HOOBEEDTNOZOFF, FORTUNE TELLER:
"I HATE MAGIC."
"I SEE THAT YOU ARE FROM A FOREIGN LAND. DIFFERENT THAN THE REST OF US."
"SHE AM UNCREDIBLE!"
THE WORLD
THE FOOL
JUSTICE
"YEAH, CAUSE YOU NEED MAGIC TO SEE THAT."
"AH, JUSTICE INVERTED. I SEE YOUR ATTEMPTS TO HELP WERE MISCONSTRUED..."
">SIGH< EVERYBODY CONSTRUE BIZARRO."
"AND THEY MADE YOU LONELY. ISOLATED. UNTIL...
"THE LIGHT OF THE NEW MOON BROUGHT RENEWAL. A NEW CYCLE. A NEW CHANCE..."
"HISSSSSSS!"
"IT AM YOU, COLIN!"
"OH PLEASE. YOU'RE NOT BUYING THIS CLAPTRAP AS WELL?"
"SHHHHHH!"
THE HERMIT
THE MOON
THE HANGED MAN
"IT BROUGHT YOU A NEW FRIEND."
"MY WORSTEST FRIEND, JIMMY OLSEN!"
"OOOO. HOW DID SHE EVER SEE THAT? MAYBE IT'S BECAUSE I'M SITTING RIGHT HERE? TELL ME SOMETHING WE DON'T KNOW, LADY."
"BEWARE! YOUR FRIEND'S MOTIVES ARE NOT AS THEY APPEAR."
"WAIT...WHAT? HOW--? SHE'S CRAZY."
"AND NOW YOU JOURNEY TOGETHER. OFF TO SEE--"
THE STAR
THE CHARIOT
MAGICIAN
">GASP< SHE AM KNOWING NOTHING!"
"THE WIZARD. YEAH, OKAY. WE'RE DONE HERE."

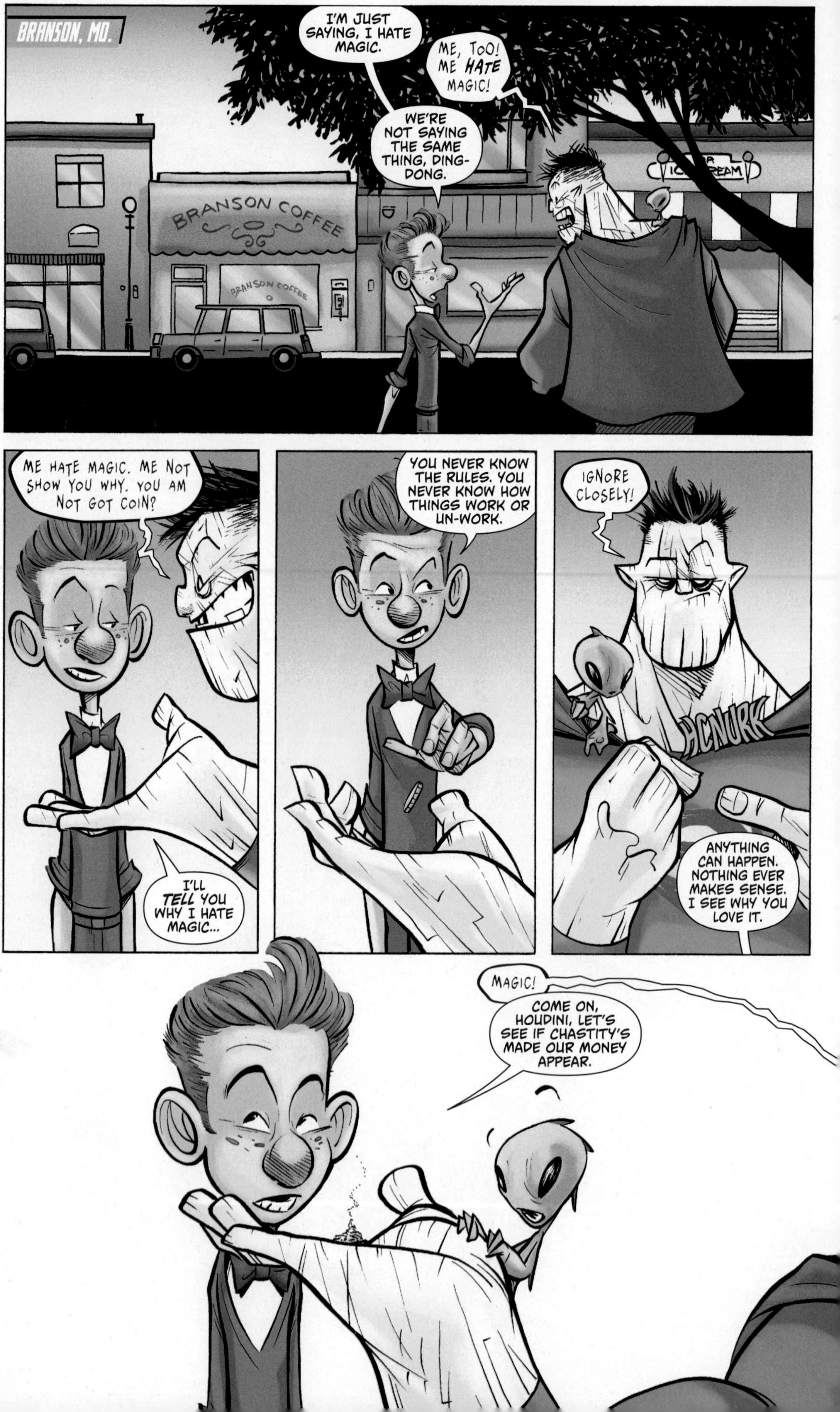
BRANSON, MO.
I'M JUST SAYING, I HATE MAGIC.
ME, TOO! ME HATE MAGIC!
WE'RE NOT SAYING THE SAME THING, DING-DONG.
BRANSON COFFEE
BRANSON COFFEE
ME HATE MAGIC. ME NOT SHOW YOU WHY. YOU AM NOT GOT COIN?
I'LL TELL YOU WHY I HATE MAGIC...
YOU NEVER KNOW THE RULES. YOU NEVER KNOW HOW THINGS WORK OR UN-WORK.
IGNORE CLOSELY!
HCNURK
ANYTHING CAN HAPPEN. NOTHING EVER MAKES SENSE. I SEE WHY YOU LOVE IT.
MAGIC!
COME ON, HOUDINI, LET'S SEE IF CHASTITY'S MADE OUR MONEY APPEAR.

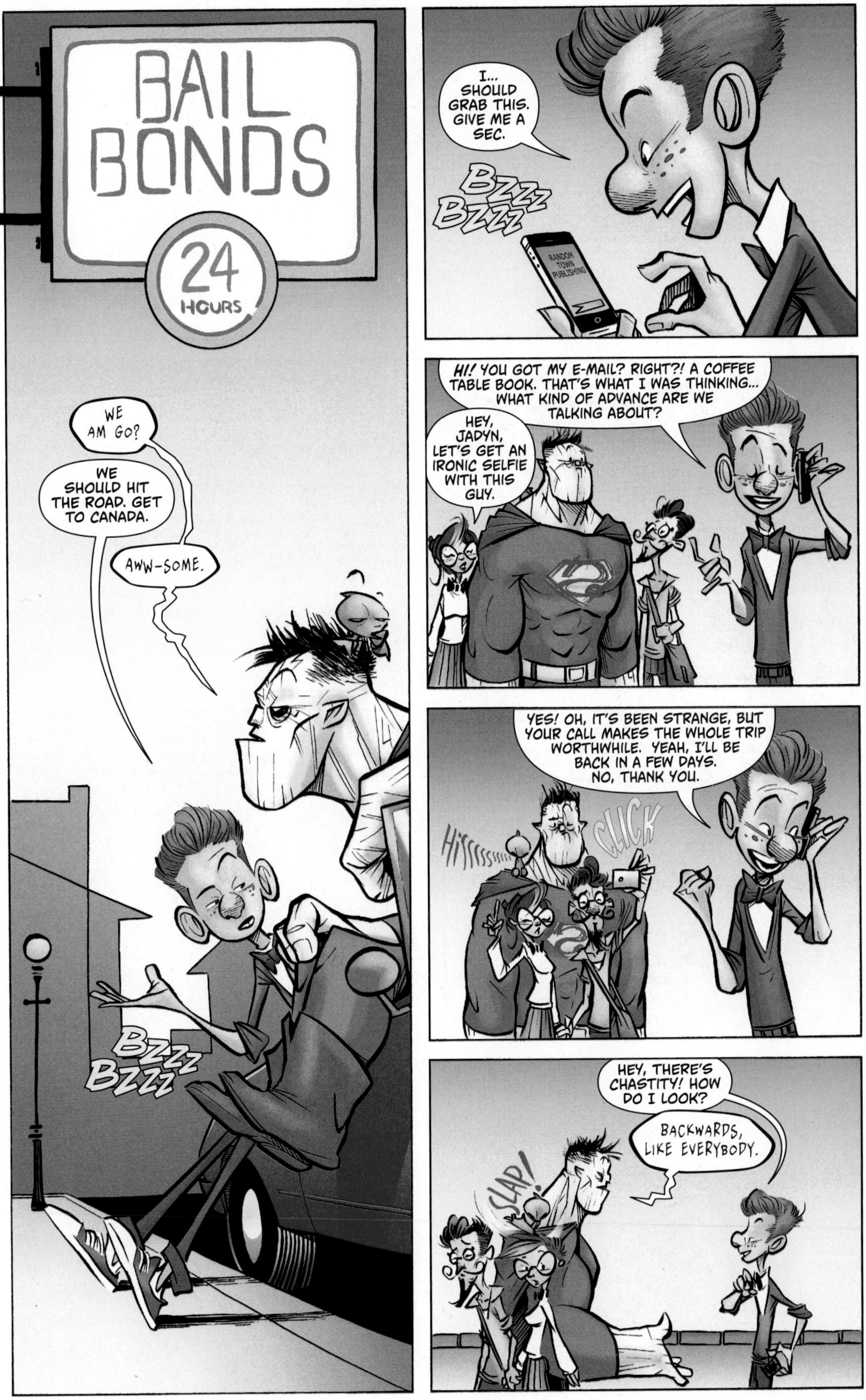
BAIL BONDS
24 HOURS
WE AM GO?
WE SHOULD HIT THE ROAD. GET TO CANADA.
AWW-SOME.
BZZZZ BZZZZ
I... SHOULD GRAB THIS. GIVE ME A SEC.
BZZZZ BZZZZ
RANDOM TOWN PUBLISHING
HI! YOU GOT MY E-MAIL? RIGHT?! A COFFEE TABLE BOOK. THAT'S WHAT I WAS THINKING... WHAT KIND OF ADVANCE ARE WE TALKING ABOUT?
HEY, JADYN, LET'S GET AN IRONIC SELFIE WITH THIS GUY.
YES! OH, IT'S BEEN STRANGE, BUT YOUR CALL MAKES THE WHOLE TRIP WORTHWHILE. YEAH, I'LL BE BACK IN A FEW DAYS. NO, THANK YOU.
HISSSSSSS
CLICK
HEY, THERE'S CHASTITY! HOW DO I LOOK?
BACKWARDS, LIKE EVERYBODY.
SLAP!

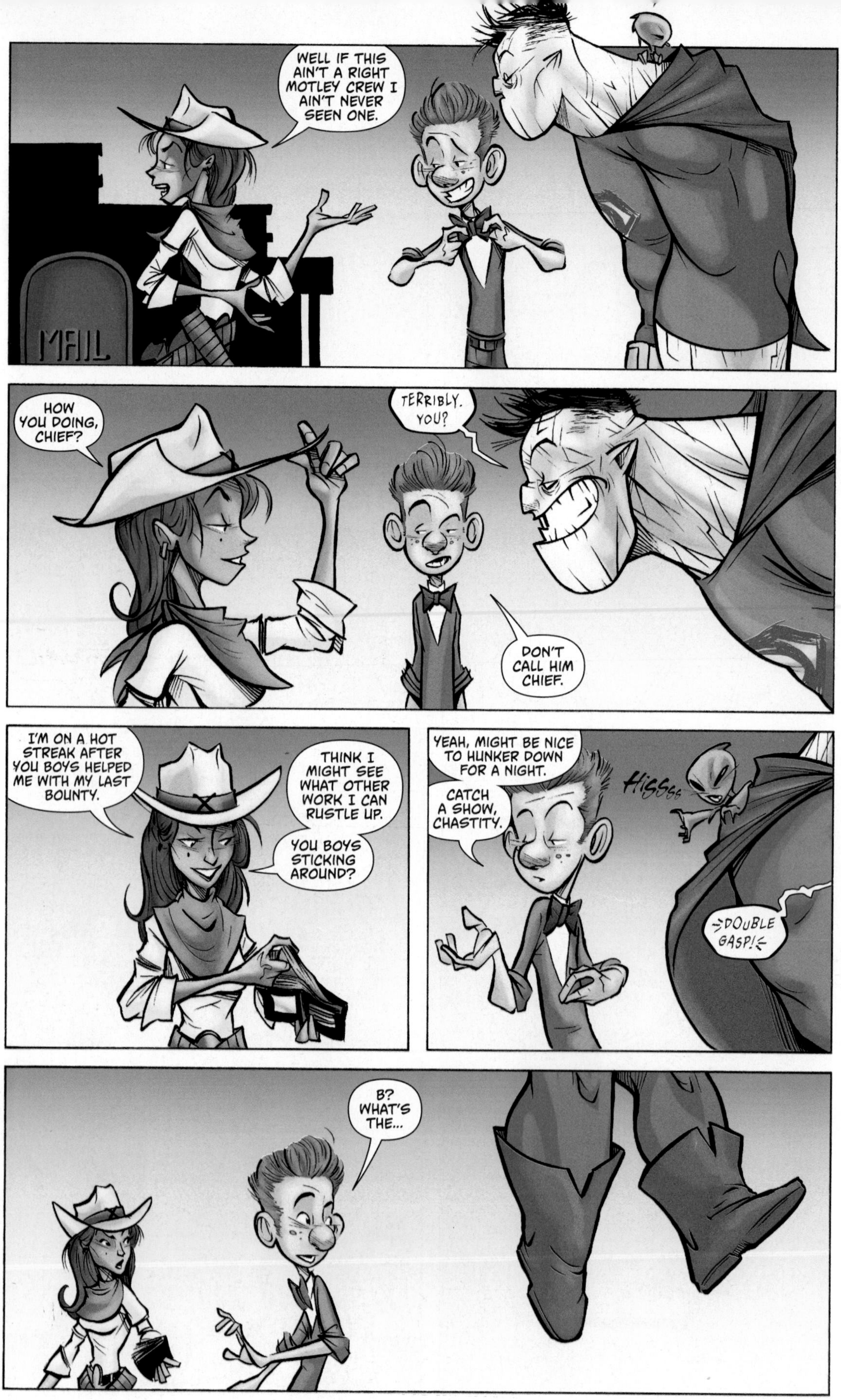
WELL IF THIS AIN'T A RIGHT MOTLEY CREW I AIN'T NEVER SEEN ONE.
MAIL
HOW YOU DOING, CHIEF?
TERRIBLY. YOU?
DON'T CALL HIM CHIEF.
I'M ON A HOT STREAK AFTER YOU BOYS HELPED ME WITH MY LAST BOUNTY.
THINK I MIGHT SEE WHAT OTHER WORK I CAN RUSTLE UP.
YOU BOYS STICKING AROUND?
YEAH, MIGHT BE NICE TO HUNKER DOWN FOR A NIGHT.
CATCH A SHOW, CHASTITY.
HISSss
DOUBLE GASP!
B? WHAT'S THE...

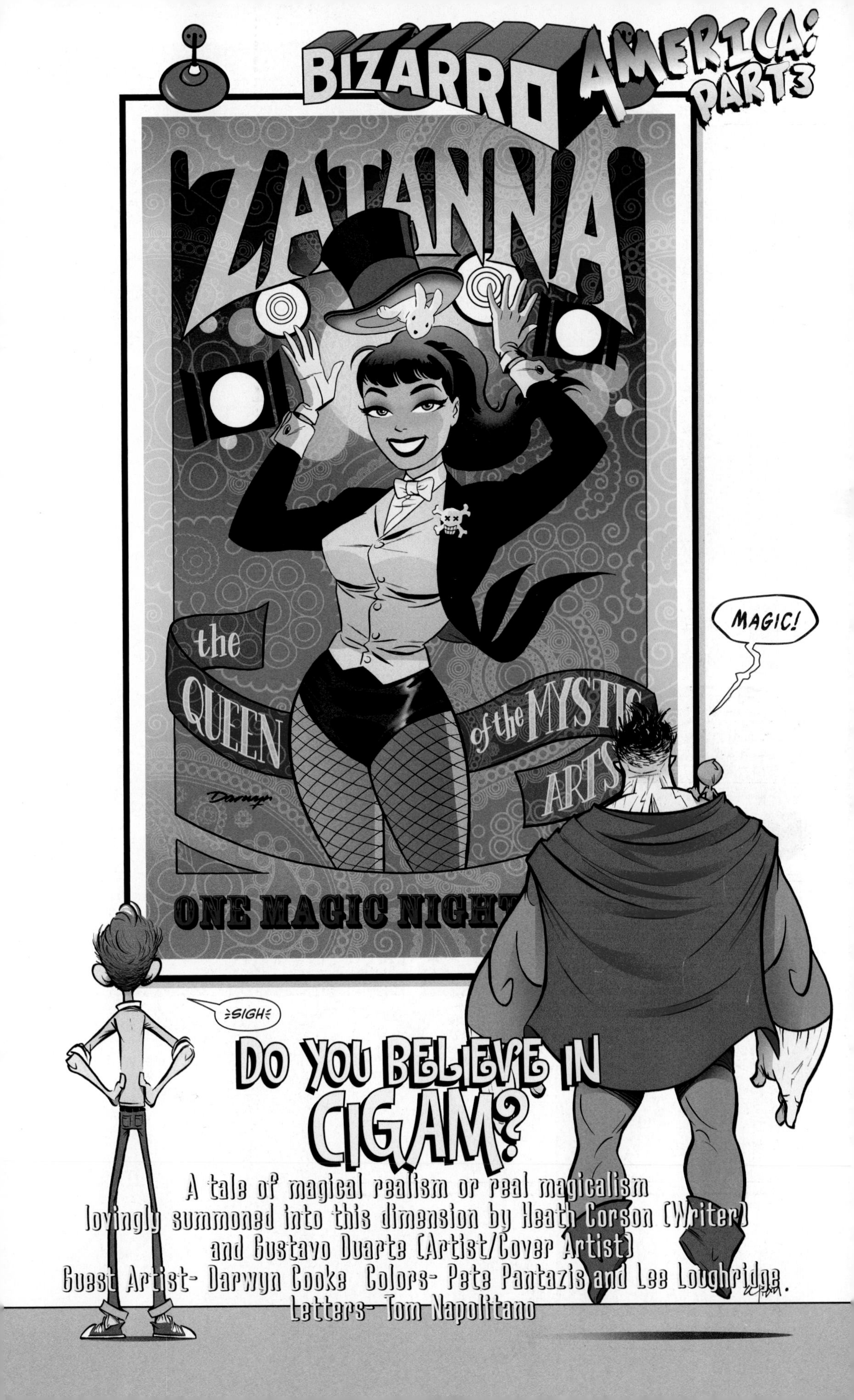
BIZARRO AMERICA: PART 3
ZATANNA
the QUEEN of the MYSTIC ARTS
ONE MAGIC NIGHT
MAGIC!
SIGH
DO YOU BELIEVE IN CIGAM?
A tale of magical realism or real magicalism
lovingly summoned into this dimension by Heath Corson (Writer)
and Gustavo Duarte (Artist/Cover Artist)
Guest Artist- Darwyn Cooke Colors- Pete Pantazis and Lee Loughridge.
Letters- Tom Napolitano

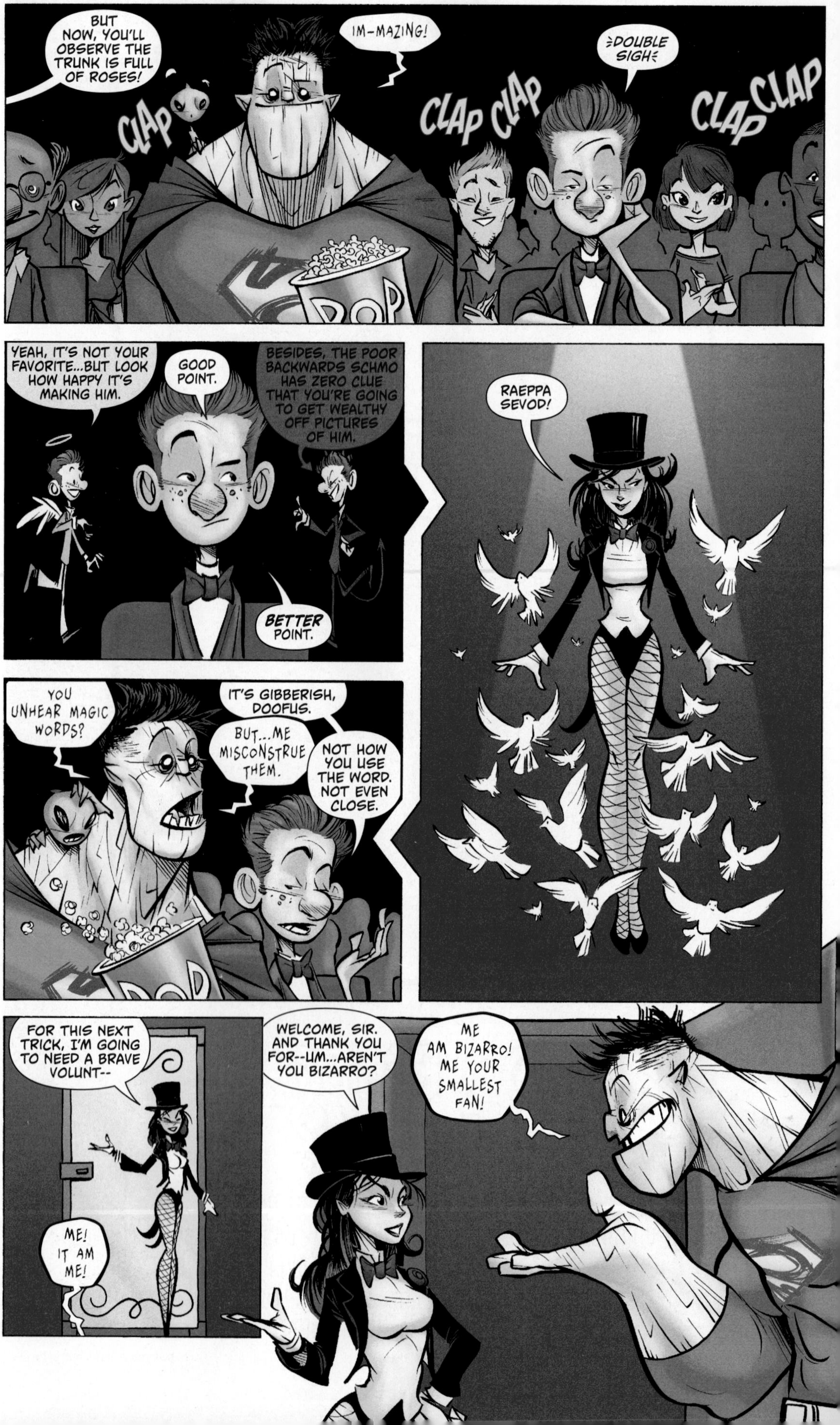
BUT NOW, YOU'LL OBSERVE THE TRUNK IS FULL OF ROSES!
IM-MAZING!
DOUBLE SIGH
CLAP
CLAP CLAP
CLAP CLAP
YEAH, IT'S NOT YOUR FAVORITE...BUT LOOK HOW HAPPY IT'S MAKING HIM.
GOOD POINT.
BESIDES, THE POOR BACKWARDS SCHMO HAS ZERO CLUE THAT YOU'RE GOING TO GET WEALTHY OFF PICTURES OF HIM.
BETTER POINT.
RAEPPA SEVOD!
YOU UNHEAR MAGIC WORDS?
IT'S GIBBERISH, DOOFUS.
BUT...ME MISCONSTRUE THEM.
NOT HOW YOU USE THE WORD. NOT EVEN CLOSE.
POP
FOR THIS NEXT TRICK, I'M GOING TO NEED A BRAVE VOLUNT--
ME! IT AM ME!
WELCOME, SIR. AND THANK YOU FOR--UM...AREN'T YOU BIZARRO?
ME AM BIZARRO! ME YOUR SMALLEST FAN!

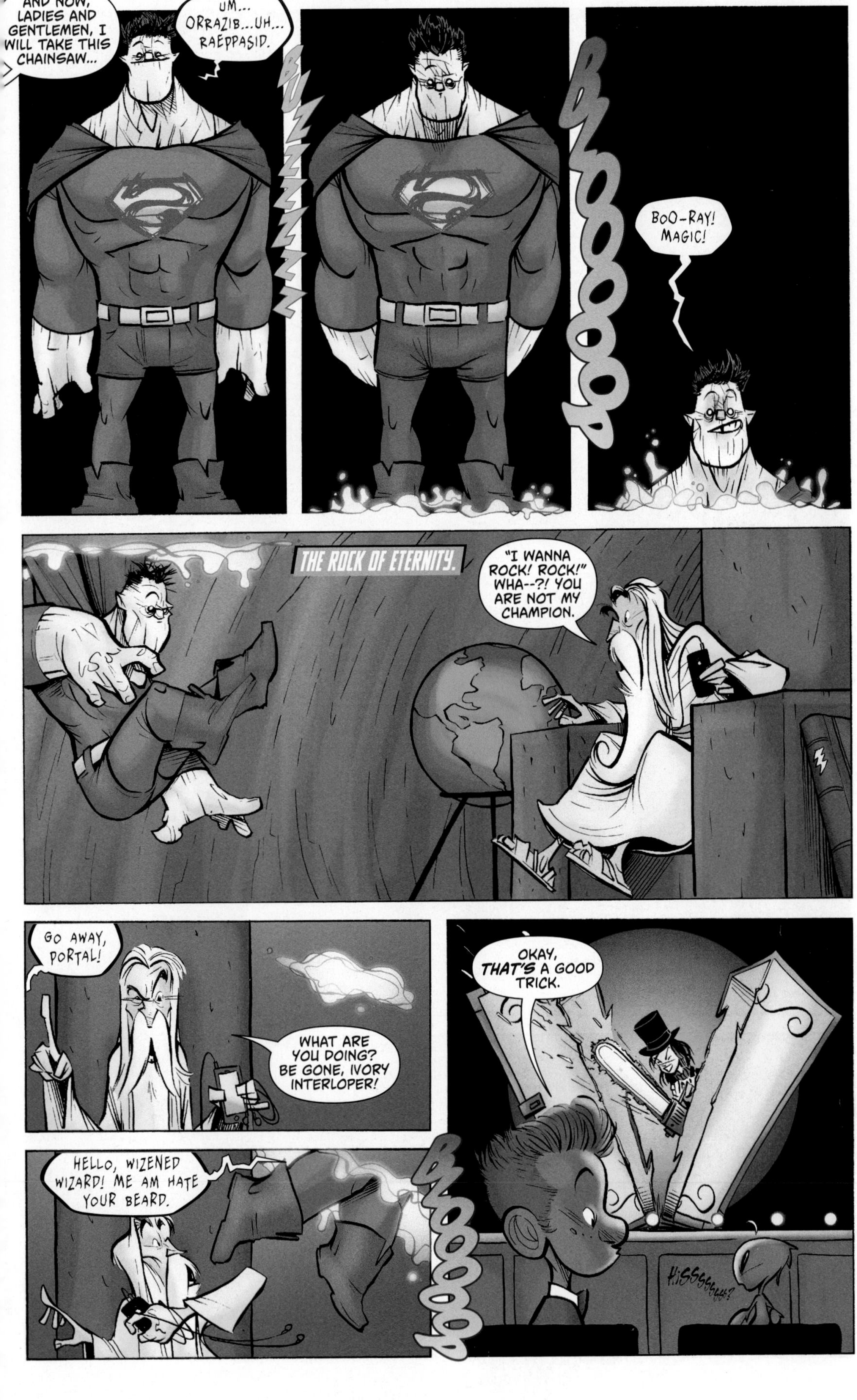
AND NOW, LADIES AND GENTLEMEN, I WILL TAKE THIS CHAINSAW...
UM... ORRAZIB...UH... RAEPPASID.
BUZZZZZZZZZ
BLOOOOOOP
BOO-RAY! MAGIC!
THE ROCK OF ETERNITY.
"I WANNA ROCK! ROCK!" WHA--?! YOU ARE NOT MY CHAMPION.
GO AWAY, PORTAL!
WHAT ARE YOU DOING? BE GONE, IVORY INTERLOPER!
HELLO, WIZENED WIZARD! ME AM HATE YOUR BEARD.
BLOOOOOP
OKAY, THAT'S A GOOD TRICK.
HISSSSSSS?

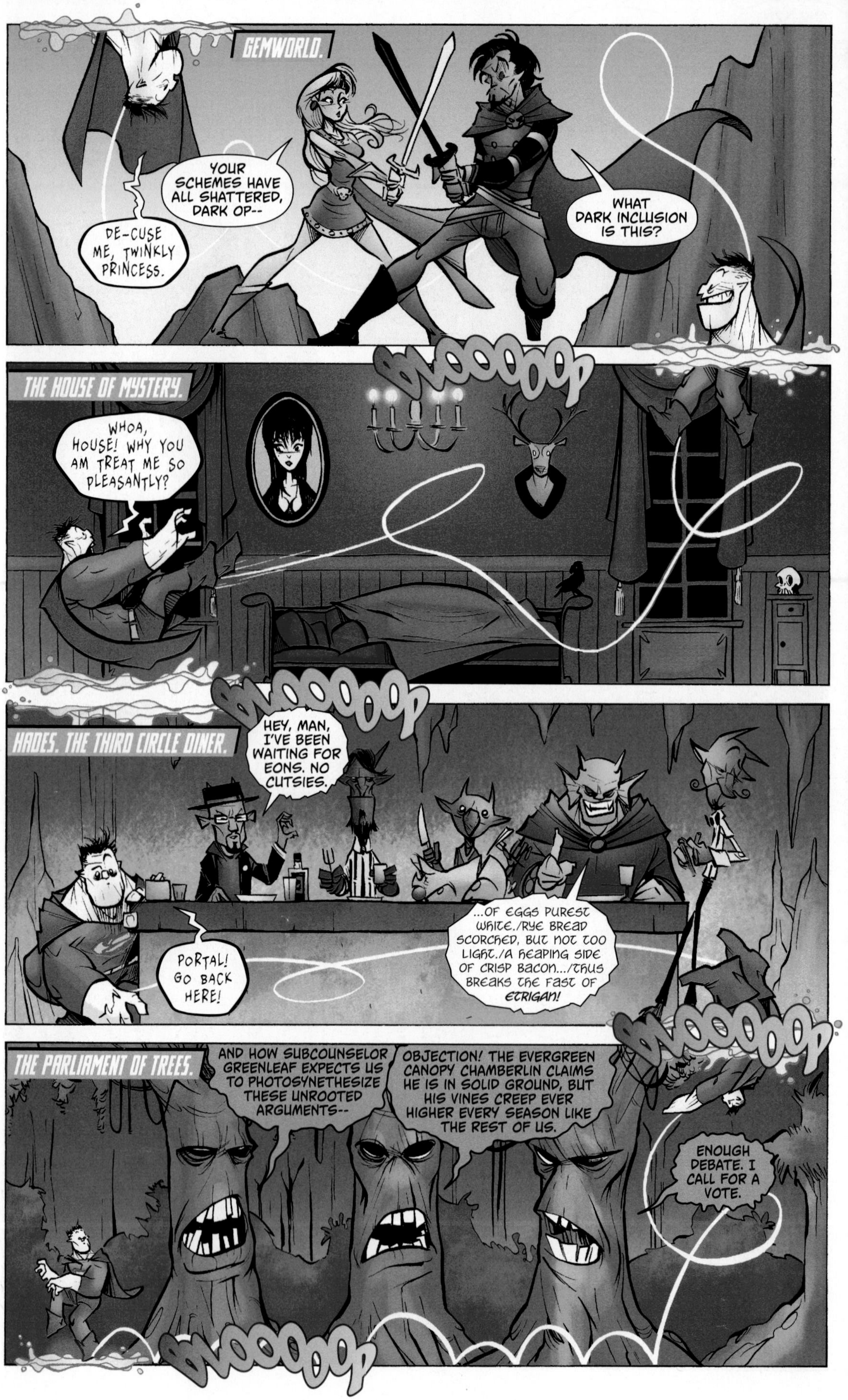
GEMWORLD.
YOUR SCHEMES HAVE ALL SHATTERED, DARK OP--
DE-CUSE ME, TWINKLY PRINCESS.
WHAT DARK INCLUSION IS THIS?
BLOOOOOP
THE HOUSE OF MYSTERY.
WHOA, HOUSE! WHY YOU AM TREAT ME SO PLEASANTLY?
BLOOOOOOP
HADES. THE THIRD CIRCLE DINER.
HEY, MAN, I'VE BEEN WAITING FOR EONS. NO CUTSIES.
...OF EGGS PUREST WHITE./RYE BREAD SCORCHED, BUT NOT TOO LIGHT./A HEAPING SIDE OF CRISP BACON.../THUS BREAKS THE FAST OF ETRIGAN!
PORTAL! GO BACK HERE!
BLOOOOOOP
THE PARLIAMENT OF TREES.
AND HOW SUBCOUNSELOR GREENLEAF EXPECTS US TO PHOTOSYNETHESIZE THESE UNROOTED ARGUMENTS--
OBJECTION! THE EVERGREEN CANOPY CHAMBERLIN CLAIMS HE IS IN SOLID GROUND, BUT HIS VINES CREEP EVER HIGHER EVERY SEASON LIKE THE REST OF US.
ENOUGH DEBATE. I CALL FOR A VOTE.
BLOOOOOP

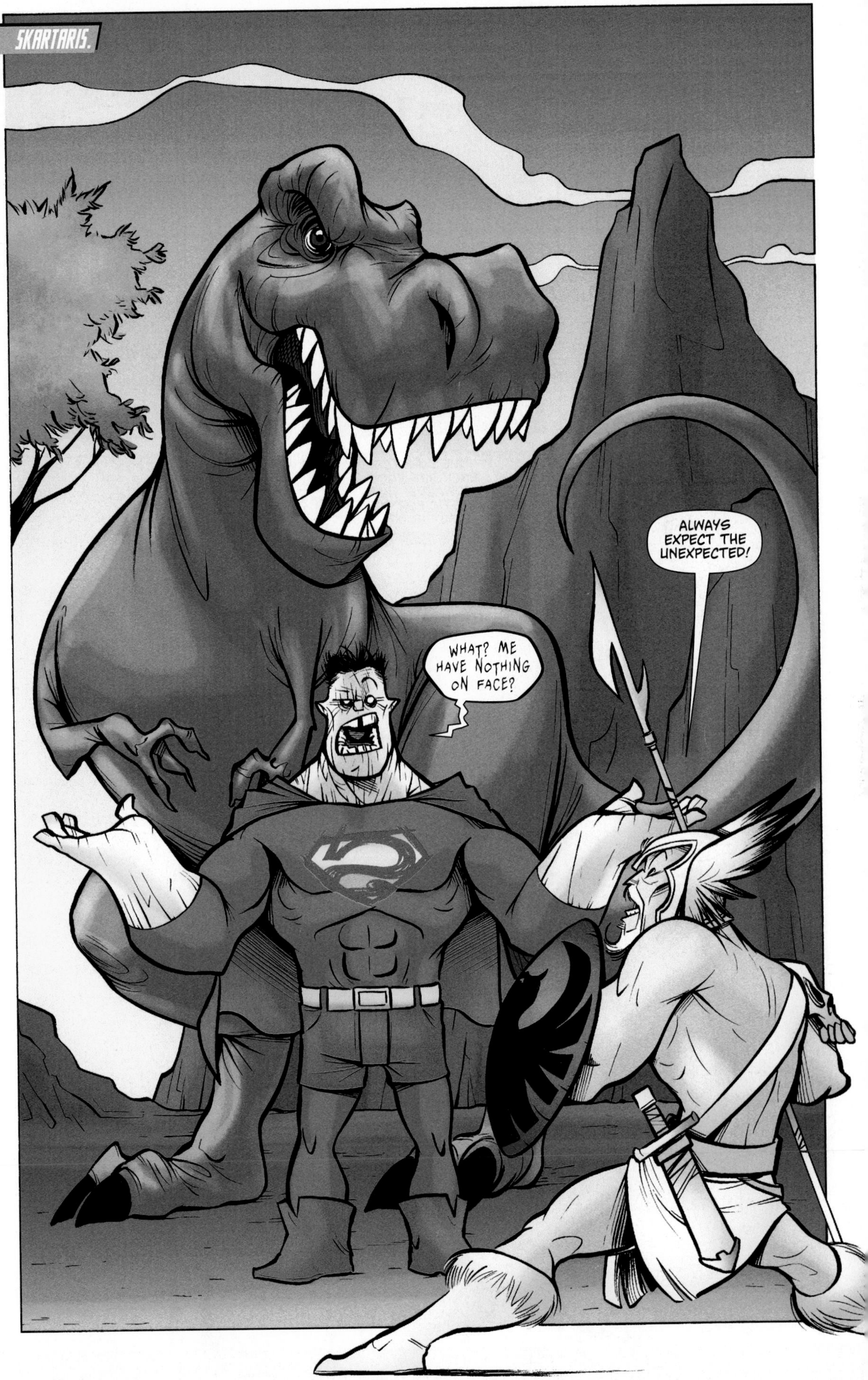
SKARTARIS.
WHAT? ME HAVE NOTHING ON FACE?
ALWAYS EXPECT THE UNEXPECTED!

COME IN, MR. OLSEN.

ZATANNA

WHA--? BUT--OH, RIGHT, *MAGIC*.

EXCUSE ME, MS. ZATANNA? THAT WAS A GREAT TRICK MAKING OUR FRIEND DISAPPEAR AND ALL...

WELL, THANK YOU. I'VE BEEN PERFORMING IT SINCE--

BUT WE WERE WONDERING, WHEN DO YOU MAKE HIM *REAPPEAR*?

WAIT... *WHAT?!*

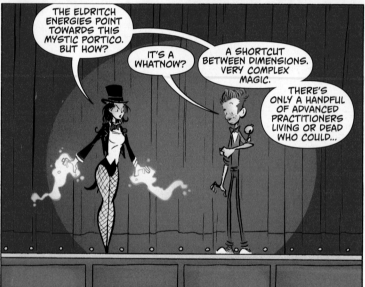

THE ELDRITCH ENERGIES POINT TOWARDS THIS MYSTIC PORTICO. BUT HOW?

IT'S A WHATNOW?

A SHORTCUT BETWEEN DIMENSIONS. VERY COMPLEX MAGIC.

THERE'S ONLY A HANDFUL OF ADVANCED PRACTITIONERS LIVING OR DEAD WHO COULD...

JIMMY, ME CAN NO DO *MAGIC!*

BLOOOGG

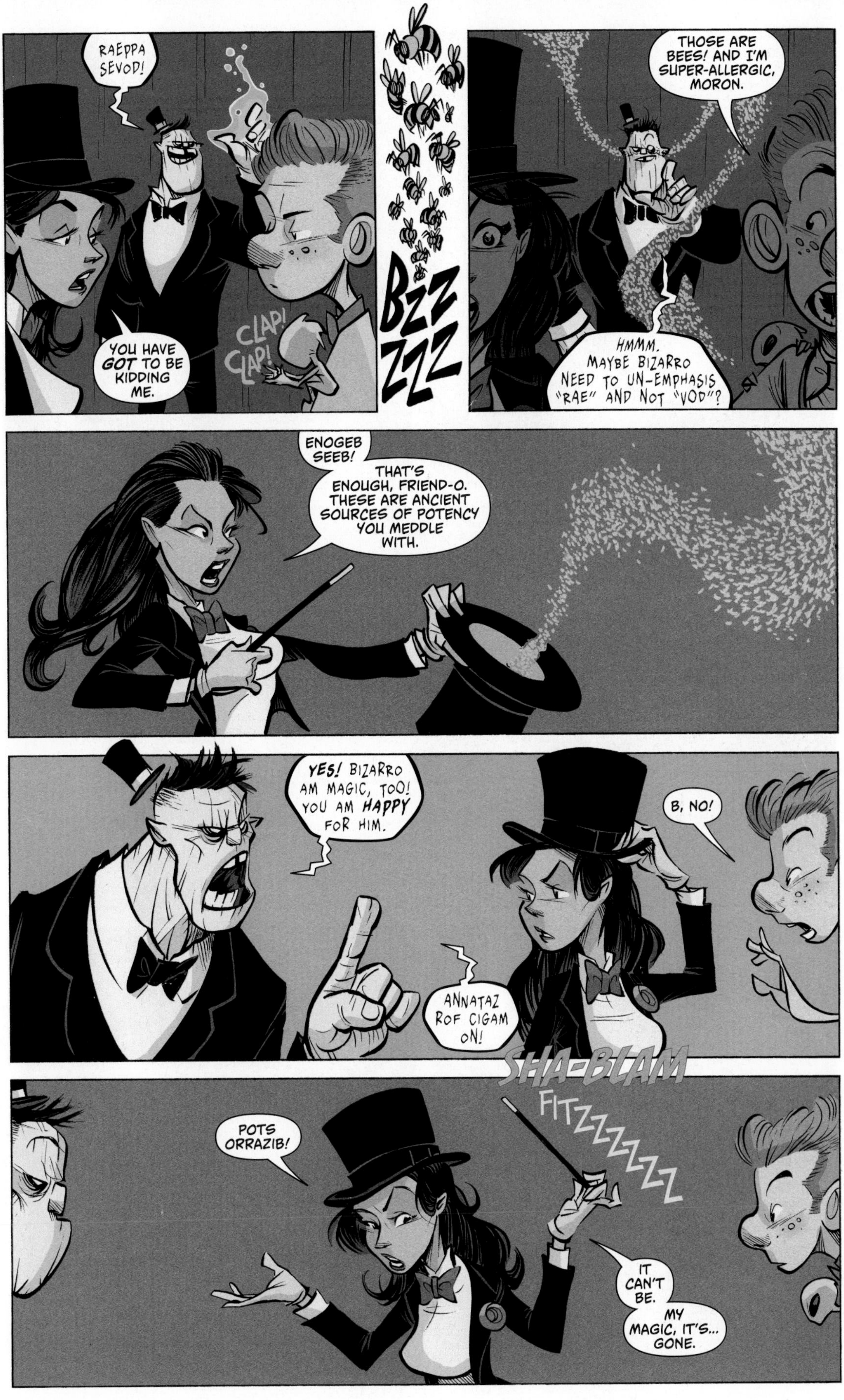
RAEPPA SEVOD!
YOU HAVE GOT TO BE KIDDING ME.
CLAP! CLAP!
BZZ ZZZ
THOSE ARE BEES! AND I'M SUPER-ALLERGIC, MORON.
HMMM. MAYBE BIZARRO NEED TO UN-EMPHASIS "RAE" AND NOT "VOD"?
ENOGEB SEEB!
THAT'S ENOUGH, FRIEND-O. THESE ARE ANCIENT SOURCES OF POTENCY YOU MEDDLE WITH.
YES! BIZARRO AM MAGIC, TOO! YOU AM HAPPY FOR HIM.
B, NO!
ANNATAZ ROF CIGAM ON!
SHA-BLAM
FITZZZZZZZ
POTS ORRAZIB!
IT CAN'T BE.
MY MAGIC, IT'S... GONE.

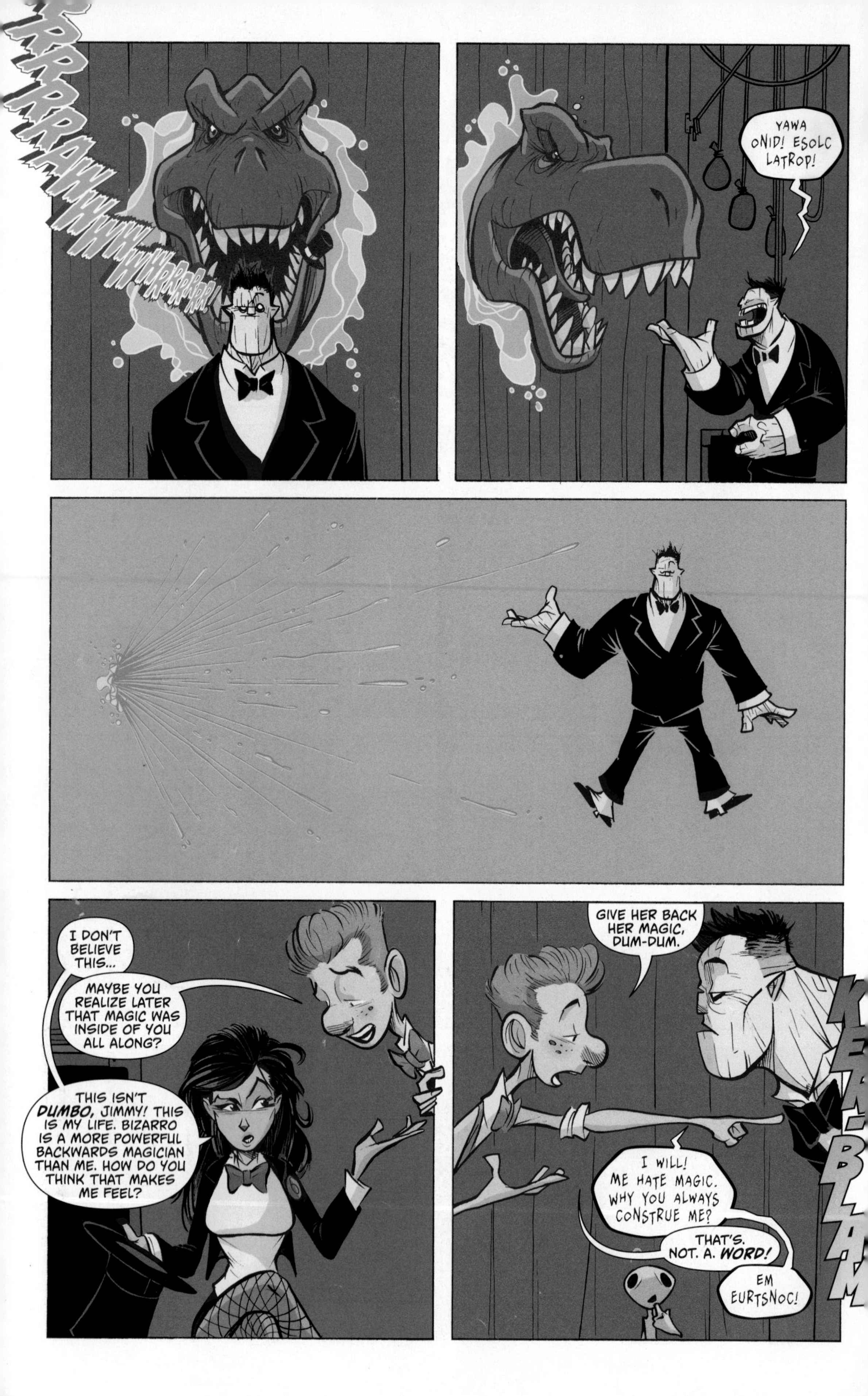
RRRRAHHHHHHRRRRRR!
YAWA ONID! ESOLC LATROP!
I DON'T BELIEVE THIS...
MAYBE YOU REALIZE LATER THAT MAGIC WAS INSIDE OF YOU ALL ALONG?
THIS ISN'T **DUMBO**, JIMMY! THIS IS MY LIFE. BIZARRO IS A MORE POWERFUL BACKWARDS MAGICIAN THAN ME. HOW DO YOU THINK THAT MAKES ME FEEL?
GIVE HER BACK HER MAGIC, DUM-DUM.
KER-BLAM
I WILL! ME HATE MAGIC. WHY YOU ALWAYS CONSTRUE ME?
THAT'S. NOT. A. **WORD!**
EM EURTSNOC!

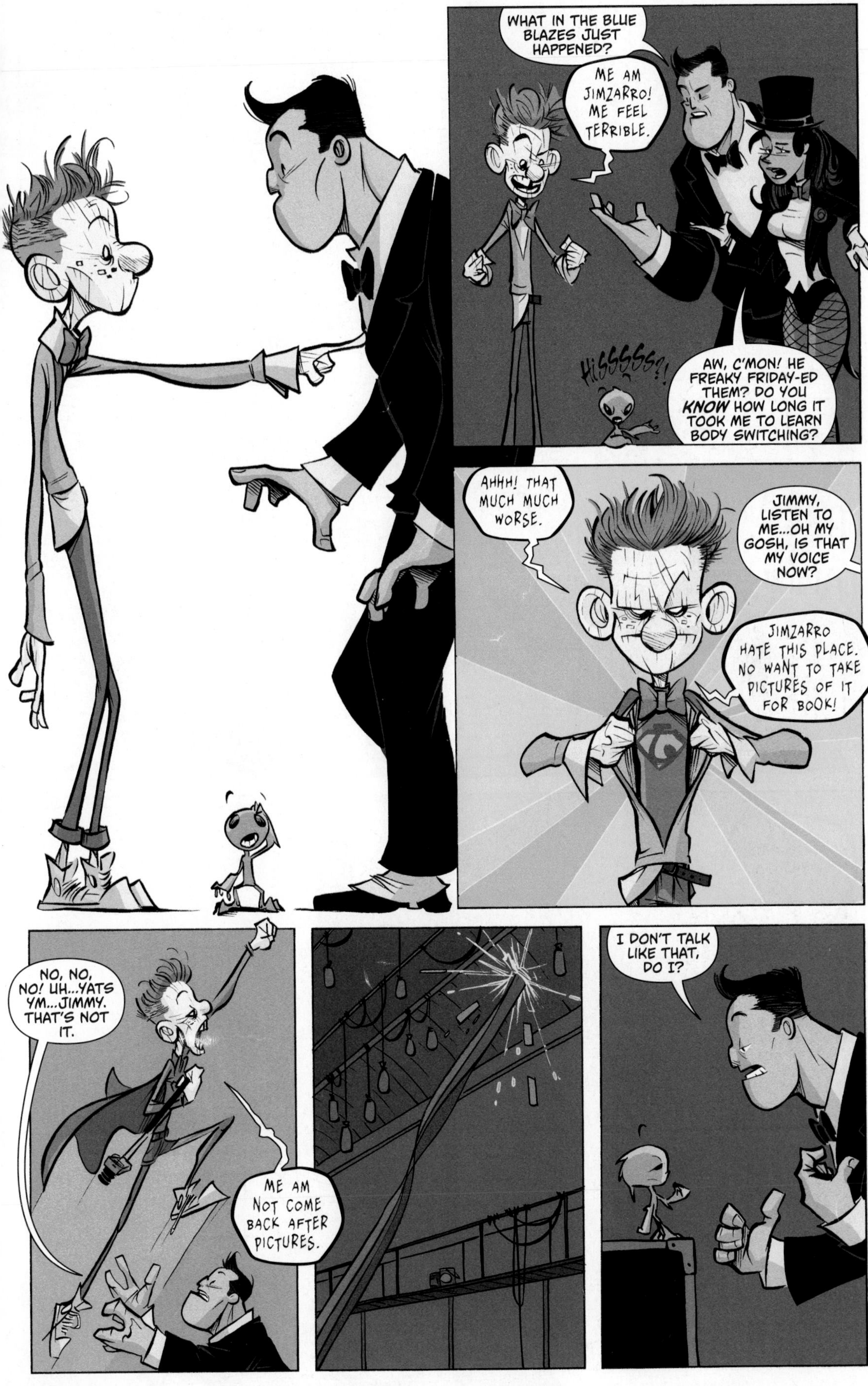
WHAT IN THE BLUE BLAZES JUST HAPPENED?
ME AM JIMZARRO! ME FEEL TERRIBLE.
HISSSSS?!
AW, C'MON! HE FREAKY FRIDAY-ED THEM? DO YOU KNOW HOW LONG IT TOOK ME TO LEARN BODY SWITCHING?
AHHH! THAT MUCH MUCH WORSE.
JIMMY, LISTEN TO ME...OH MY GOSH, IS THAT MY VOICE NOW?
JIMZARRO HATE THIS PLACE. NO WANT TO TAKE PICTURES OF IT FOR BOOK!
NO, NO, NO! UH...YATS YM...JIMMY. THAT'S NOT IT.
ME AM NOT COME BACK AFTER PICTURES.
I DON'T TALK LIKE THAT, DO I?

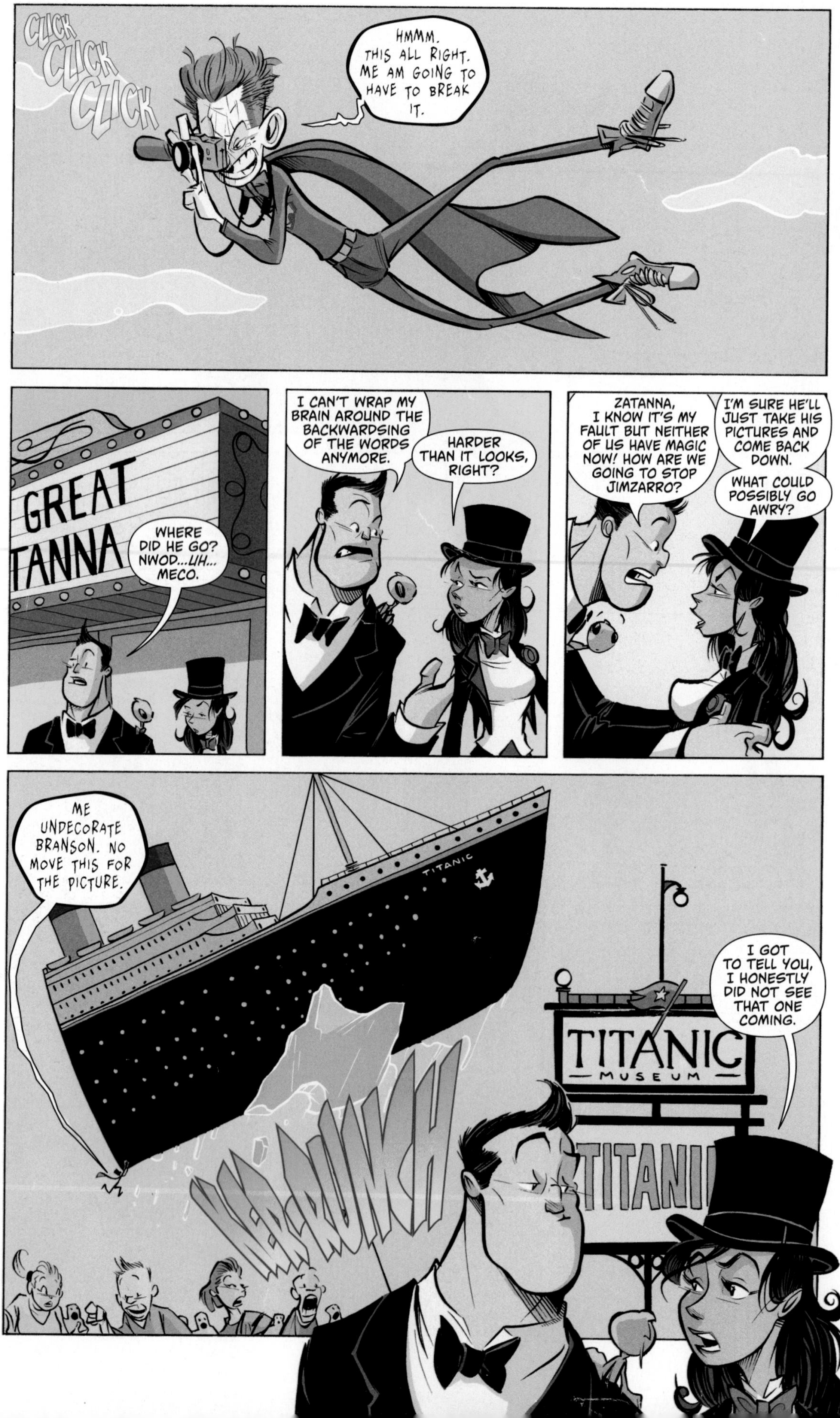
CLICK CLICK CLICK
HMMM. THIS ALL RIGHT. ME AM GOING TO HAVE TO BREAK IT.
GREAT
TANNA
WHERE DID HE GO? NWOD...UH... MECO.
I CAN'T WRAP MY BRAIN AROUND THE BACKWARDSING OF THE WORDS ANYMORE.
HARDER THAN IT LOOKS, RIGHT?
ZATANNA, I KNOW IT'S MY FAULT BUT NEITHER OF US HAVE MAGIC NOW! HOW ARE WE GOING TO STOP JIMZARRO?
I'M SURE HE'LL JUST TAKE HIS PICTURES AND COME BACK DOWN.
WHAT COULD POSSIBLY GO AWRY?
ME UNDECORATE BRANSON. NO MOVE THIS FOR THE PICTURE.
TITANIC
TITANIC
MUSEUM
TITANI
I GOT TO TELL YOU, I HONESTLY DID NOT SEE THAT ONE COMING.

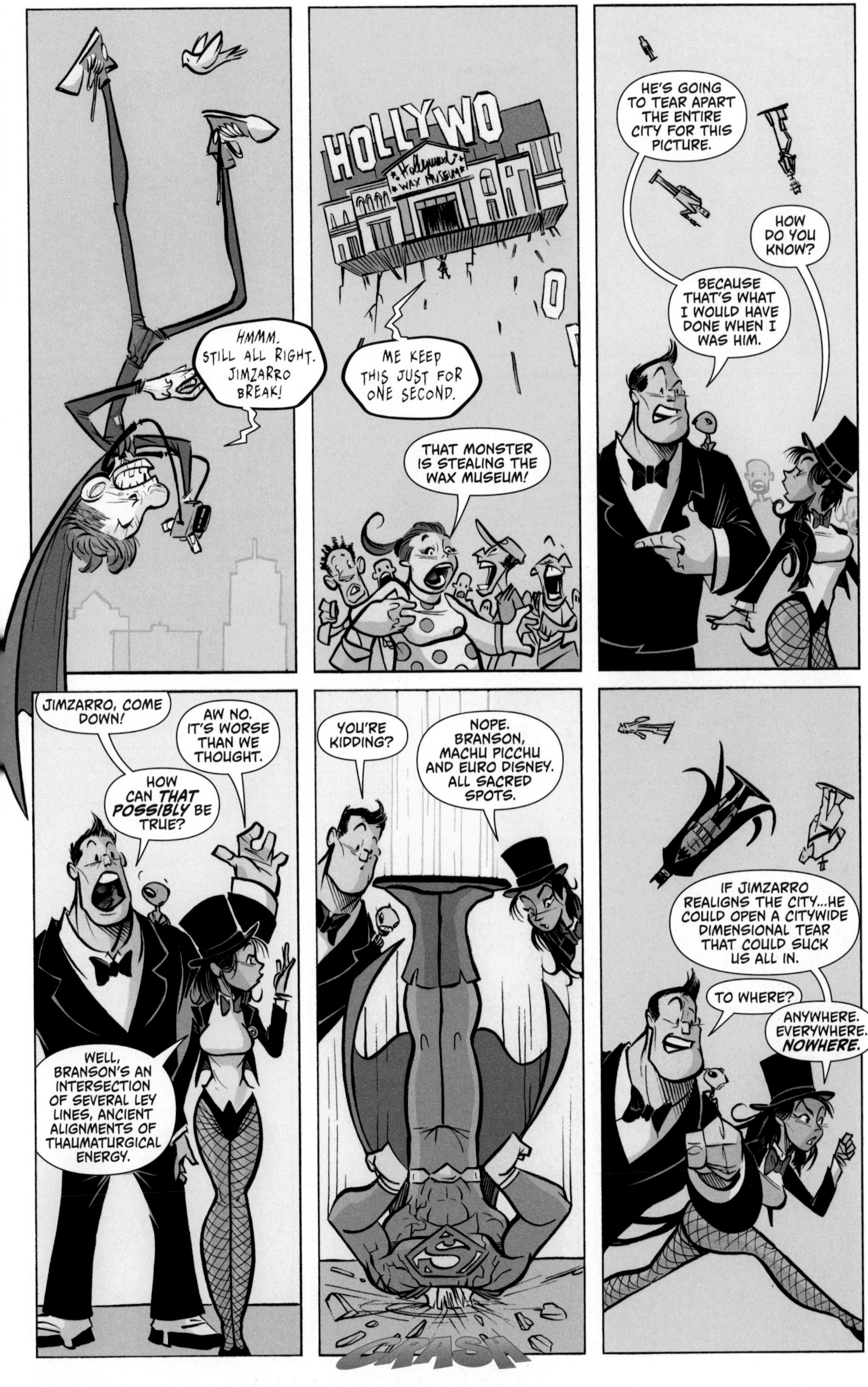
HMMM. STILL ALL RIGHT. JIMZARRO BREAK!
HOLLYWO
Hollywood WAX MUSEUM
ME KEEP THIS JUST FOR ONE SECOND.
THAT MONSTER IS STEALING THE WAX MUSEUM!
HE'S GOING TO TEAR APART THE ENTIRE CITY FOR THIS PICTURE.
HOW DO YOU KNOW?
BECAUSE THAT'S WHAT I WOULD HAVE DONE WHEN I WAS HIM.
JIMZARRO, COME DOWN!
AW NO. IT'S WORSE THAN WE THOUGHT.
HOW CAN THAT POSSIBLY BE TRUE?
WELL, BRANSON'S AN INTERSECTION OF SEVERAL LEY LINES, ANCIENT ALIGNMENTS OF THAUMATURGICAL ENERGY.
YOU'RE KIDDING?
NOPE. BRANSON, MACHU PICCHU AND EURO DISNEY. ALL SACRED SPOTS.
CRASH
IF JIMZARRO REALIGNS THE CITY...HE COULD OPEN A CITYWIDE DIMENSIONAL TEAR THAT COULD SUCK US ALL IN.
TO WHERE?
ANYWHERE. EVERYWHERE. NOWHERE.

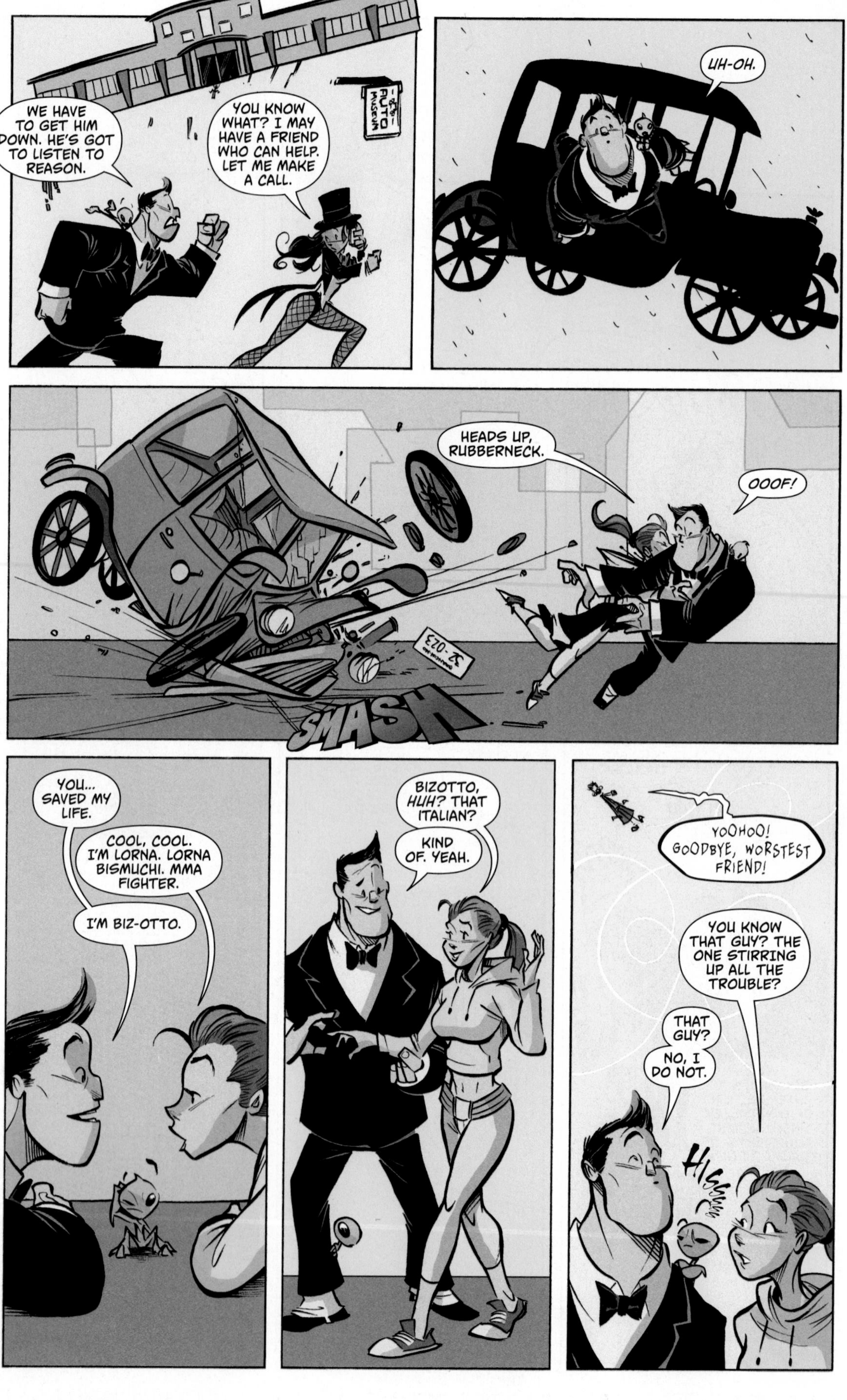
AUTO MUSEUM
WE HAVE TO GET HIM DOWN. HE'S GOT TO LISTEN TO REASON.
YOU KNOW WHAT? I MAY HAVE A FRIEND WHO CAN HELP. LET ME MAKE A CALL.
UH-OH.
HEADS UP, RUBBERNECK.
OOOF!
SMASH
YOU... SAVED MY LIFE.
COOL, COOL. I'M LORNA. LORNA BISMUCHI. MMA FIGHTER.
I'M BIZ-OTTO.
BIZOTTO, HUH? THAT ITALIAN?
KIND OF. YEAH.
YOOHOO! GOODBYE, WORSTEST FRIEND!
YOU KNOW THAT GUY? THE ONE STIRRING UP ALL THE TROUBLE?
THAT GUY?
NO, I DO NOT.
HISSSS

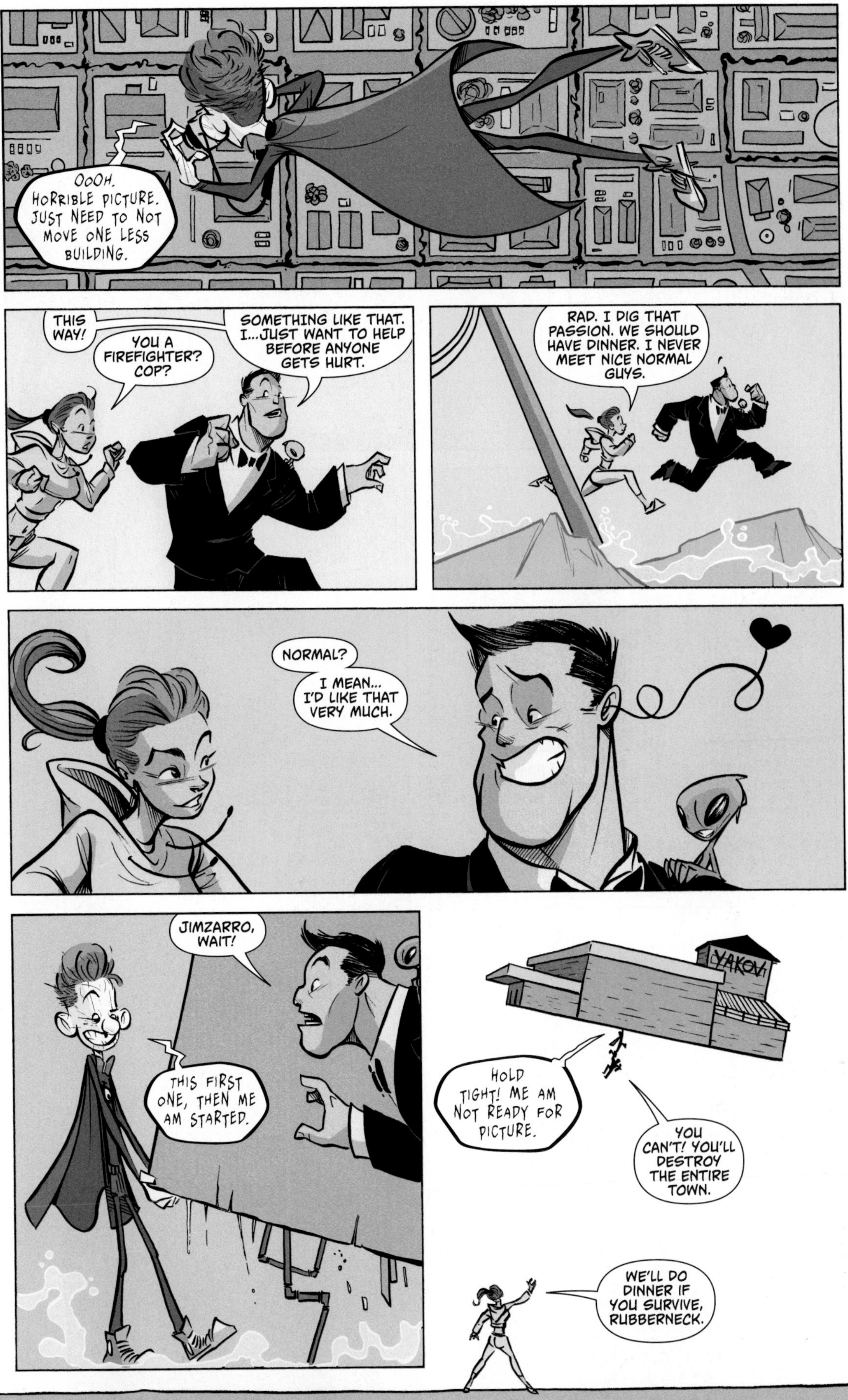
OOOH. HORRIBLE PICTURE. JUST NEED TO NOT MOVE ONE LESS BUILDING.
THIS WAY!
YOU A FIREFIGHTER? COP?
SOMETHING LIKE THAT. I...JUST WANT TO HELP BEFORE ANYONE GETS HURT.
RAD. I DIG THAT PASSION. WE SHOULD HAVE DINNER. I NEVER MEET NICE NORMAL GUYS.
NORMAL?
I MEAN... I'D LIKE THAT VERY MUCH.
JIMZARRO, WAIT!
THIS FIRST ONE, THEN ME AM STARTED.
YAKOV
HOLD TIGHT! ME AM NOT READY FOR PICTURE.
YOU CAN'T! YOU'LL DESTROY THE ENTIRE TOWN.
WE'LL DO DINNER IF YOU SURVIVE, RUBBERNECK.

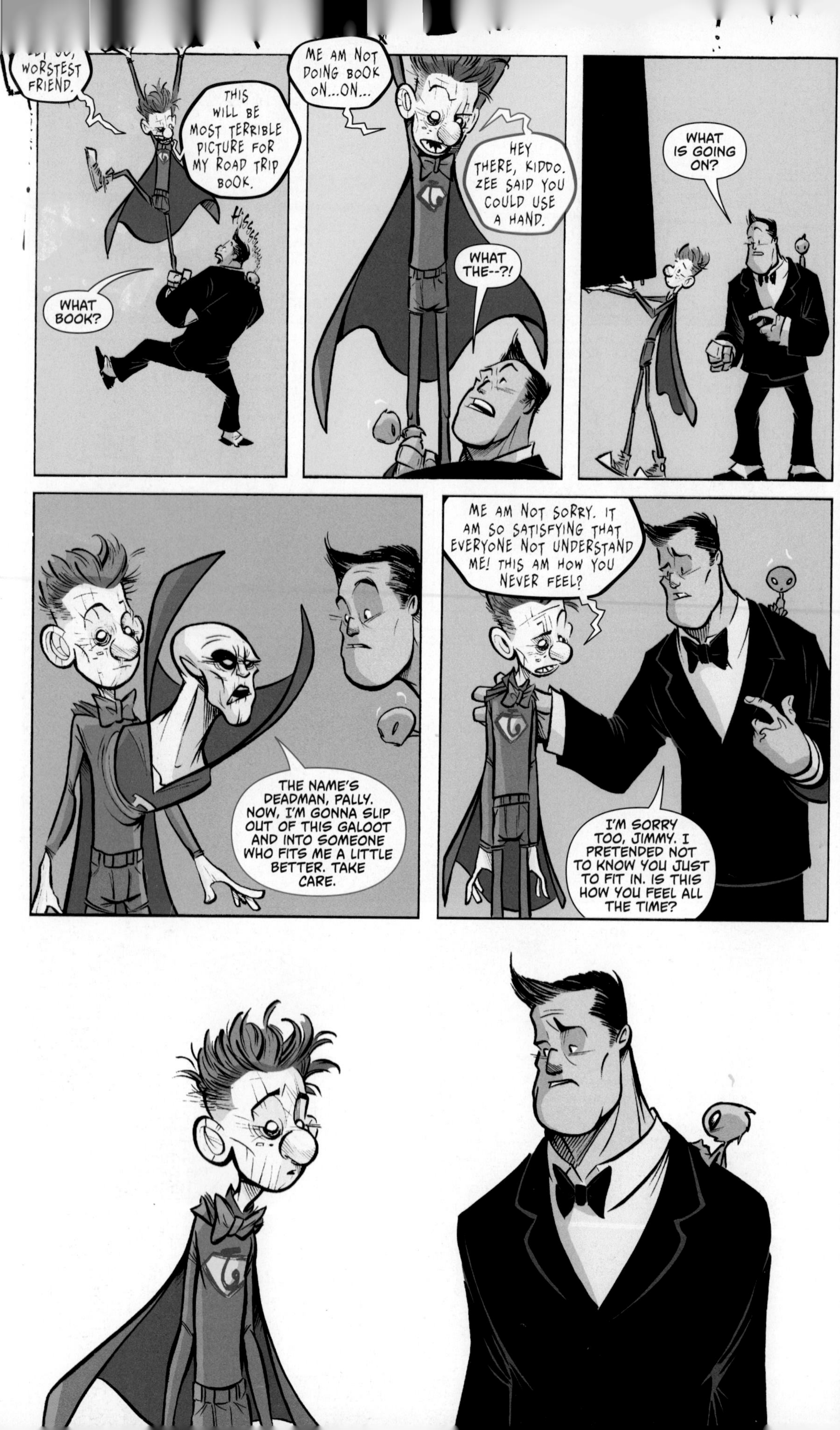
WORSTEST FRIEND.
THIS WILL BE MOST TERRIBLE PICTURE FOR MY ROAD TRIP BOOK.
WHAT BOOK?
ME AM NOT DOING BOOK ON...ON...
HEY THERE, KIDDO. ZEE SAID YOU COULD USE A HAND.
WHAT THE--?!
WHAT IS GOING ON?
THE NAME'S DEADMAN, PALLY. NOW, I'M GONNA SLIP OUT OF THIS GALOOT AND INTO SOMEONE WHO FITS ME A LITTLE BETTER. TAKE CARE.
ME AM NOT SORRY. IT AM SO SATISFYING THAT EVERYONE NOT UNDERSTAND ME! THIS AM HOW YOU NEVER FEEL?
I'M SORRY TOO, JIMMY. I PRETENDED NOT TO KNOW YOU JUST TO FIT IN. IS THIS HOW YOU FEEL ALL THE TIME?

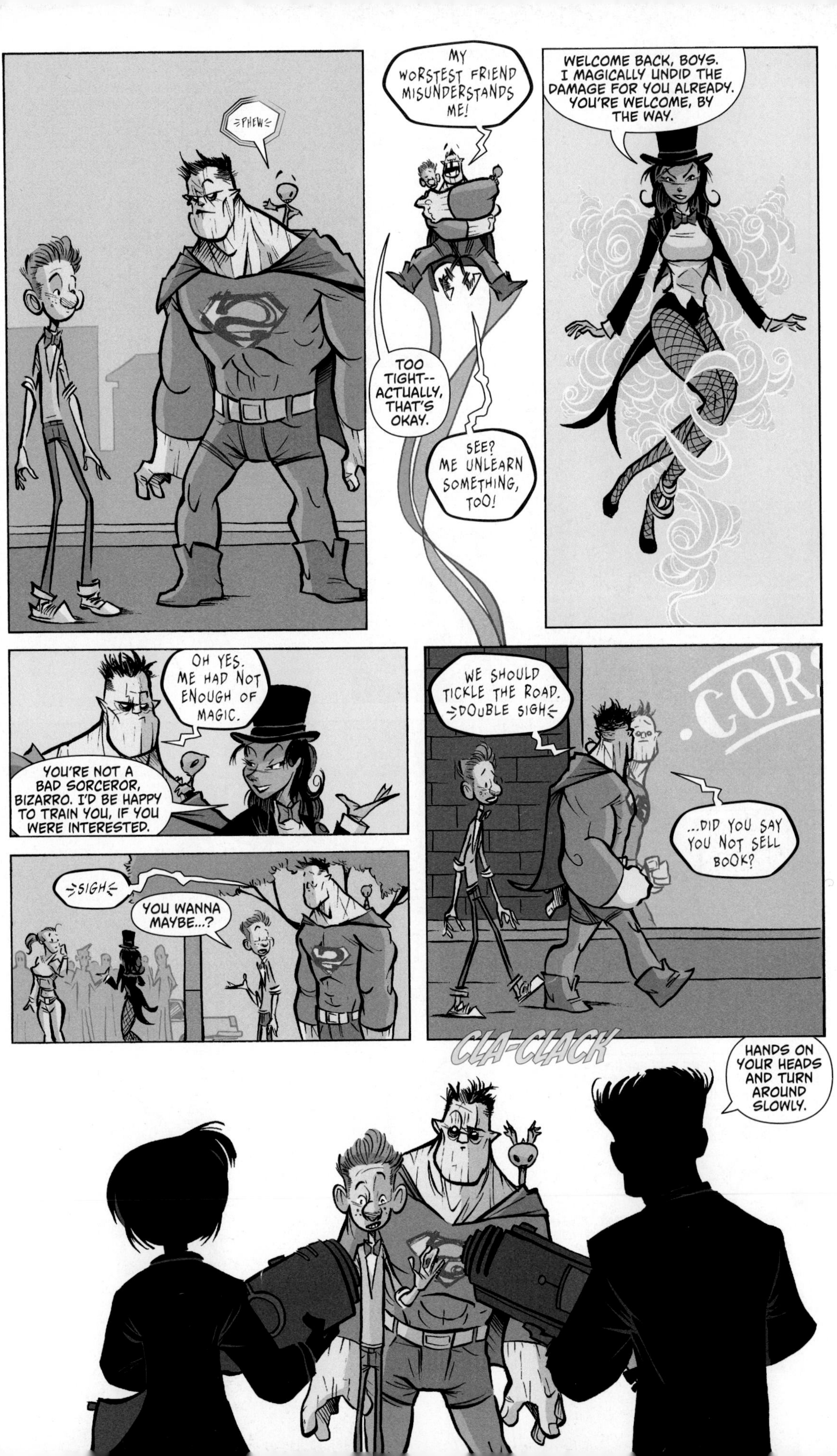

⇒PHEW⇐
MY WORSTEST FRIEND MISUNDERSTANDS ME!
TOO TIGHT-- ACTUALLY, THAT'S OKAY.
SEE? ME UNLEARN SOMETHING, TOO!
WELCOME BACK, BOYS. I MAGICALLY UNDID THE DAMAGE FOR YOU ALREADY. YOU'RE WELCOME, BY THE WAY.
YOU'RE NOT A BAD SORCEROR, BIZARRO. I'D BE HAPPY TO TRAIN YOU, IF YOU WERE INTERESTED.
OH YES. ME HAD NOT ENOUGH OF MAGIC.
⇒SIGH⇐
YOU WANNA MAYBE...?
WE SHOULD TICKLE THE ROAD. ⇒DOUBLE SIGH⇐
...DID YOU SAY YOU NOT SELL BOOK?
.CORS
CLA-CLACK
HANDS ON YOUR HEADS AND TURN AROUND SLOWLY.

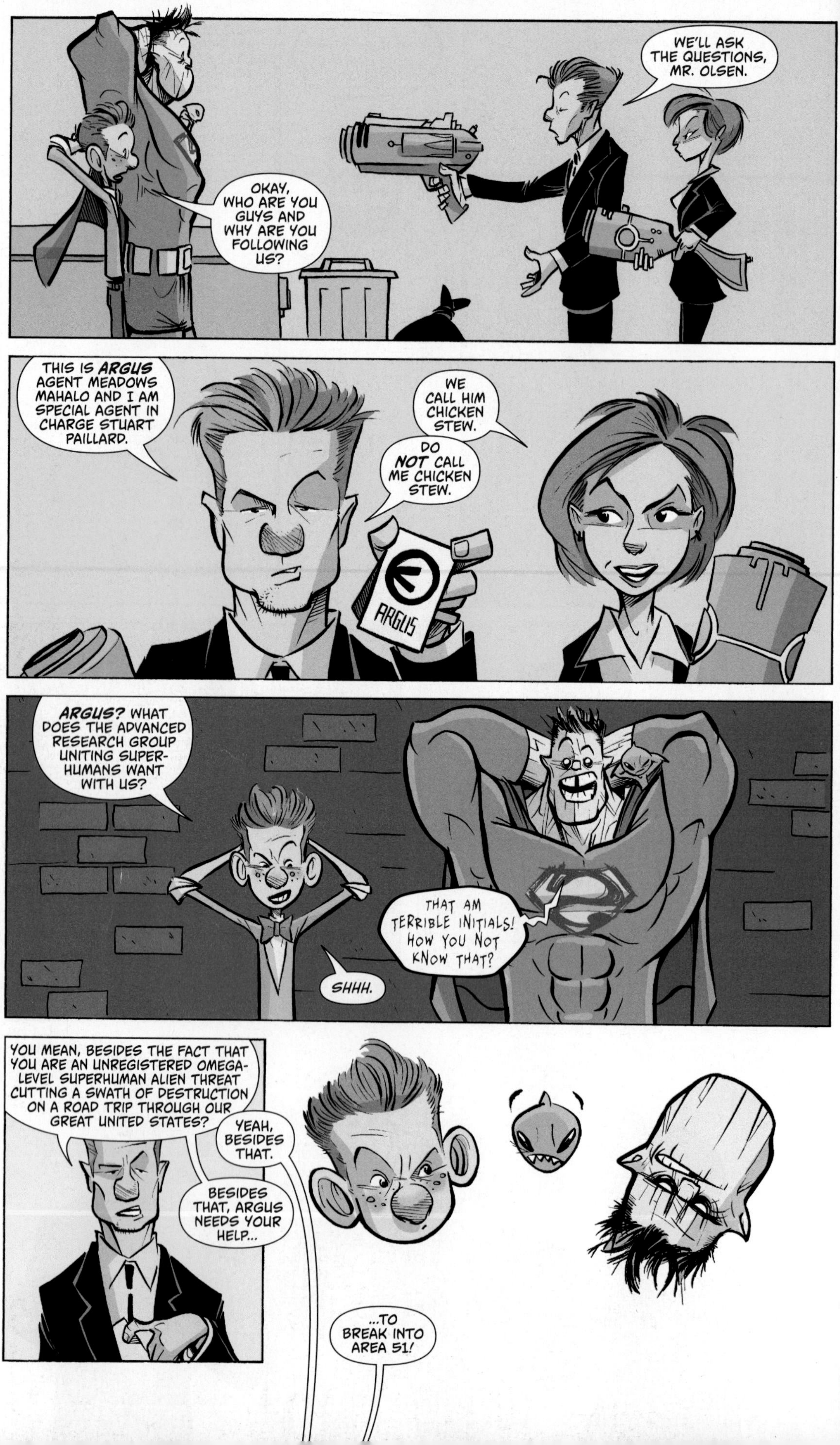
WE'LL ASK THE QUESTIONS, MR. OLSEN.
OKAY, WHO ARE YOU GUYS AND WHY ARE YOU FOLLOWING US?
THIS IS ARGUS AGENT MEADOWS MAHALO AND I AM SPECIAL AGENT IN CHARGE STUART PAILLARD.
WE CALL HIM CHICKEN STEW.
DO NOT CALL ME CHICKEN STEW.
ARGUS
ARGUS? WHAT DOES THE ADVANCED RESEARCH GROUP UNITING SUPER-HUMANS WANT WITH US?
THAT AM TERRIBLE INITIALS! HOW YOU NOT KNOW THAT?
SHHH.
YOU MEAN, BESIDES THE FACT THAT YOU ARE AN UNREGISTERED OMEGA-LEVEL SUPERHUMAN ALIEN THREAT CUTTING A SWATH OF DESTRUCTION ON A ROAD TRIP THROUGH OUR GREAT UNITED STATES?
YEAH, BESIDES THAT.
BESIDES THAT, ARGUS NEEDS YOUR HELP...
...TO BREAK INTO AREA 51!

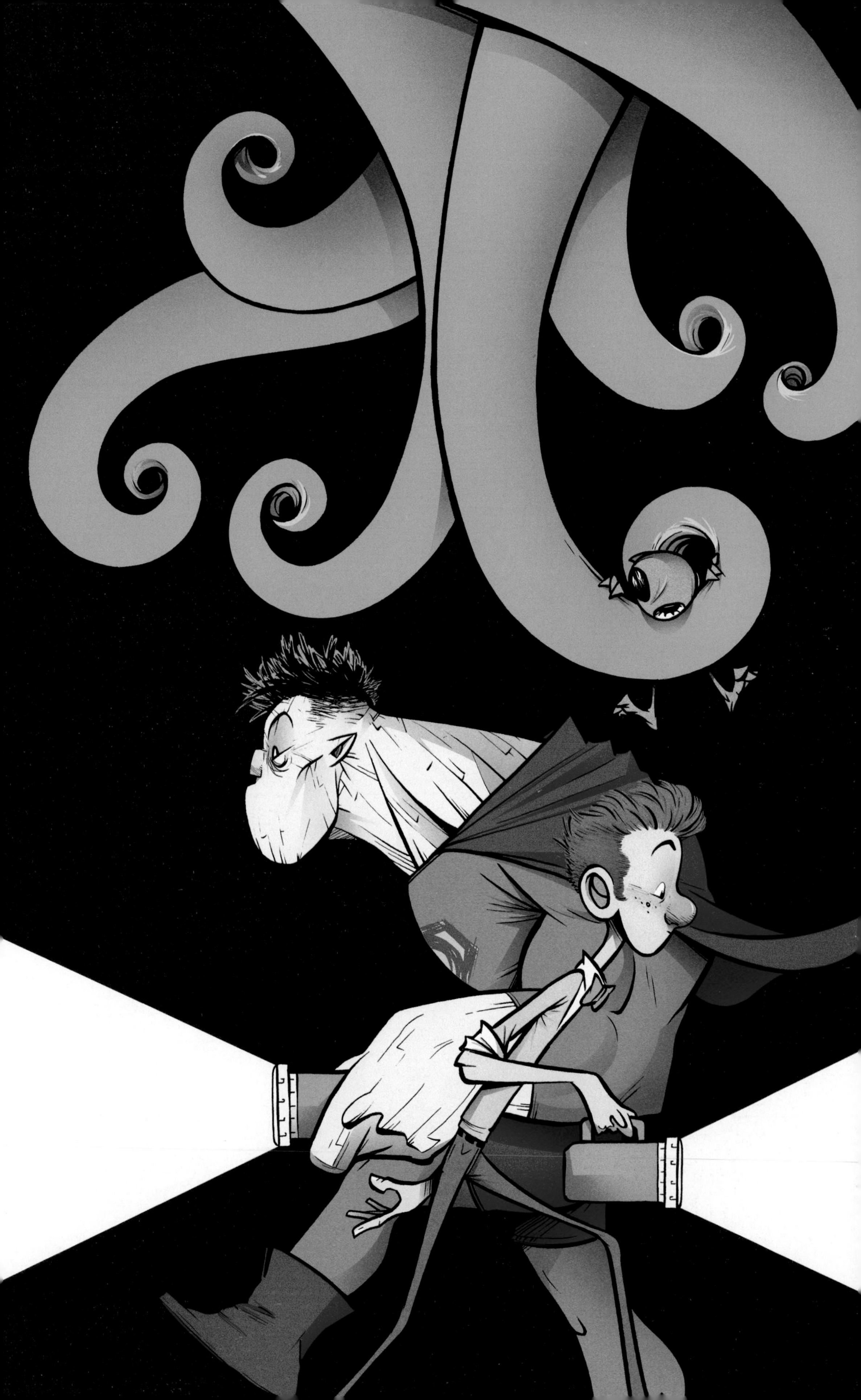

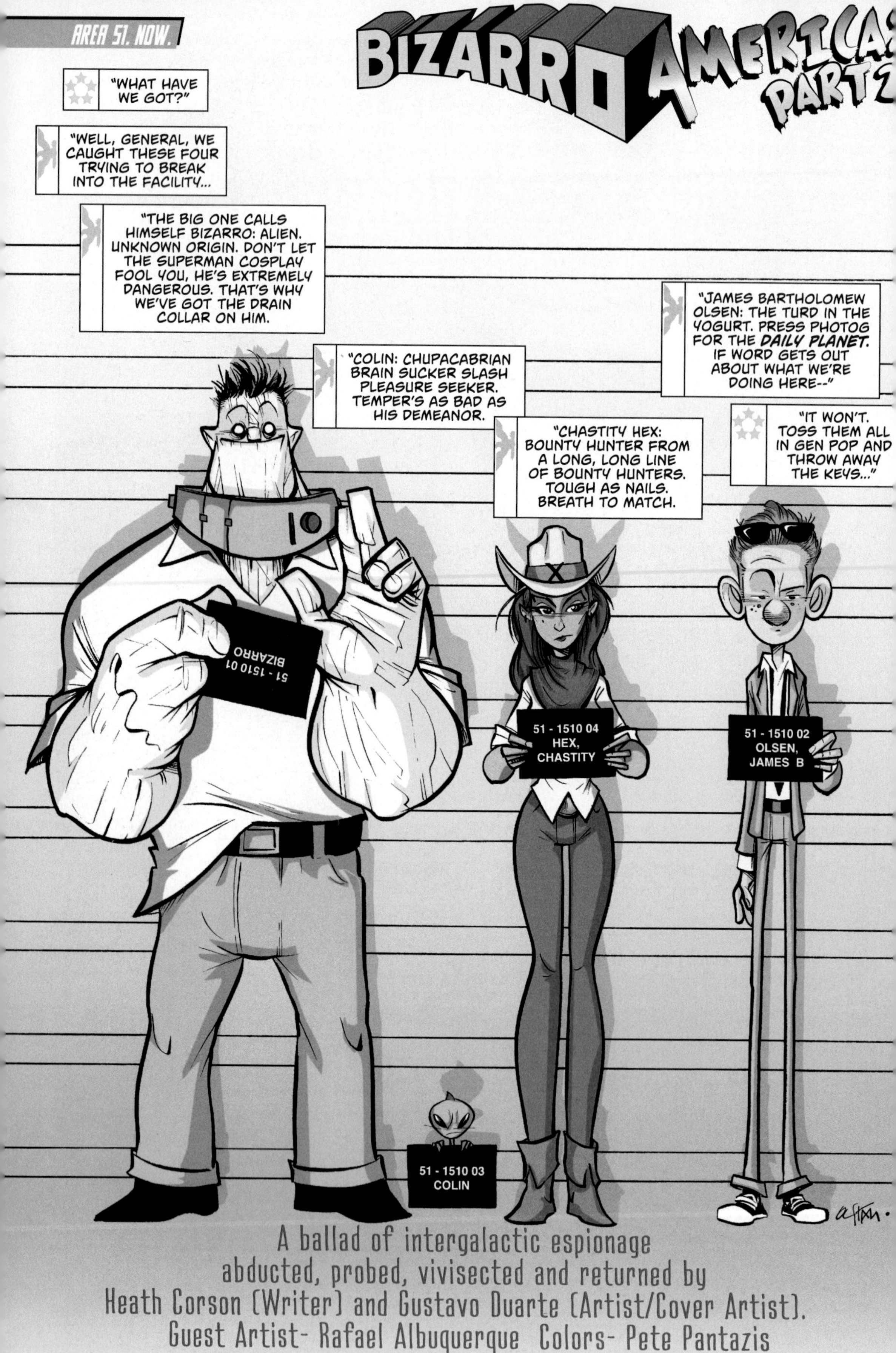
AREA 51. NOW.
BIZARRO AMERICA PART 2
"WHAT HAVE WE GOT?"
"WELL, GENERAL, WE CAUGHT THESE FOUR TRYING TO BREAK INTO THE FACILITY...
"THE BIG ONE CALLS HIMSELF BIZARRO: ALIEN. UNKNOWN ORIGIN. DON'T LET THE SUPERMAN COSPLAY FOOL YOU, HE'S EXTREMELY DANGEROUS. THAT'S WHY WE'VE GOT THE DRAIN COLLAR ON HIM.
"COLIN: CHUPACABRIAN BRAIN SUCKER SLASH PLEASURE SEEKER. TEMPER'S AS BAD AS HIS DEMEANOR.
"CHASTITY HEX: BOUNTY HUNTER FROM A LONG, LONG LINE OF BOUNTY HUNTERS. TOUGH AS NAILS. BREATH TO MATCH.
"JAMES BARTHOLOMEW OLSEN: THE TURD IN THE YOGURT. PRESS PHOTOG FOR THE *DAILY PLANET.* IF WORD GETS OUT ABOUT WHAT WE'RE DOING HERE--"
"IT WON'T. TOSS THEM ALL IN GEN POP AND THROW AWAY THE KEYS..."
51 - 1510 01 BIZARRO
51 - 1510 04 HEX, CHASTITY
51 - 1510 02 OLSEN, JAMES B
51 - 1510 03 COLIN

A ballad of intergalactic espionage
abducted, probed, vivisected and returned by
Heath Corson (Writer) and Gustavo Duarte (Artist/Cover Artist).
Guest Artist- Rafael Albuquerque Colors- Pete Pantazis
Letters- Tom Napolitano

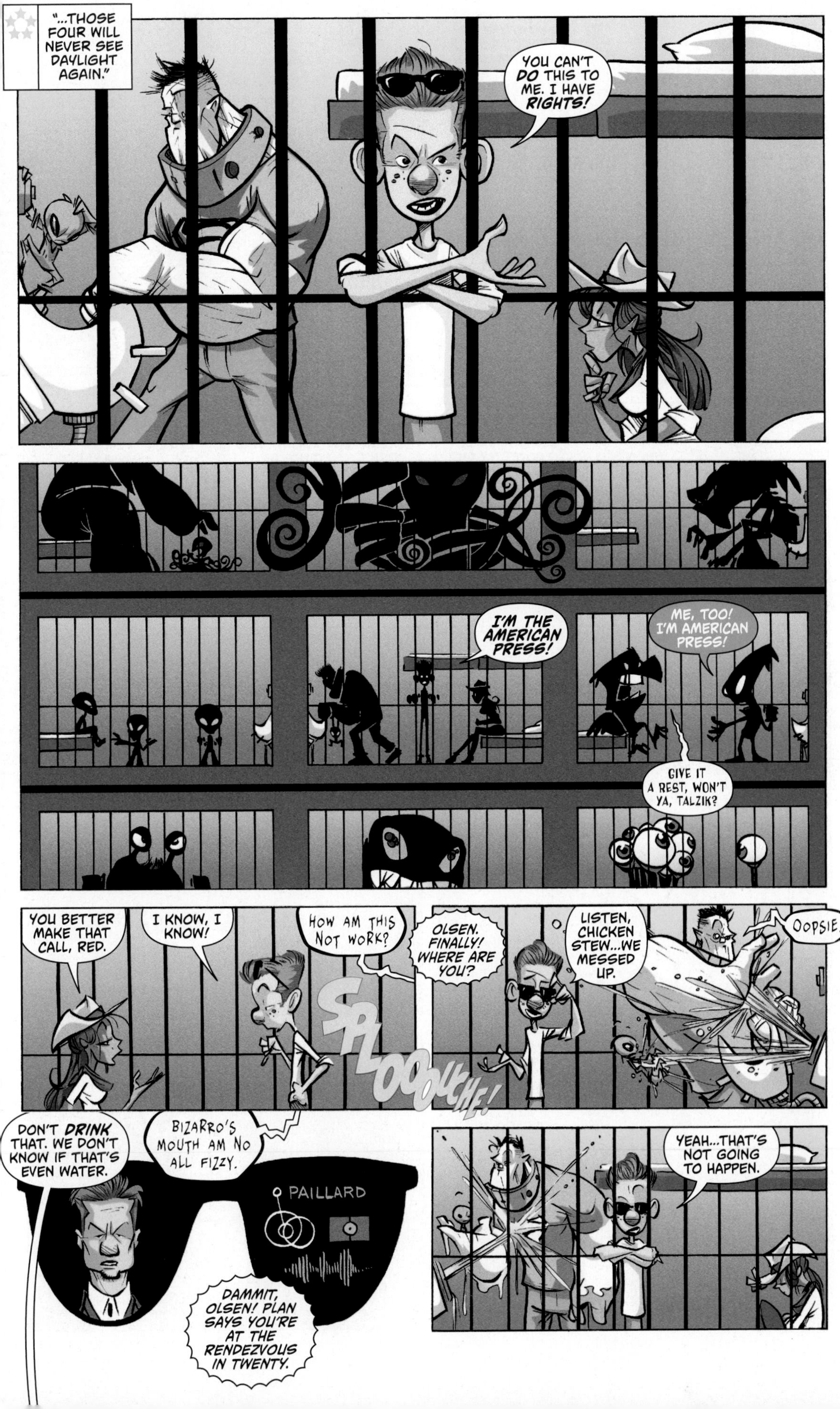
"...THOSE FOUR WILL NEVER SEE DAYLIGHT AGAIN."
YOU CAN'T DO THIS TO ME. I HAVE RIGHTS!
I'M THE AMERICAN PRESS!
ME, TOO! I'M AMERICAN PRESS!
GIVE IT A REST, WON'T YA, TALZIK?
YOU BETTER MAKE THAT CALL, RED.
I KNOW, I KNOW!
HOW AM THIS NOT WORK?
SPLOOOUCHE!
OLSEN. FINALLY! WHERE ARE YOU?
LISTEN, CHICKEN STEW...WE MESSED UP.
OOPSIE.
DON'T DRINK THAT. WE DON'T KNOW IF THAT'S EVEN WATER.
BIZARRO'S MOUTH AM NO ALL FIZZY.
PAILLARD
DAMMIT, OLSEN! PLAN SAYS YOU'RE AT THE RENDEZVOUS IN TWENTY.
YEAH...THAT'S NOT GOING TO HAPPEN.

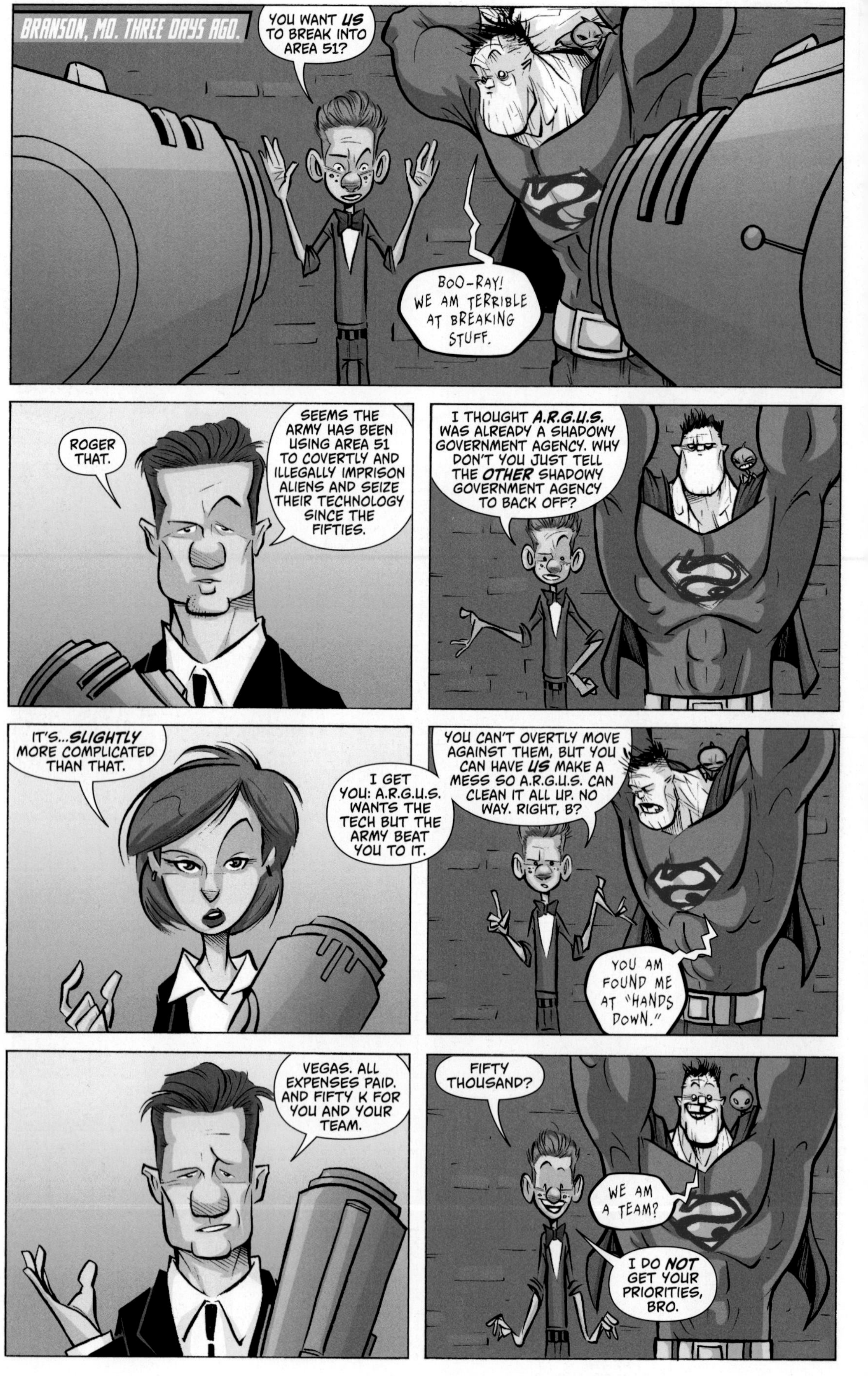
BRANSON, MO. THREE DAYS AGO.
YOU WANT US TO BREAK INTO AREA 51?
BOO-RAY! WE AM TERRIBLE AT BREAKING STUFF.
ROGER THAT.
SEEMS THE ARMY HAS BEEN USING AREA 51 TO COVERTLY AND ILLEGALLY IMPRISON ALIENS AND SEIZE THEIR TECHNOLOGY SINCE THE FIFTIES.
I THOUGHT A.R.G.U.S. WAS ALREADY A SHADOWY GOVERNMENT AGENCY. WHY DON'T YOU JUST TELL THE OTHER SHADOWY GOVERNMENT AGENCY TO BACK OFF?
IT'S...SLIGHTLY MORE COMPLICATED THAN THAT.
I GET YOU: A.R.G.U.S. WANTS THE TECH BUT THE ARMY BEAT YOU TO IT.
YOU CAN'T OVERTLY MOVE AGAINST THEM, BUT YOU CAN HAVE US MAKE A MESS SO A.R.G.U.S. CAN CLEAN IT ALL UP. NO WAY. RIGHT, B?
YOU AM FOUND ME AT "HANDS DOWN."
VEGAS. ALL EXPENSES PAID. AND FIFTY K FOR YOU AND YOUR TEAM.
FIFTY THOUSAND?
WE AM A TEAM?
I DO NOT GET YOUR PRIORITIES, BRO.

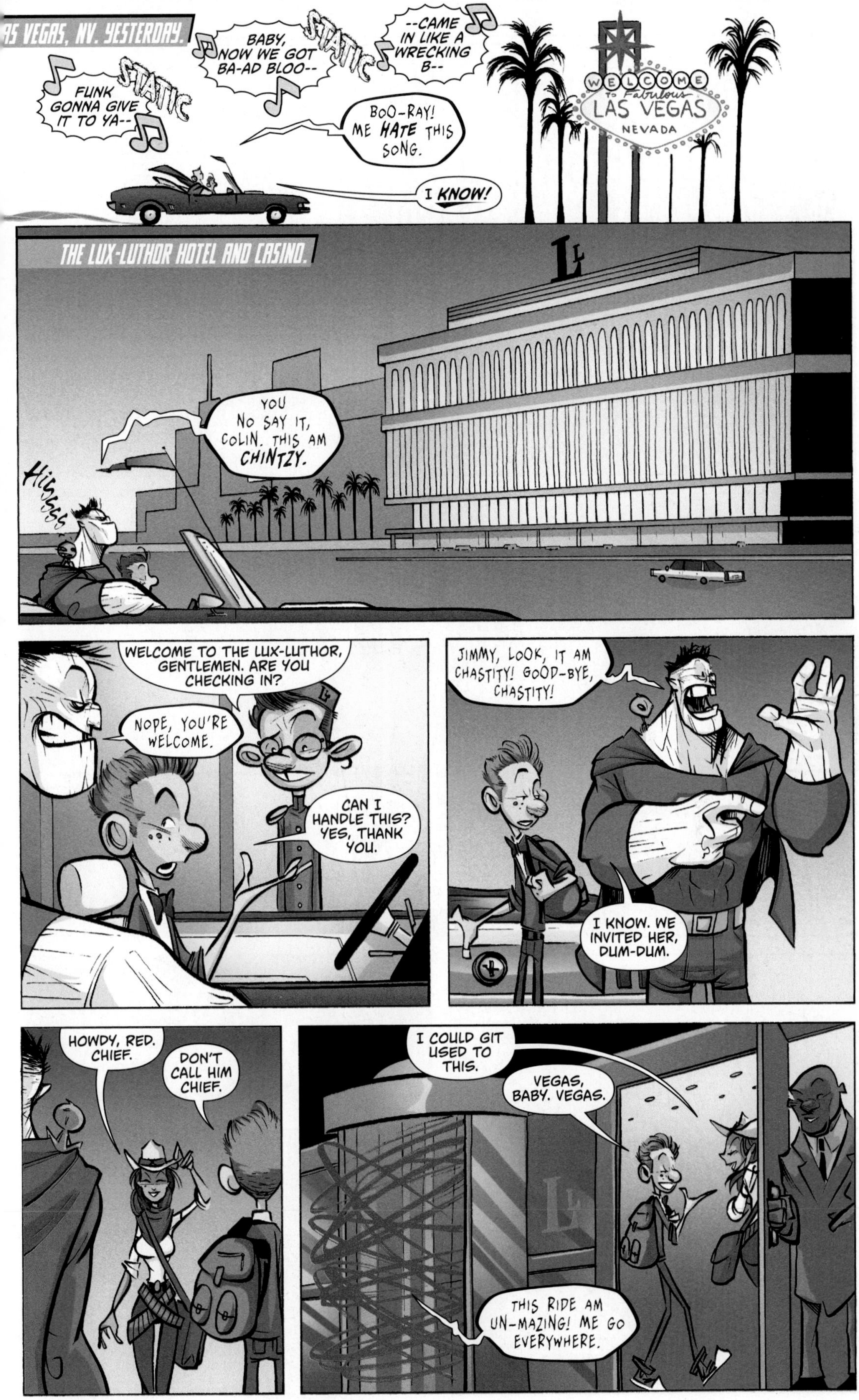
AS VEGAS, NV. YESTERDAY.
FUNK GONNA GIVE IT TO YA--
STATIC
BABY, NOW WE GOT BA-AD BLOO--
STATIC
--CAME IN LIKE A WRECKING B--
BOO-RAY! ME HATE THIS SONG.
I KNOW!
WELCOME to Fabulous LAS VEGAS NEVADA
THE LUX-LUTHOR HOTEL AND CASINO.
YOU NO SAY IT, COLIN. THIS AM CHINTZY.
HISSSS
WELCOME TO THE LUX-LUTHOR, GENTLEMEN. ARE YOU CHECKING IN?
NOPE, YOU'RE WELCOME.
CAN I HANDLE THIS? YES, THANK YOU.
JIMMY, LOOK, IT AM CHASTITY! GOOD-BYE, CHASTITY!
I KNOW. WE INVITED HER, DUM-DUM.
HOWDY, RED. CHIEF.
DON'T CALL HIM CHIEF.
I COULD GIT USED TO THIS.
VEGAS, BABY. VEGAS.
THIS RIDE AM UN-MAZING! ME GO EVERYWHERE.

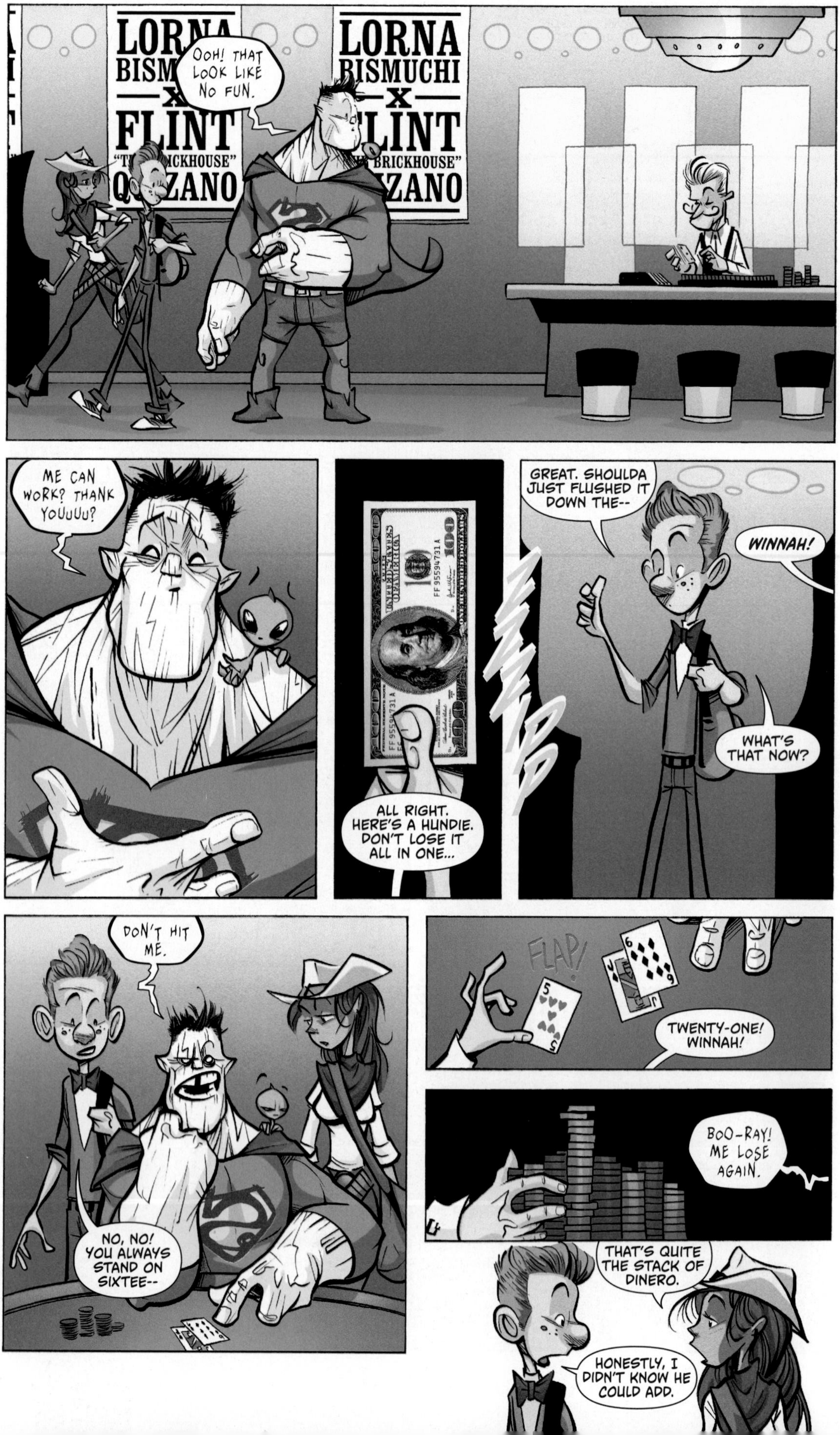
LORNA BISMUCHI X FLINT "THE BRICKHOUSE" QUIZANO
OOH! THAT LOOK LIKE NO FUN.
ME CAN WORK? THANK YOUUUU?
ALL RIGHT. HERE'S A HUNDIE. DON'T LOSE IT ALL IN ONE...
GREAT. SHOULDA JUST FLUSHED IT DOWN THE--
WINNAH!
WHAT'S THAT NOW?
DON'T HIT ME.
NO, NO! YOU ALWAYS STAND ON SIXTEE--
FLAP!
TWENTY-ONE! WINNAH!
BOO-RAY! ME LOSE AGAIN.
THAT'S QUITE THE STACK OF DINERO.
HONESTLY, I DIDN'T KNOW HE COULD ADD.

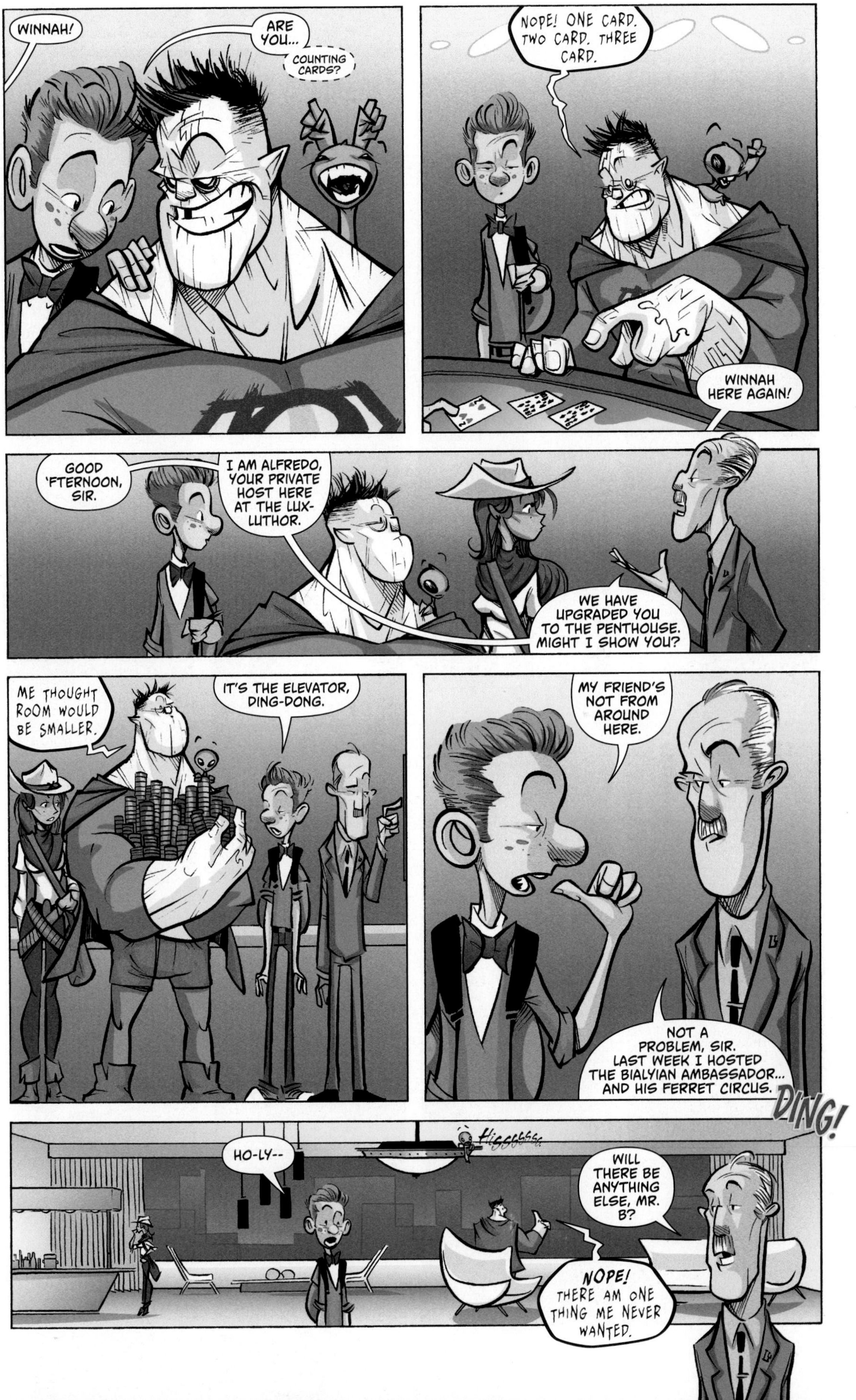
WINNAH!
ARE YOU...
COUNTING CARDS?
NOPE! ONE CARD. TWO CARD. THREE CARD.
WINNAH HERE AGAIN!
GOOD 'FTERNOON, SIR.
I AM ALFREDO, YOUR PRIVATE HOST HERE AT THE LUX-LUTHOR.
WE HAVE UPGRADED YOU TO THE PENTHOUSE. MIGHT I SHOW YOU?
ME THOUGHT ROOM WOULD BE SMALLER.
IT'S THE ELEVATOR, DING-DONG.
MY FRIEND'S NOT FROM AROUND HERE.
NOT A PROBLEM, SIR. LAST WEEK I HOSTED THE BIALYIAN AMBASSADOR... AND HIS FERRET CIRCUS.
DING!
HO-LY--
WILL THERE BE ANYTHING ELSE, MR. B?
NOPE! THERE AM ONE THING ME NEVER WANTED.

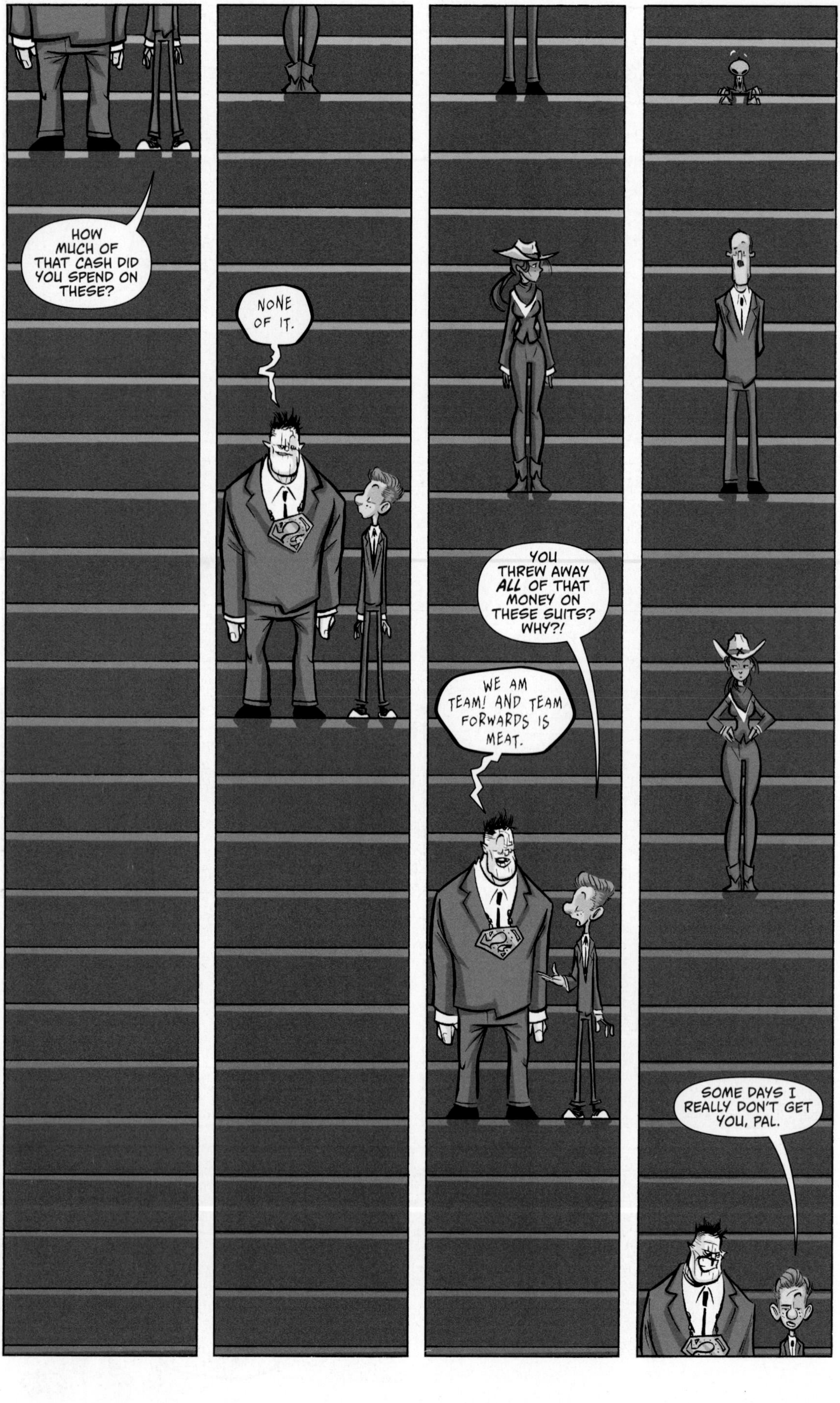
HOW MUCH OF THAT CASH DID YOU SPEND ON THESE?
NONE OF IT.
YOU THREW AWAY ALL OF THAT MONEY ON THESE SUITS? WHY?!
WE AM TEAM! AND TEAM FORWARDS IS MEAT.
SOME DAYS I REALLY DON'T GET YOU, PAL.

"ONCE IN, YOU CONNECT WITH BIG MUNK. TOP GUY IN THE PRISON. NOTHING HAPPENS WITHOUT HIS SAY-SO."

WHERE AM WE END?

'F IT WERE ME, I'D GRAB THE BIGGEST, MEANEST ALIEN HERE AND RATTLE THEIR CAGE 'TIL THEY TOOK US TO THE BOSSMAN.

TERRIBLE IDEA, WORSTEST FRIEND CHASTITY.

WHAT?! HOLD UP...

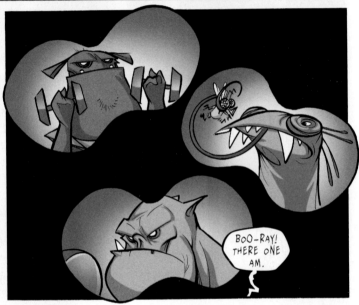

BOO-RAY! THERE ONE AM.

SLOW YOUR ROLL HERE, B. THAT COLLAR EQUALS *NO POWERS.* DON'T BE LOOKING FOR TROUBLE WITH IT *ON.*

ME AM EXCITED OF LISTENING TO YOU, JIMMY OLSEN!

ME? WHAT DID I DO?

YOU! YOU AM NO OOZING ALL OVER MY SPOT.

HERE WE GO...

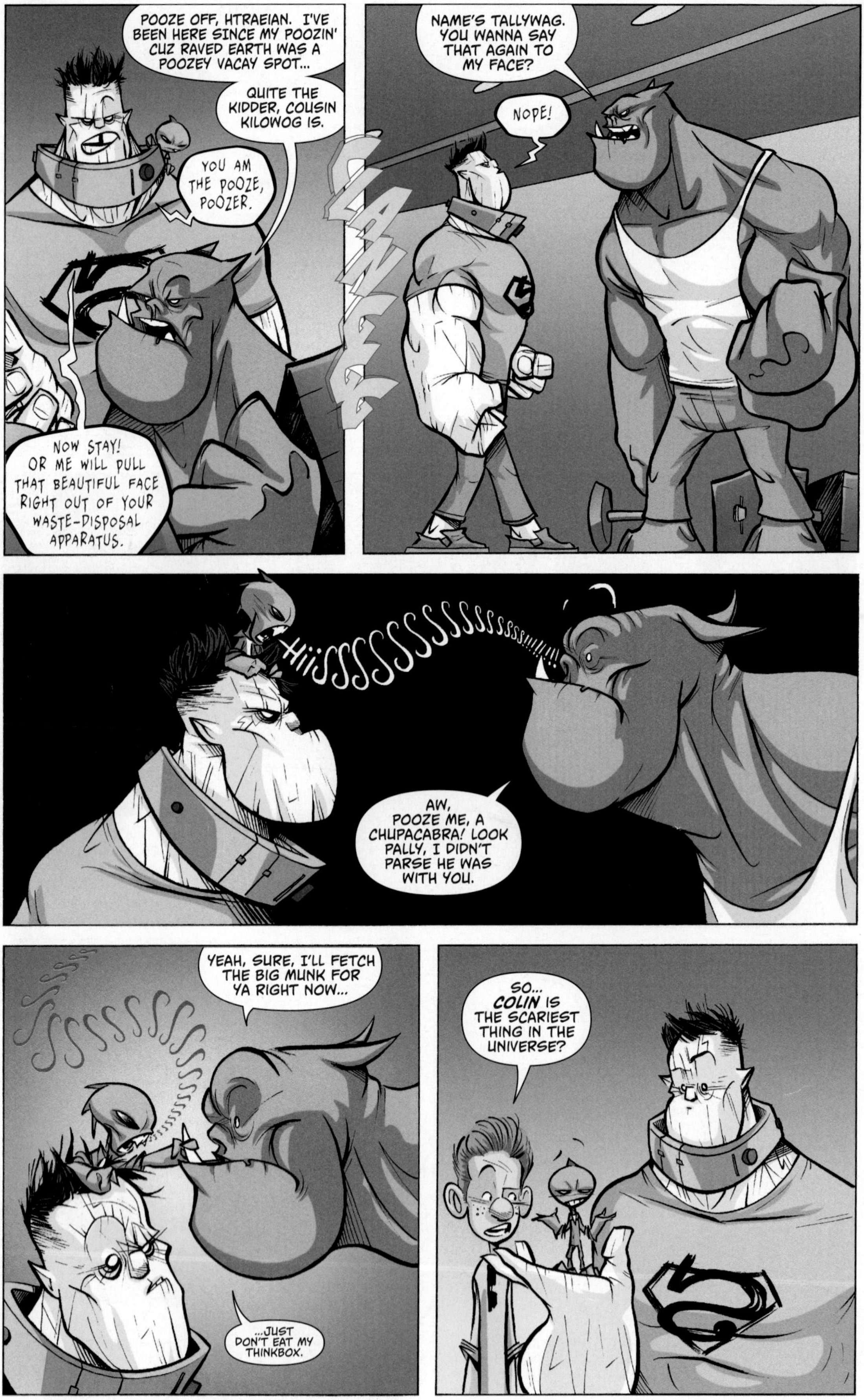
POOZE OFF, HTRAEIAN. I'VE BEEN HERE SINCE MY POOZIN' CUZ RAVED EARTH WAS A POOZEY VACAY SPOT...
QUITE THE KIDDER, COUSIN KILOWOG IS.
YOU AM THE POOZE, POOZER.
NOW STAY! OR ME WILL PULL THAT BEAUTIFUL FACE RIGHT OUT OF YOUR WASTE-DISPOSAL APPARATUS.
CLANGGG
NAME'S TALLYWAG. YOU WANNA SAY THAT AGAIN TO MY FACE?
NOPE!
HIISSSSSSSSSSSSSSSSSS!!!!!!!
AW, POOZE ME, A CHUPACABRA! LOOK PALLY, I DIDN'T PARSE HE WAS WITH YOU.
YEAH, SURE, I'LL FETCH THE BIG MUNK FOR YA RIGHT NOW...
...JUST DON'T EAT MY THINKBOX.
SO... COLIN IS THE SCARIEST THING IN THE UNIVERSE?

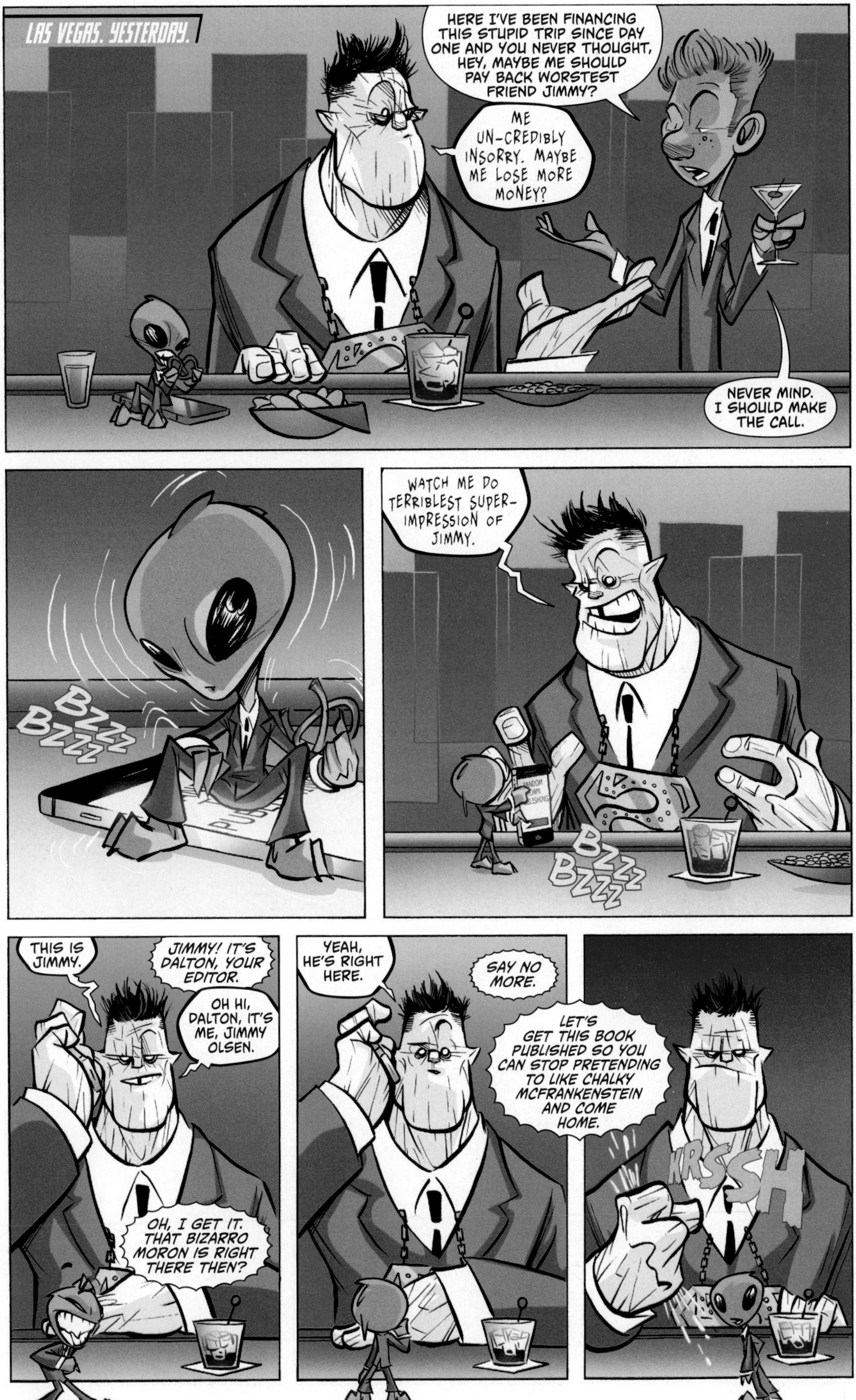
LAS VEGAS. YESTERDAY.
HERE I'VE BEEN FINANCING THIS STUPID TRIP SINCE DAY ONE AND YOU NEVER THOUGHT, HEY, MAYBE ME SHOULD PAY BACK WORSTEST FRIEND JIMMY?
ME UN-CREDIBLY INSORRY. MAYBE ME LOSE MORE MONEY?
NEVER MIND. I SHOULD MAKE THE CALL.
BZZZ BZZZZ
WATCH ME DO TERRIBLEST SUPER-IMPRESSION OF JIMMY.
BZZZ BZZZZ
THIS IS JIMMY.
JIMMY! IT'S DALTON, YOUR EDITOR.
OH HI, DALTON, IT'S ME, JIMMY OLSEN.
OH, I GET IT. THAT BIZARRO MORON IS RIGHT THERE THEN?
YEAH, HE'S RIGHT HERE.
SAY NO MORE.
LET'S GET THIS BOOK PUBLISHED SO YOU CAN STOP PRETENDING TO LIKE CHALKY MCFRANKENSTEIN AND COME HOME.
KRSSH

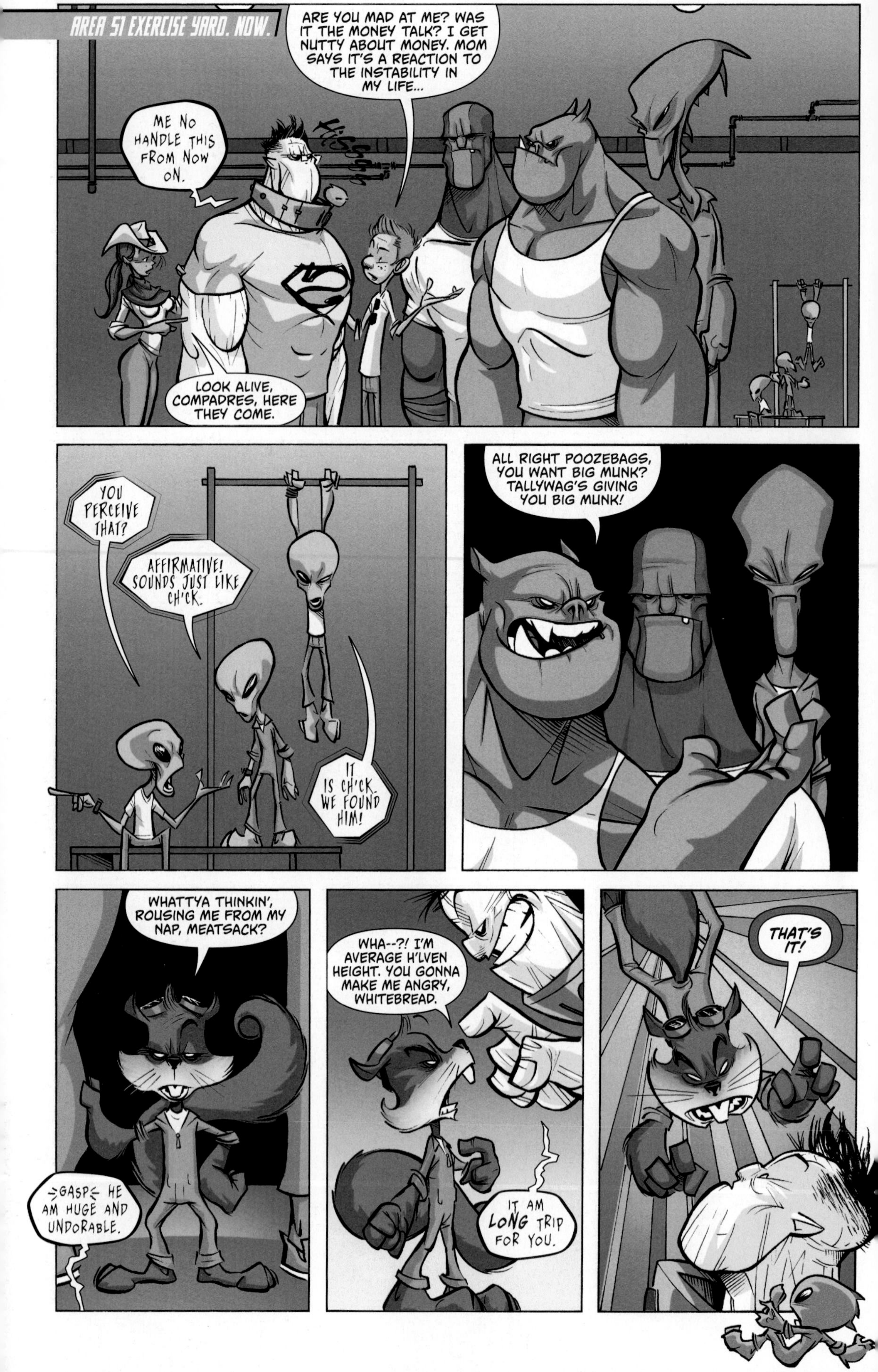
AREA 51 EXERCISE YARD. NOW.
ARE YOU MAD AT ME? WAS IT THE MONEY TALK? I GET NUTTY ABOUT MONEY. MOM SAYS IT'S A REACTION TO THE INSTABILITY IN MY LIFE...
ME NO HANDLE THIS FROM NOW ON.
HISSSS
LOOK ALIVE, COMPADRES, HERE THEY COME.
YOU PERCEIVE THAT?
AFFIRMATIVE! SOUNDS JUST LIKE CH'CK.
IT IS CH'CK. WE FOUND HIM!
ALL RIGHT POOZEBAGS, YOU WANT BIG MUNK? TALLYWAG'S GIVING YOU BIG MUNK!
WHATTYA THINKIN', ROUSING ME FROM MY NAP, MEATSACK?
GASP HE AM HUGE AND UNDORABLE.
WHA--?! I'M AVERAGE H'LVEN HEIGHT. YOU GONNA MAKE ME ANGRY, WHITEBREAD.
IT AM LONG TRIP FOR YOU.
THAT'S IT!

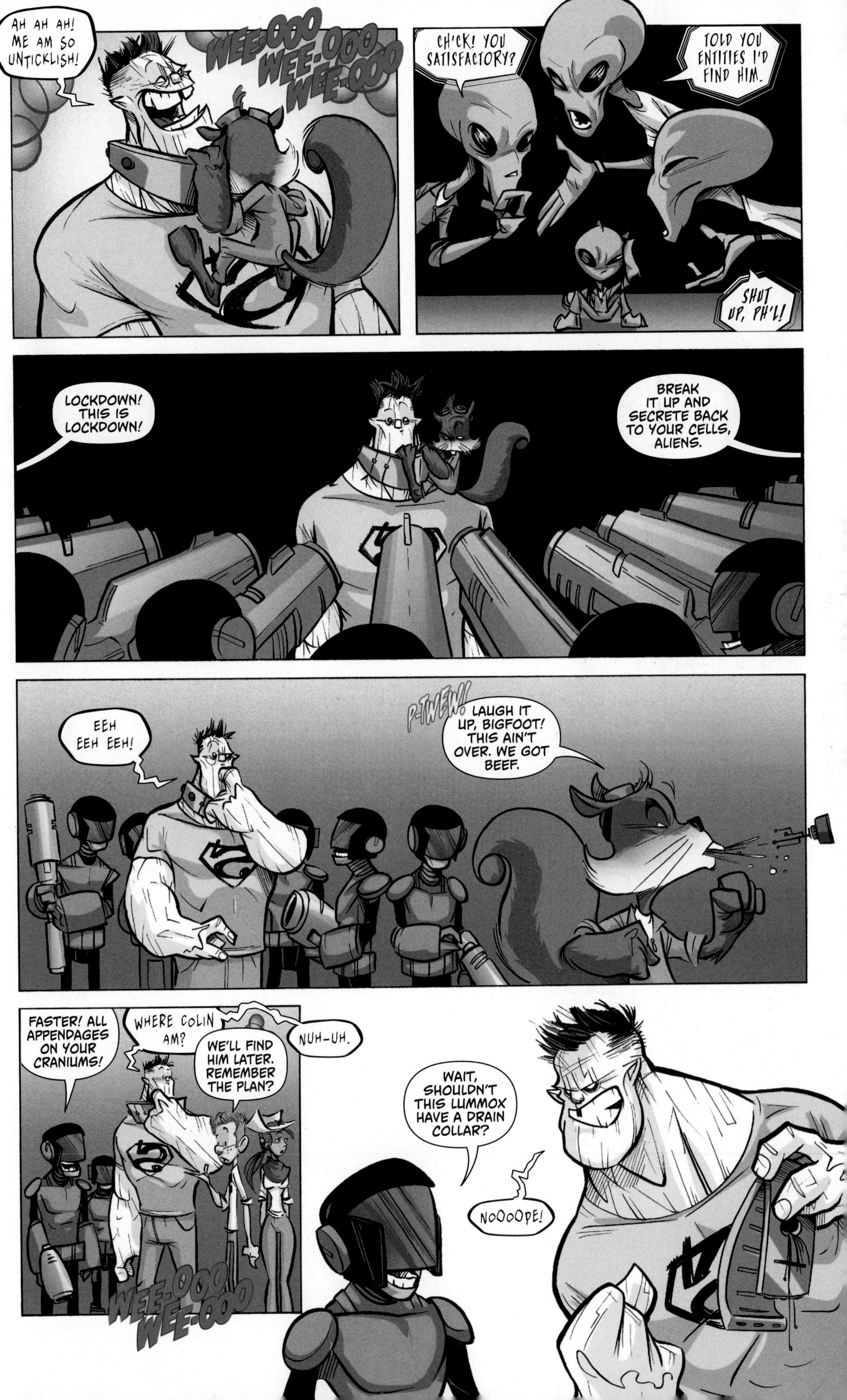
AH AH AH! ME AM SO UNTICKLISH!
WEE-OOO WEE-OOO WEE-OOO
CH'CK! YOU SATISFACTORY?
TOLD YOU ENTITIES I'D FIND HIM.
SHUT UP, PH'L!
LOCKDOWN! THIS IS LOCKDOWN!
BREAK IT UP AND SECRETE BACK TO YOUR CELLS, ALIENS.
EEH EEH EEH!
P-TWEW!
LAUGH IT UP, BIGFOOT! THIS AIN'T OVER. WE GOT BEEF.
FASTER! ALL APPENDAGES ON YOUR CRANIUMS!
WHERE COLIN AM?
WE'LL FIND HIM LATER. REMEMBER THE PLAN?
NUH-UH.
WEE-OOO WEE-OOO
WAIT, SHOULDN'T THIS LUMMOX HAVE A DRAIN COLLAR?
NOOOOPE!

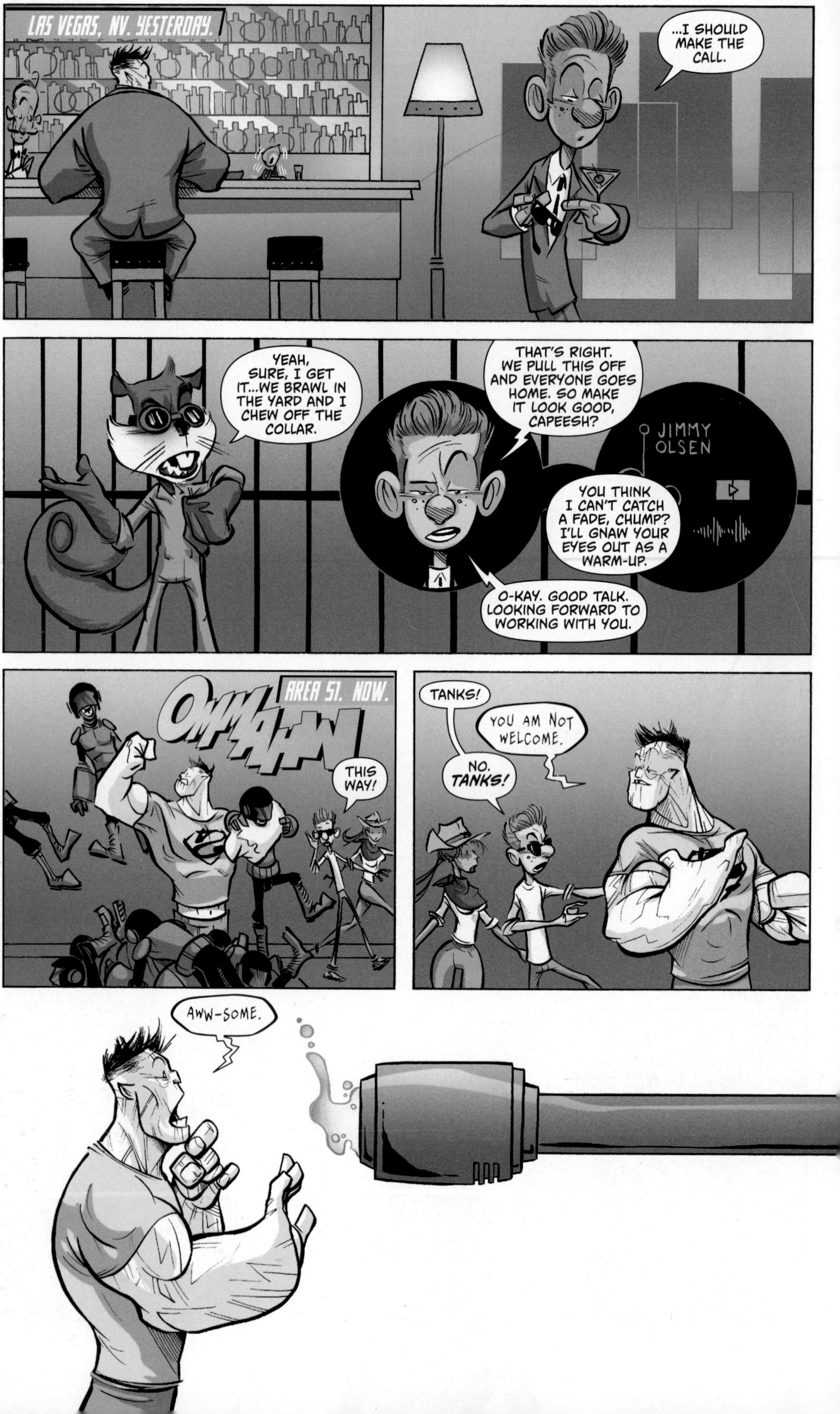
LAS VEGAS, NV. YESTERDAY.
...I SHOULD MAKE THE CALL.
YEAH, SURE, I GET IT...WE BRAWL IN THE YARD AND I CHEW OFF THE COLLAR.
THAT'S RIGHT. WE PULL THIS OFF AND EVERYONE GOES HOME. SO MAKE IT LOOK GOOD, CAPEESH?
JIMMY OLSEN
YOU THINK I CAN'T CATCH A FADE, CHUMP? I'LL GNAW YOUR EYES OUT AS A WARM-UP.
O-KAY. GOOD TALK. LOOKING FORWARD TO WORKING WITH YOU.
AREA 51. NOW.
OHHAHHH
THIS WAY!
TANKS!
YOU AM NOT WELCOME.
NO. TANKS!
AWW-SOME.

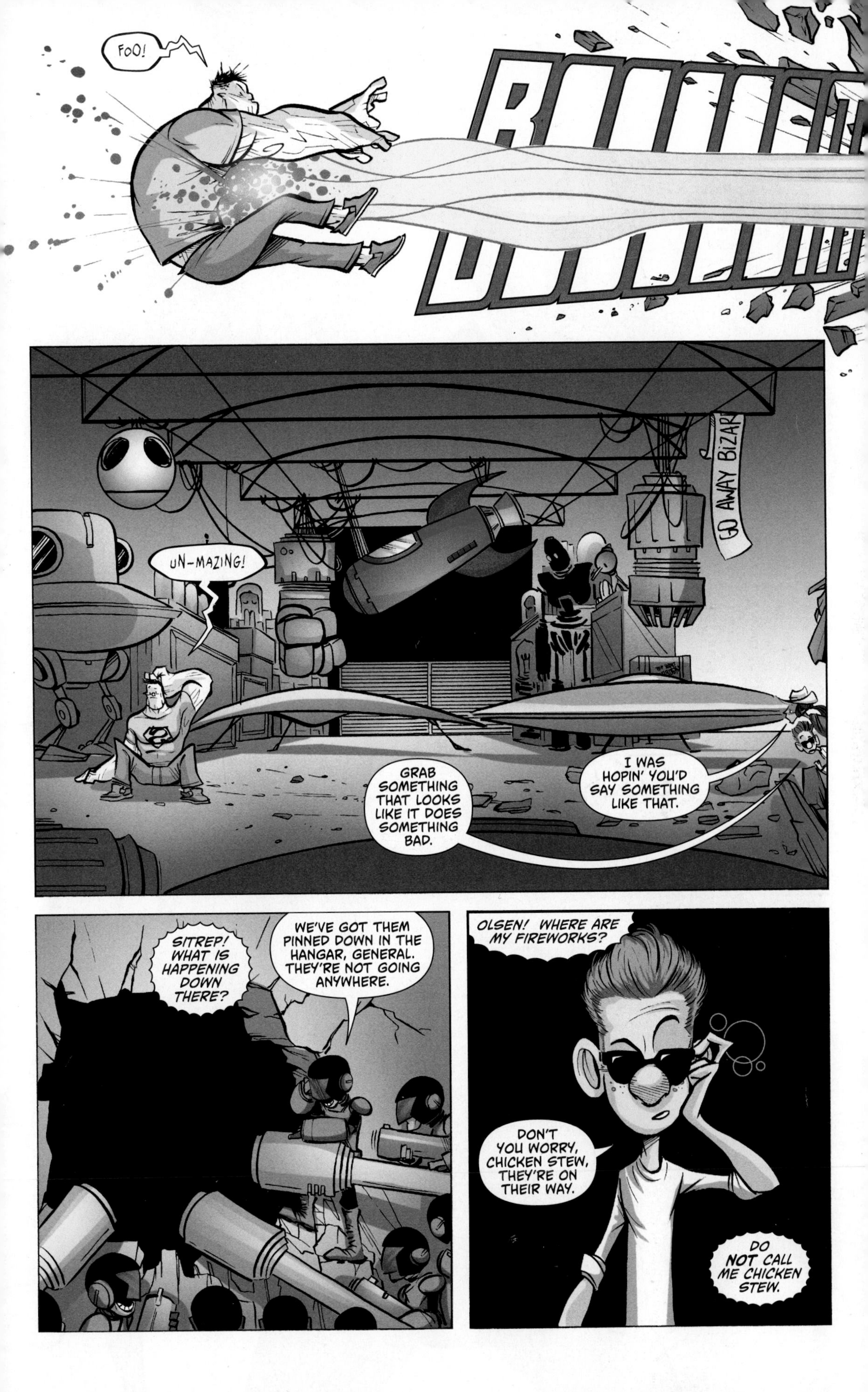
FOO!
UN-MAZING!
GO AWAY BIZAR
GRAB SOMETHING THAT LOOKS LIKE IT DOES SOMETHING BAD.
I WAS HOPIN' YOU'D SAY SOMETHING LIKE THAT.
SITREP! WHAT IS HAPPENING DOWN THERE?
WE'VE GOT THEM PINNED DOWN IN THE HANGAR, GENERAL. THEY'RE NOT GOING ANYWHERE.
OLSEN! WHERE ARE MY FIREWORKS?
DON'T YOU WORRY, CHICKEN STEW, THEY'RE ON THEIR WAY.
DO NOT CALL ME CHICKEN STEW.

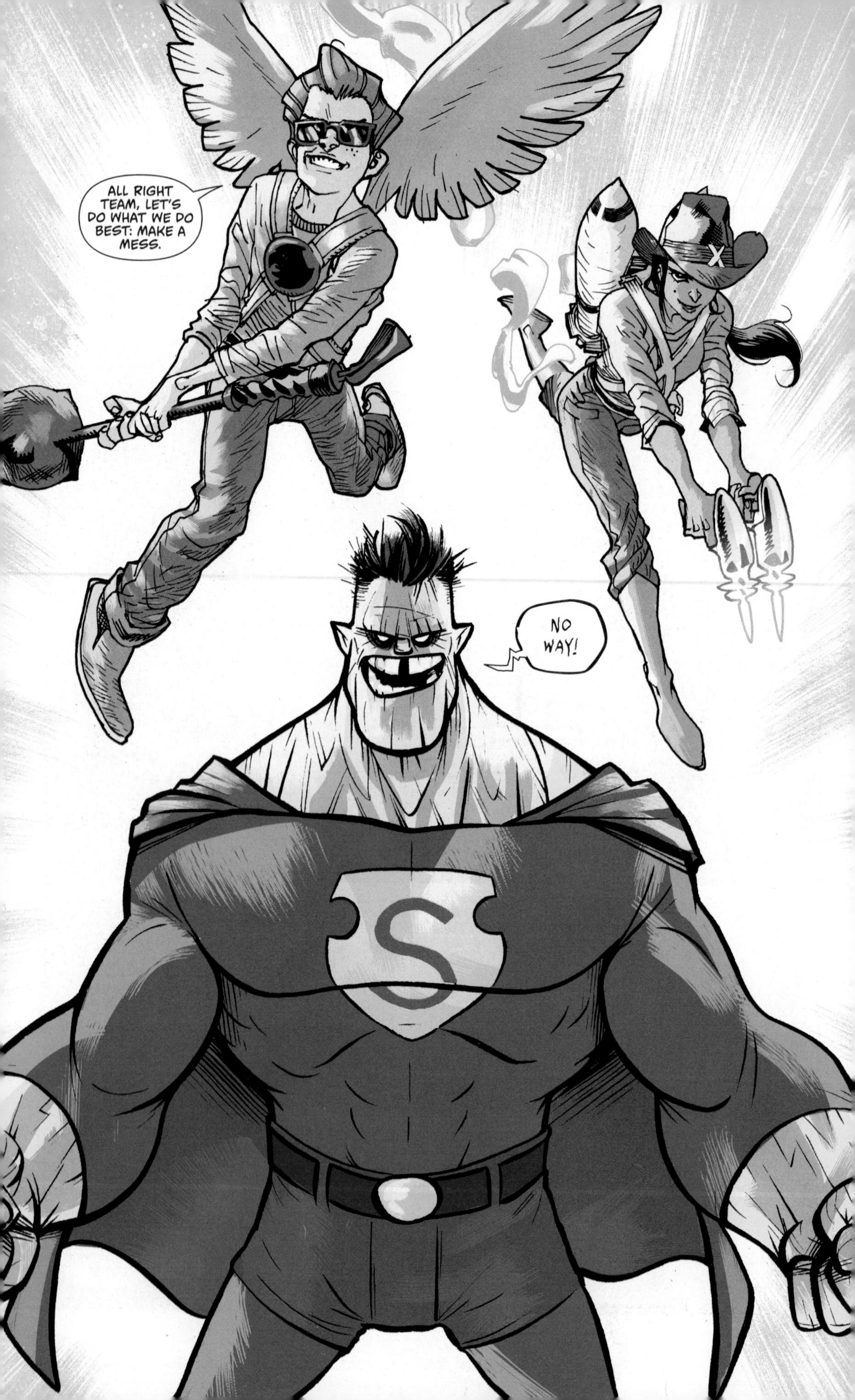
ALL RIGHT TEAM, LET'S DO WHAT WE DO BEST: MAKE A MESS.
NO WAY!

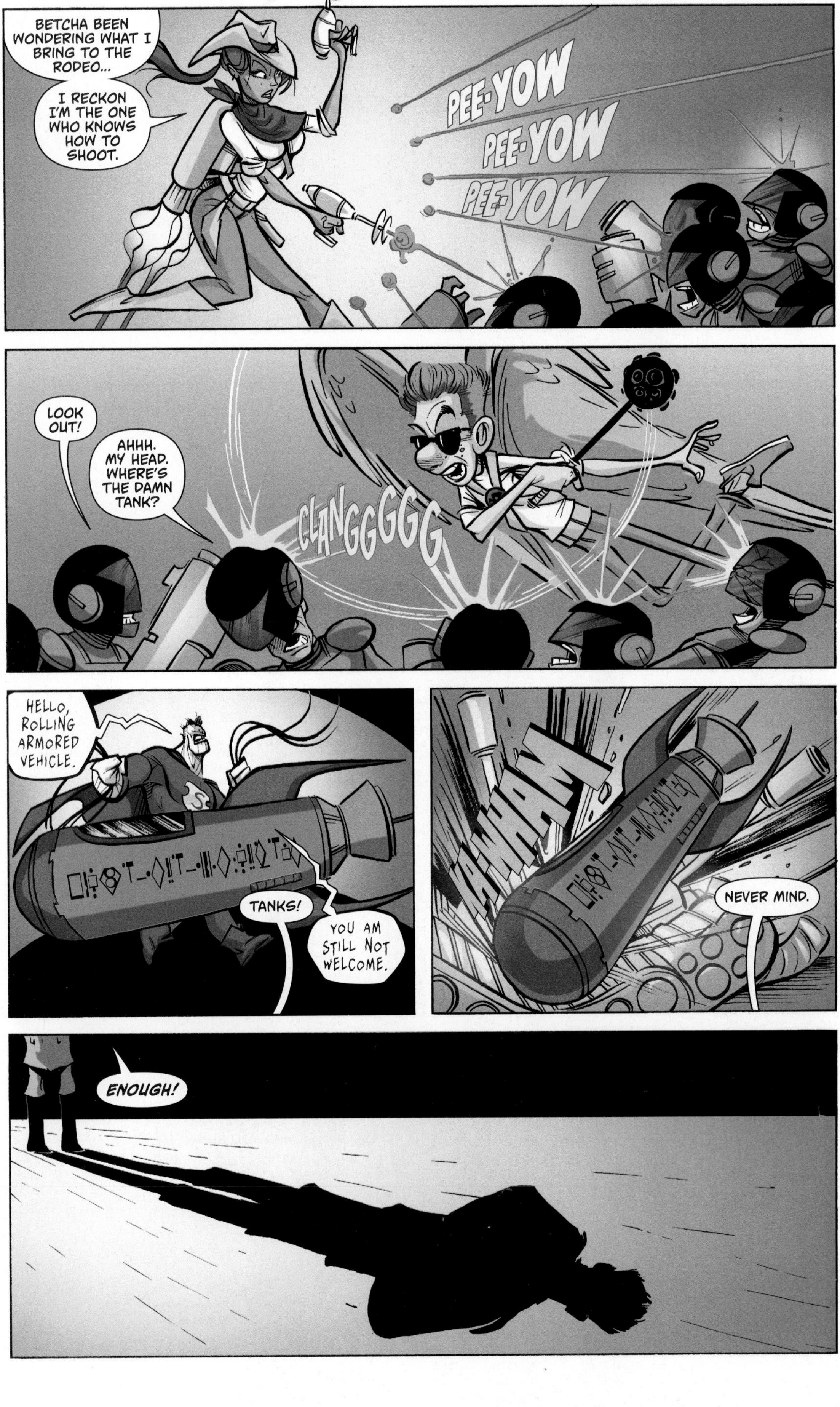
BETCHA BEEN WONDERING WHAT I BRING TO THE RODEO...
I RECKON I'M THE ONE WHO KNOWS HOW TO SHOOT.
PEE-YOW
PEE-YOW
PEE-YOW
LOOK OUT!
AHHH. MY HEAD. WHERE'S THE DAMN TANK?
CLANGGGGG
HELLO, ROLLING ARMORED VEHICLE.
TANKS!
YOU AM STILL NOT WELCOME.
NEVER MIND.
ENOUGH!

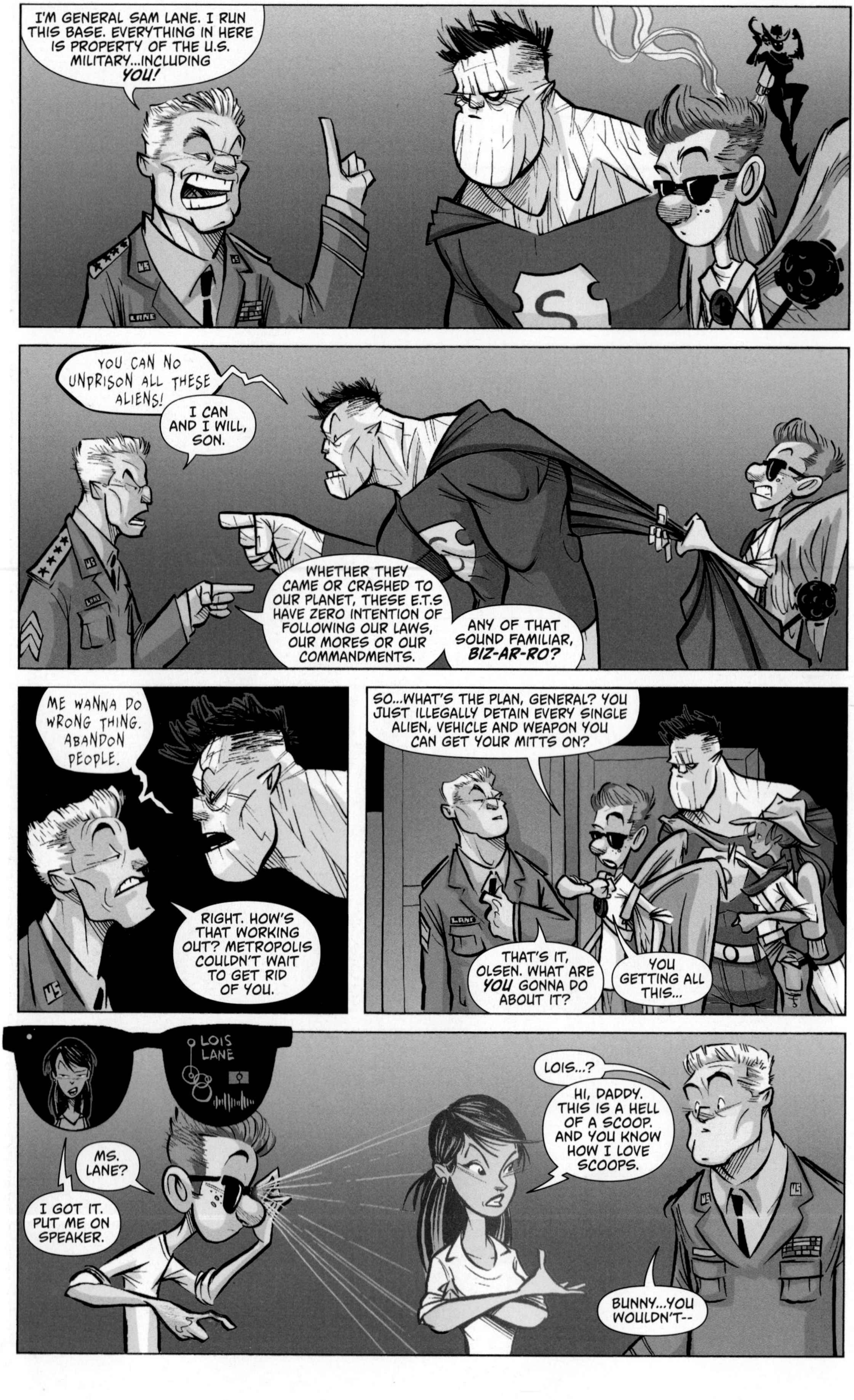

I'M GENERAL SAM LANE. I RUN THIS BASE. EVERYTHING IN HERE IS PROPERTY OF THE U.S. MILITARY...INCLUDING YOU!
YOU CAN NO UNPRISON ALL THESE ALIENS!
I CAN AND I WILL, SON.
WHETHER THEY CAME OR CRASHED TO OUR PLANET, THESE E.T.S HAVE ZERO INTENTION OF FOLLOWING OUR LAWS, OUR MORES OR OUR COMMANDMENTS.
ANY OF THAT SOUND FAMILIAR, BIZ-AR-RO?
ME WANNA DO WRONG THING. ABANDON PEOPLE.
RIGHT. HOW'S THAT WORKING OUT? METROPOLIS COULDN'T WAIT TO GET RID OF YOU.
SO...WHAT'S THE PLAN, GENERAL? YOU JUST ILLEGALLY DETAIN EVERY SINGLE ALIEN, VEHICLE AND WEAPON YOU CAN GET YOUR MITTS ON?
THAT'S IT, OLSEN. WHAT ARE YOU GONNA DO ABOUT IT?
YOU GETTING ALL THIS...
LOIS LANE
MS. LANE?
I GOT IT. PUT ME ON SPEAKER.
LOIS...?
HI, DADDY. THIS IS A HELL OF A SCOOP. AND YOU KNOW HOW I LOVE SCOOPS.
BUNNY...YOU WOULDN'T--

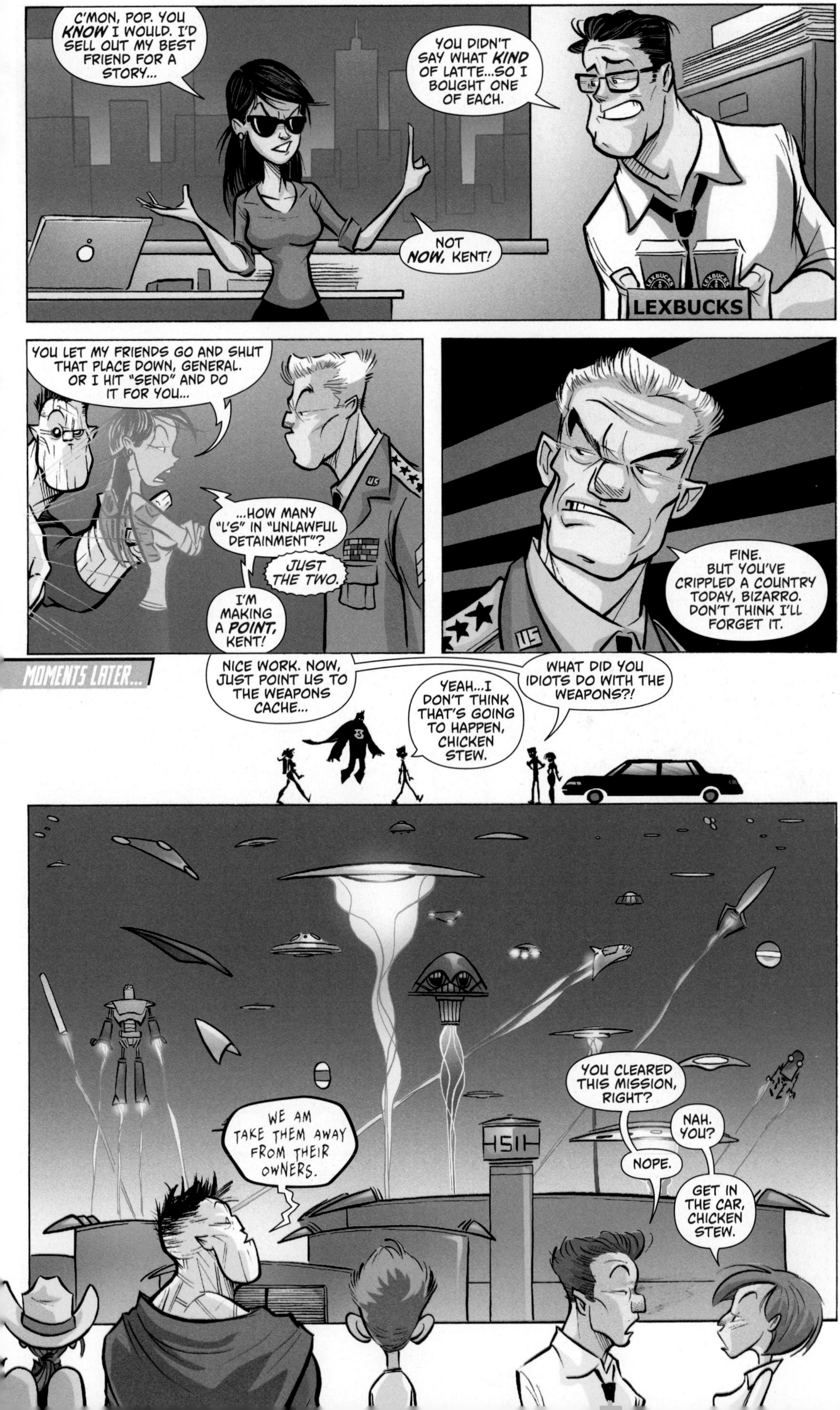
C'MON, POP. YOU KNOW I WOULD. I'D SELL OUT MY BEST FRIEND FOR A STORY...
YOU DIDN'T SAY WHAT KIND OF LATTE...SO I BOUGHT ONE OF EACH.
NOT NOW, KENT!
LEXBUCKS
YOU LET MY FRIENDS GO AND SHUT THAT PLACE DOWN, GENERAL. OR I HIT "SEND" AND DO IT FOR YOU...
...HOW MANY "L'S" IN "UNLAWFUL DETAINMENT"?
JUST THE TWO.
I'M MAKING A POINT, KENT!
FINE. BUT YOU'VE CRIPPLED A COUNTRY TODAY, BIZARRO. DON'T THINK I'LL FORGET IT.
MOMENTS LATER...
NICE WORK. NOW, JUST POINT US TO THE WEAPONS CACHE...
YEAH...I DON'T THINK THAT'S GOING TO HAPPEN, CHICKEN STEW.
WHAT DID YOU IDIOTS DO WITH THE WEAPONS?!
WE AM TAKE THEM AWAY FROM THEIR OWNERS.
YOU CLEARED THIS MISSION, RIGHT?
NOPE.
NAH. YOU?
GET IN THE CAR, CHICKEN STEW.
H51

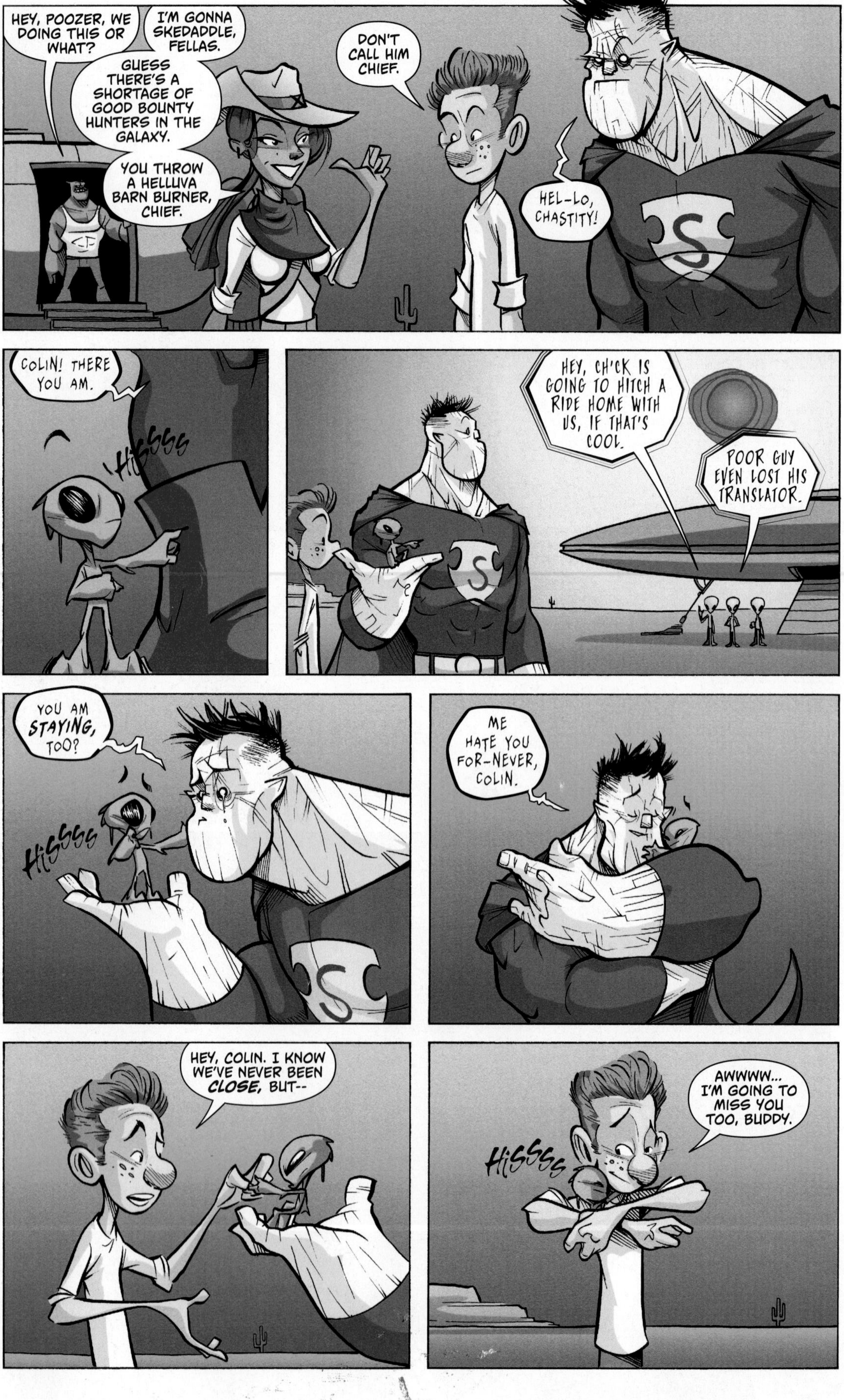
HEY, POOZER, WE DOING THIS OR WHAT?
I'M GONNA SKEDADDLE, FELLAS.
GUESS THERE'S A SHORTAGE OF GOOD BOUNTY HUNTERS IN THE GALAXY.
YOU THROW A HELLUVA BARN BURNER, CHIEF.
DON'T CALL HIM CHIEF.
HEL-LO, CHASTITY!
COLIN! THERE YOU AM.
HISSSS
HEY, CH'CK IS GOING TO HITCH A RIDE HOME WITH US, IF THAT'S COOL.
POOR GUY EVEN LOST HIS TRANSLATOR.
YOU AM STAYING, TOO?
HISSSS
ME HATE YOU FOR-NEVER, COLIN.
HEY, COLIN. I KNOW WE'VE NEVER BEEN CLOSE, BUT--
AWWWW... I'M GOING TO MISS YOU TOO, BUDDY.
HISSSS

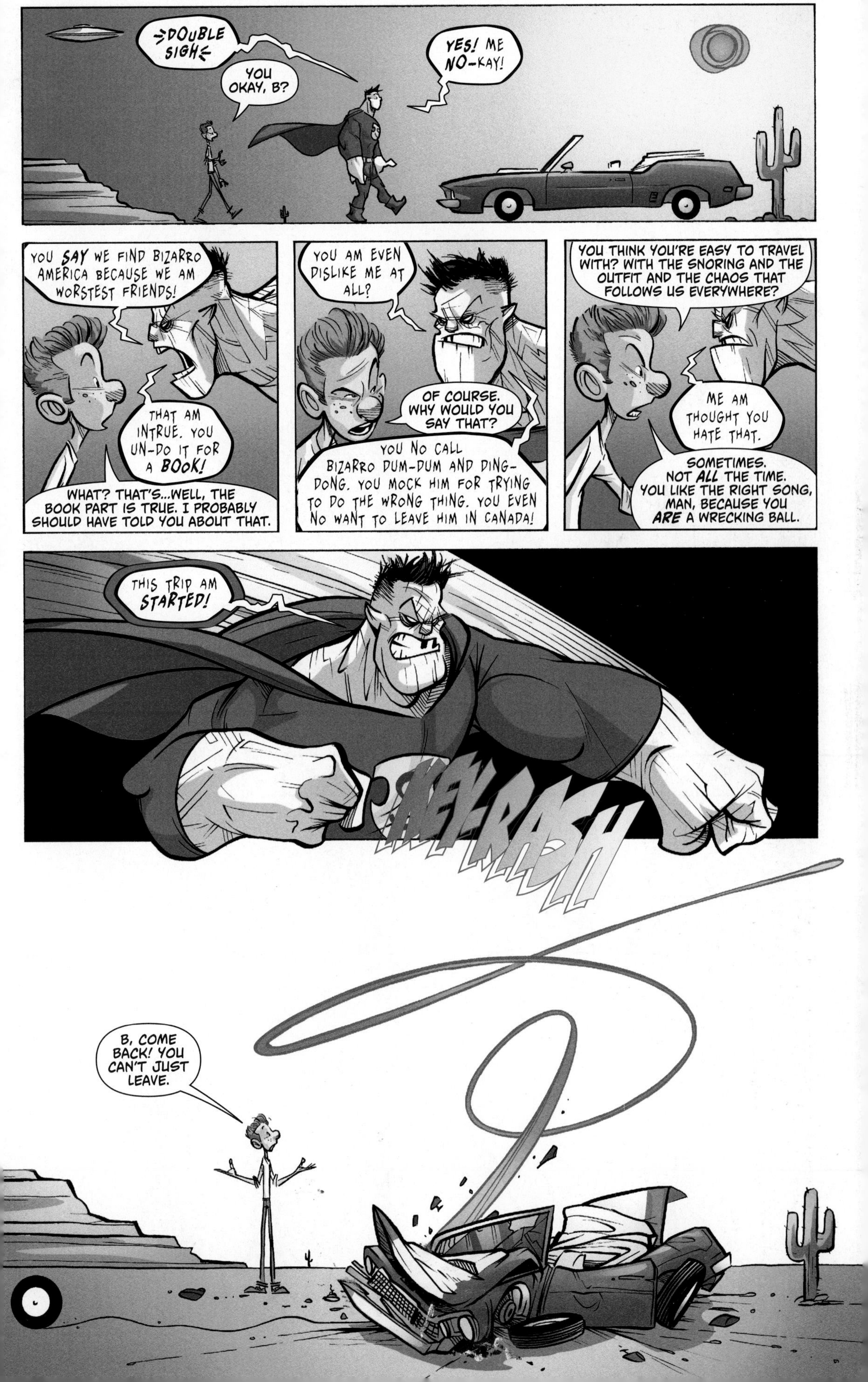

>DOUBLE SIGH<
YOU OKAY, B?
YES! ME NO-KAY!
YOU SAY WE FIND BIZARRO AMERICA BECAUSE WE AM WORSTEST FRIENDS!
THAT AM INTRUE. YOU UN-DO IT FOR A BOOK!
WHAT? THAT'S...WELL, THE BOOK PART IS TRUE. I PROBABLY SHOULD HAVE TOLD YOU ABOUT THAT.
YOU AM EVEN DISLIKE ME AT ALL?
OF COURSE. WHY WOULD YOU SAY THAT?
YOU NO CALL BIZARRO DUM-DUM AND DING-DONG. YOU MOCK HIM FOR TRYING TO DO THE WRONG THING. YOU EVEN NO WANT TO LEAVE HIM IN CANADA!
YOU THINK YOU'RE EASY TO TRAVEL WITH? WITH THE SNORING AND THE OUTFIT AND THE CHAOS THAT FOLLOWS US EVERYWHERE?
ME AM THOUGHT YOU HATE THAT.
SOMETIMES. NOT ALL THE TIME. YOU LIKE THE RIGHT SONG, MAN, BECAUSE YOU ARE A WRECKING BALL.
THIS TRIP AM STARTED!
KEY-RASH
B, COME BACK! YOU CAN'T JUST LEAVE.

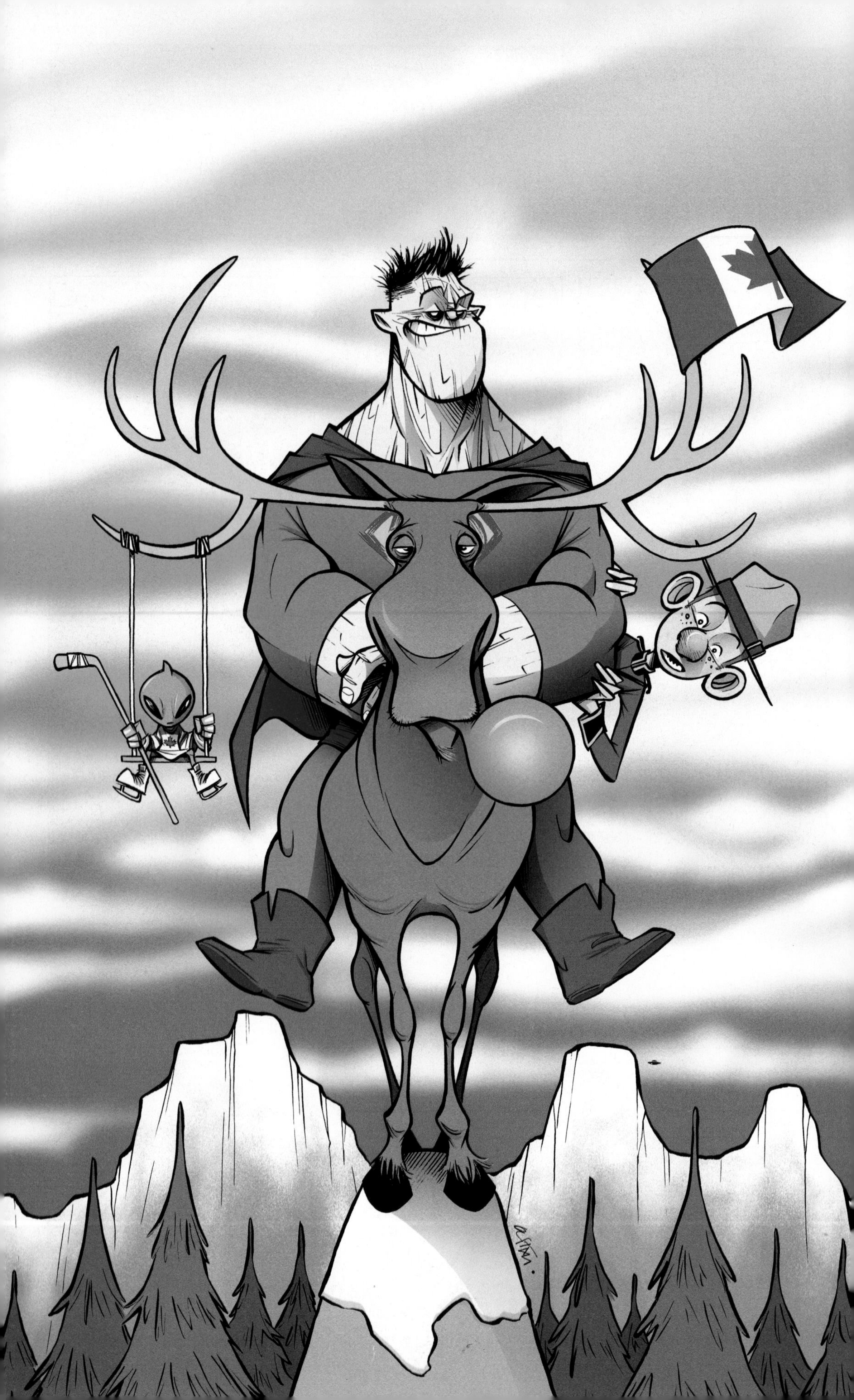

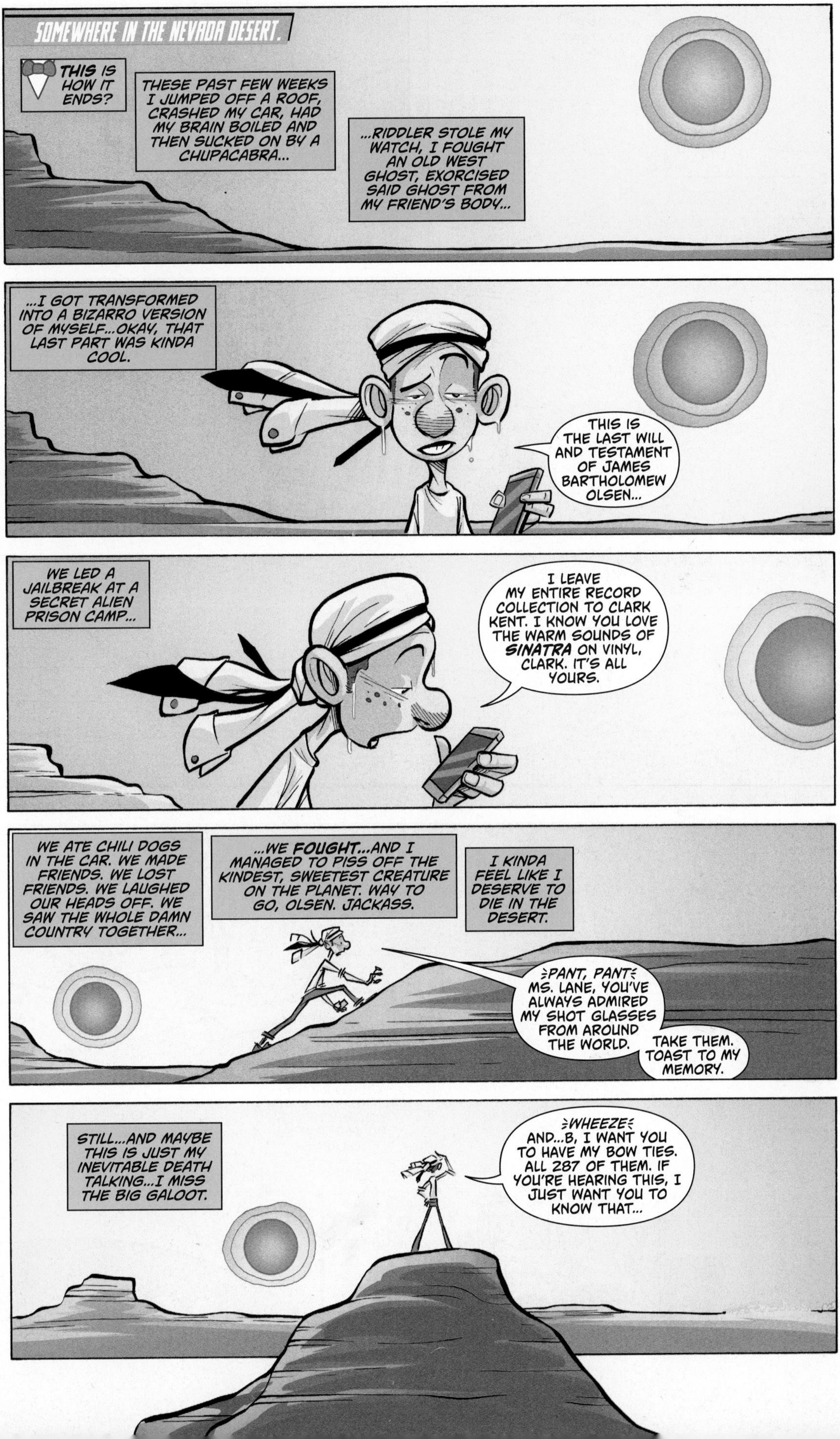

SOMEWHERE IN THE NEVADA DESERT.
THIS IS HOW IT ENDS?
THESE PAST FEW WEEKS I JUMPED OFF A ROOF, CRASHED MY CAR, HAD MY BRAIN BOILED AND THEN SUCKED ON BY A CHUPACABRA...
...RIDDLER STOLE MY WATCH, I FOUGHT AN OLD WEST GHOST, EXORCISED SAID GHOST FROM MY FRIEND'S BODY...
...I GOT TRANSFORMED INTO A BIZARRO VERSION OF MYSELF...OKAY, THAT LAST PART WAS KINDA COOL.
THIS IS THE LAST WILL AND TESTAMENT OF JAMES BARTHOLOMEW OLSEN...
WE LED A JAILBREAK AT A SECRET ALIEN PRISON CAMP...
I LEAVE MY ENTIRE RECORD COLLECTION TO CLARK KENT. I KNOW YOU LOVE THE WARM SOUNDS OF SINATRA ON VINYL, CLARK. IT'S ALL YOURS.
WE ATE CHILI DOGS IN THE CAR. WE MADE FRIENDS. WE LOST FRIENDS. WE LAUGHED OUR HEADS OFF. WE SAW THE WHOLE DAMN COUNTRY TOGETHER...
...WE FOUGHT...AND I MANAGED TO PISS OFF THE KINDEST, SWEETEST CREATURE ON THE PLANET. WAY TO GO, OLSEN. JACKASS.
I KINDA FEEL LIKE I DESERVE TO DIE IN THE DESERT.
PANT, PANT MS. LANE, YOU'VE ALWAYS ADMIRED MY SHOT GLASSES FROM AROUND THE WORLD.
TAKE THEM. TOAST TO MY MEMORY.
STILL...AND MAYBE THIS IS JUST MY INEVITABLE DEATH TALKING...I MISS THE BIG GALOOT.
WHEEZE AND...B, I WANT YOU TO HAVE MY BOW TIES. ALL 287 OF THEM. IF YOU'RE HEARING THIS, I JUST WANT YOU TO KNOW THAT...

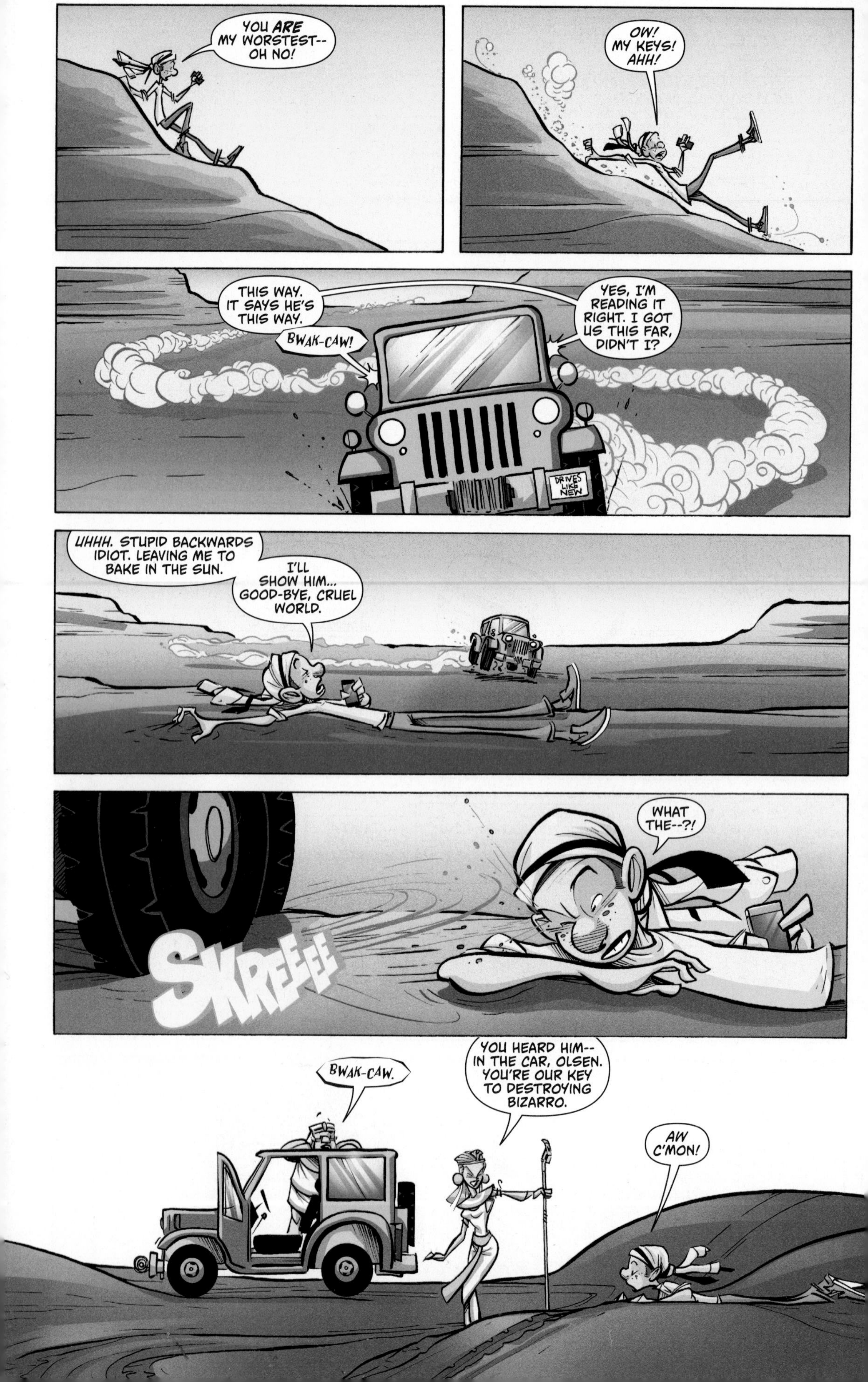
YOU ARE MY WORSTEST-- OH NO!
OW! MY KEYS! AHH!
THIS WAY. IT SAYS HE'S THIS WAY.
BWAK-CAW!
YES, I'M READING IT RIGHT. I GOT US THIS FAR, DIDN'T I?
DRIVES LIKE NEW
UHHH. STUPID BACKWARDS IDIOT. LEAVING ME TO BAKE IN THE SUN.
I'LL SHOW HIM... GOOD-BYE, CRUEL WORLD.
WHAT THE--?!
SKREEEE
BWAK-CAW.
YOU HEARD HIM-- IN THE CAR, OLSEN. YOU'RE OUR KEY TO DESTROYING BIZARRO.
AW C'MON!

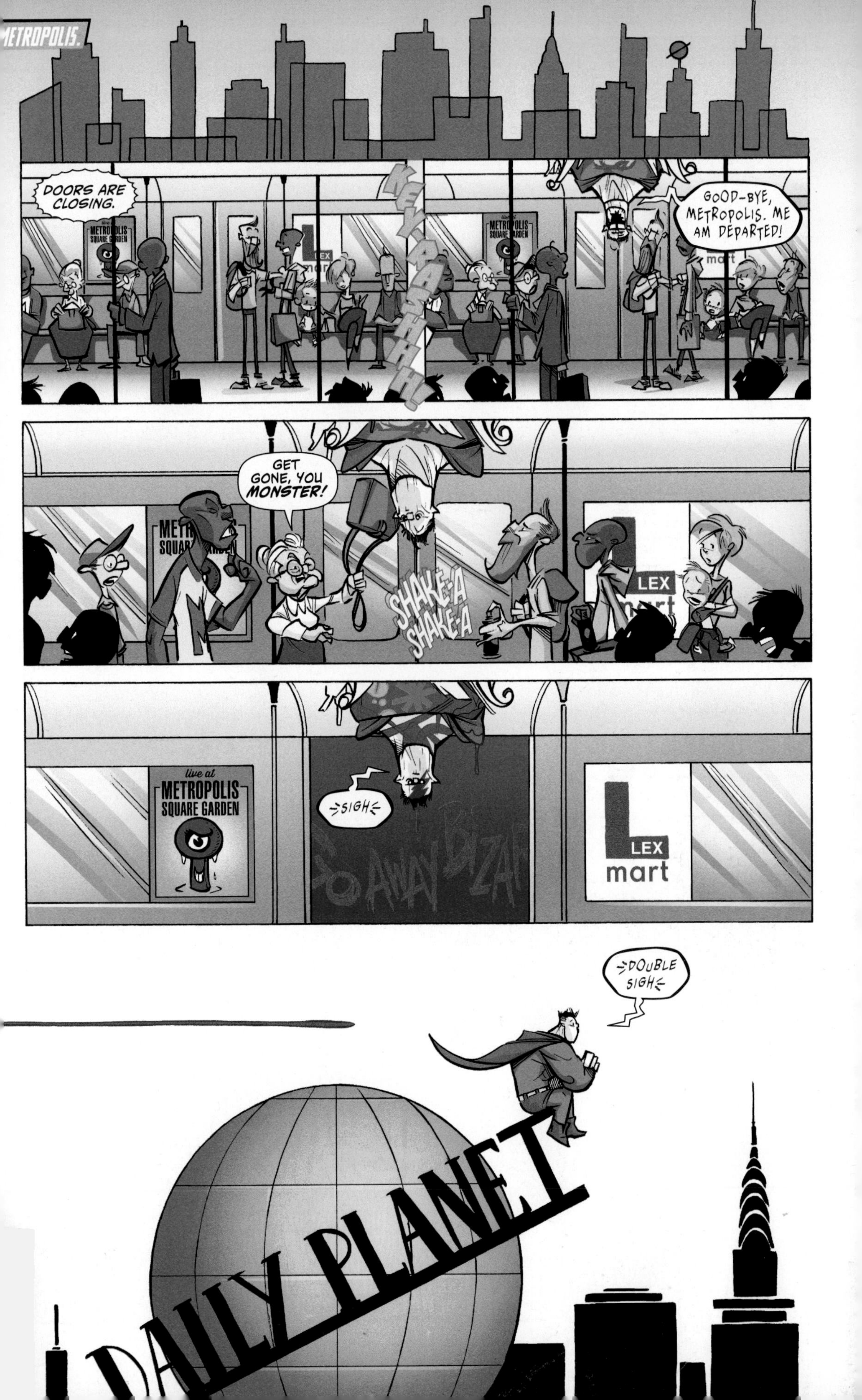
METROPOLIS.
DOORS ARE CLOSING.
live at METROPOLIS SQUARE GARDEN
LEX mart
KEYRASHHHH!
GOOD-BYE, METROPOLIS. ME AM DEPARTED!
GET GONE, YOU MONSTER!
METROPOLIS SQUARE GARDEN
LEX mart
SHAKE-A SHAKE-A
live at METROPOLIS SQUARE GARDEN
SIGH
LEX mart
DOUBLE SIGH
DAILY PLANET

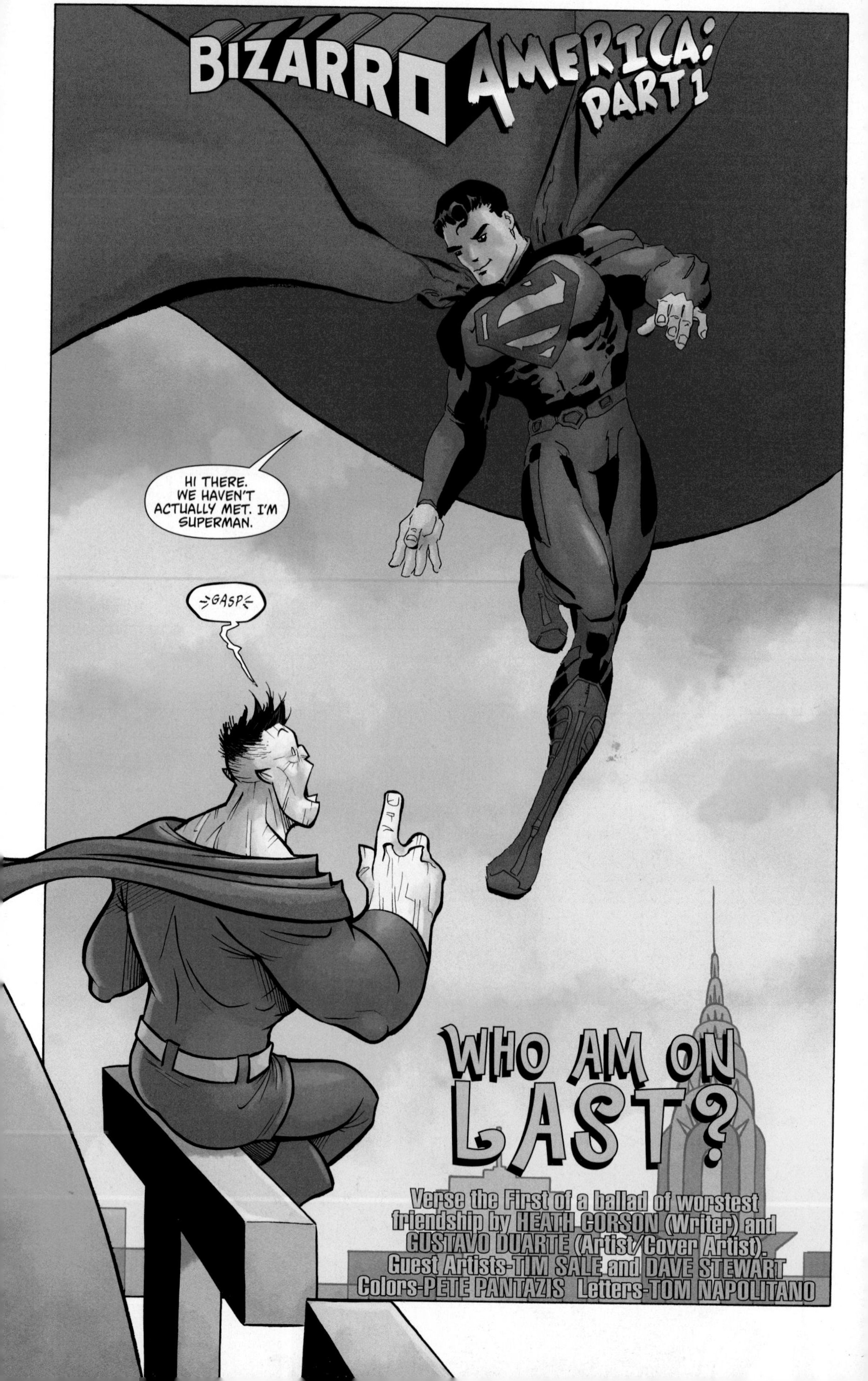

BIZARRO AMERICA: PART 1
HI THERE. WE HAVEN'T ACTUALLY MET. I'M SUPERMAN.
GASP
WHO AM ON LAST?
Verse the First of a ballad of worstest friendship by HEATH CORSON (Writer) and GUSTAVO DUARTE (Artist/Cover Artist). Guest Artists-TIM SALE and DAVE STEWART Colors-PETE PANTAZIS Letters-TOM NAPOLITANO

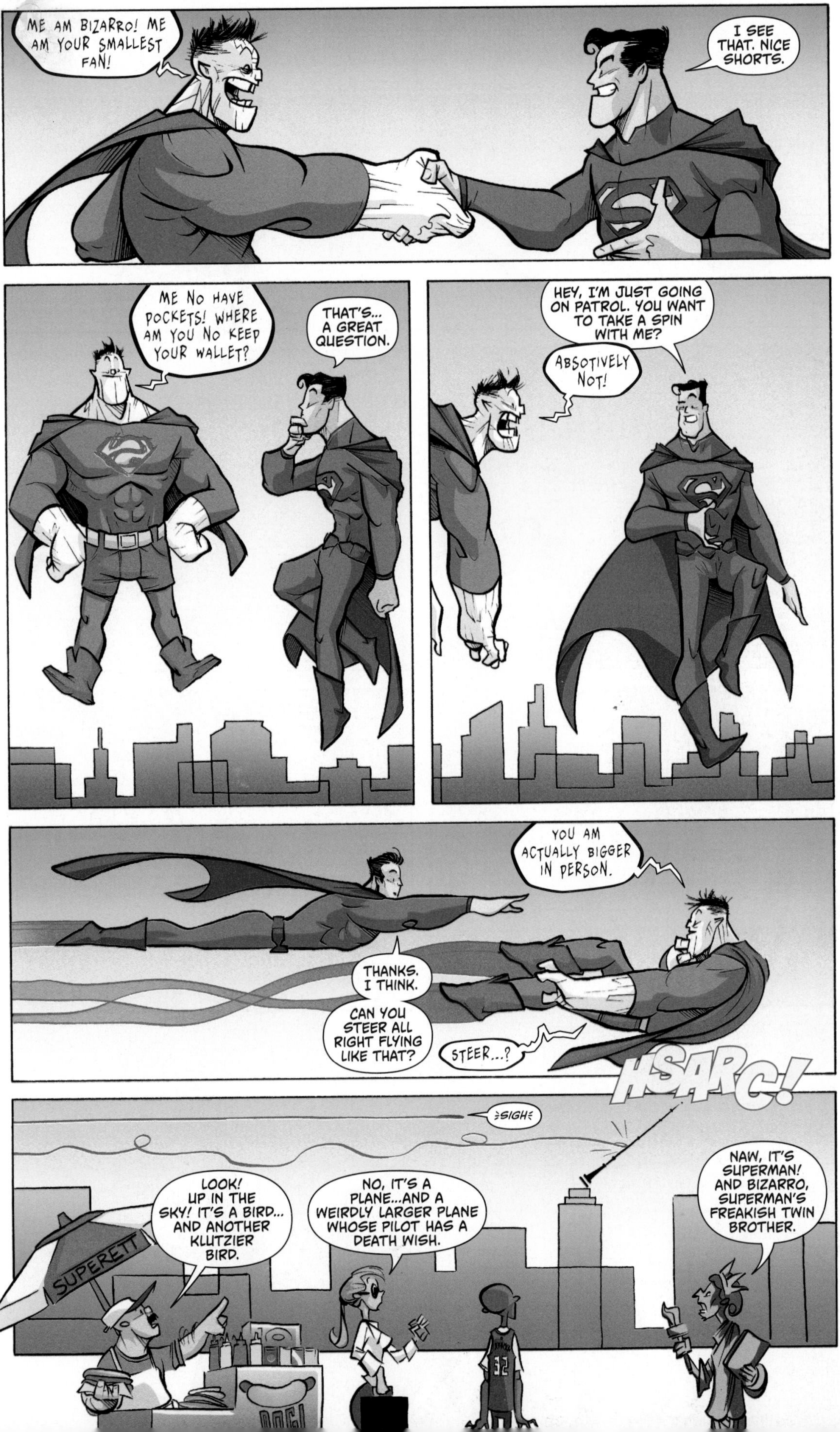

ME AM BIZARRO! ME AM YOUR SMALLEST FAN!
I SEE THAT. NICE SHORTS.
ME NO HAVE POCKETS! WHERE AM YOU NO KEEP YOUR WALLET?
THAT'S... A GREAT QUESTION.
HEY, I'M JUST GOING ON PATROL. YOU WANT TO TAKE A SPIN WITH ME?
ABSOTIVELY NOT!
YOU AM ACTUALLY BIGGER IN PERSON.
THANKS. I THINK.
CAN YOU STEER ALL RIGHT FLYING LIKE THAT?
STEER...?
HSARC!
SIGH
LOOK! UP IN THE SKY! IT'S A BIRD... AND ANOTHER KLUTZIER BIRD.
NO, IT'S A PLANE...AND A WEIRDLY LARGER PLANE WHOSE PILOT HAS A DEATH WISH.
NAW, IT'S SUPERMAN! AND BIZARRO, SUPERMAN'S FREAKISH TWIN BROTHER.
SUPERETT

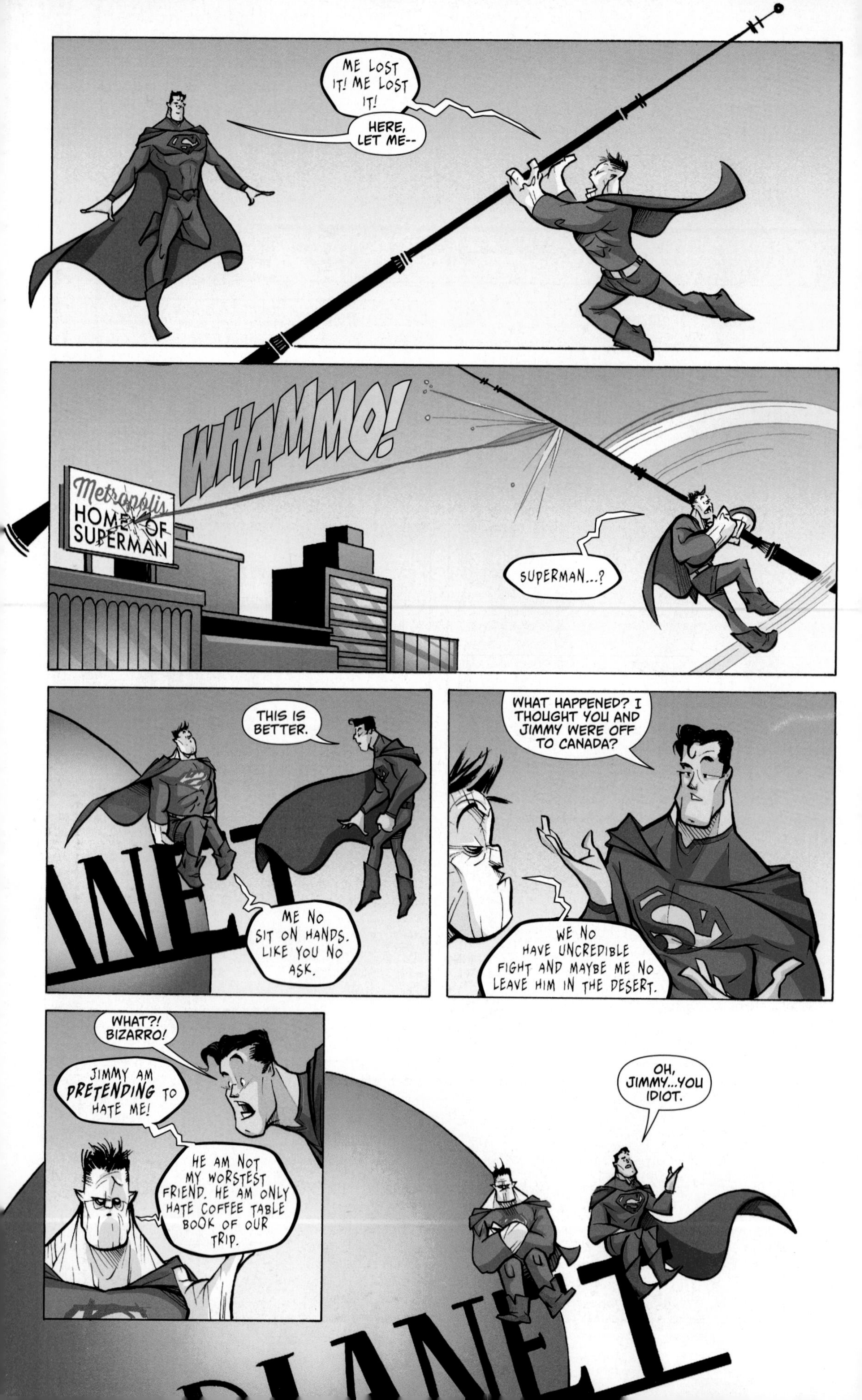
ME LOST IT! ME LOST IT!
HERE, LET ME--
WHAMMO!
Metropolis HOME OF SUPERMAN
SUPERMAN...?
THIS IS BETTER.
ME NO SIT ON HANDS. LIKE YOU NO ASK.
WHAT HAPPENED? I THOUGHT YOU AND JIMMY WERE OFF TO CANADA?
WE NO HAVE UNCREDIBLE FIGHT AND MAYBE ME NO LEAVE HIM IN THE DESERT.
WHAT?! BIZARRO!
JIMMY AM PRETENDING TO HATE ME!
HE AM NOT MY WORSTEST FRIEND. HE AM ONLY HATE COFFEE TABLE BOOK OF OUR TRIP.
OH, JIMMY...YOU IDIOT.

HE'S NOT COMING.

HE'LL COME. HE'S YOUR BEST FRIEND.

I TOLD YOU: WE HAD A FIGHT. AND I SAID SOME-- OW!

BWAK-CAW!

QUIT PECKING ME!

I'LL HANDLE THIS, DAD. WHY ISN'T HE COMING?

WELL, IT'S NOT THE EASIEST OF ROAD TRIPS.

BIZARRO IS A WHIRLING DERVISH OF CHAOS.

HE'S GOT ZERO MONEY... AND HE NEVER CAN PICK A STATION.

BWA-CAWWWW.

OKAY, I DID LIE TO HIM. AT FIRST. NOW I LIKE THE BIG GALOOT.

BWAK-CAW.

I KNOW. I SHOULD BE TELLING HIM.

ENOUGH! IF HE WON'T COME FOR YOU, WE'LL MAKE HIM A DEAL HE CAN'T REFUSE.

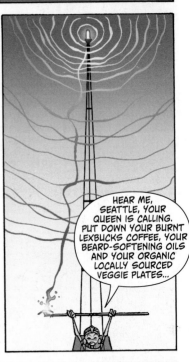

HEAR ME, SEATTLE, YOUR QUEEN IS CALLING. PUT DOWN YOUR BURNT LEXBUCKS COFFEE, YOUR BEARD-SOFTENING OILS AND YOUR ORGANIC LOCALLY SOURCED VEGGIE PLATES...

SUMMON THE MONSTER FOR ME. CALL FOR BIZARRO!

BIZ-ZAR-O! BIZ-ZAR-O! BIZ-ZAR-O!

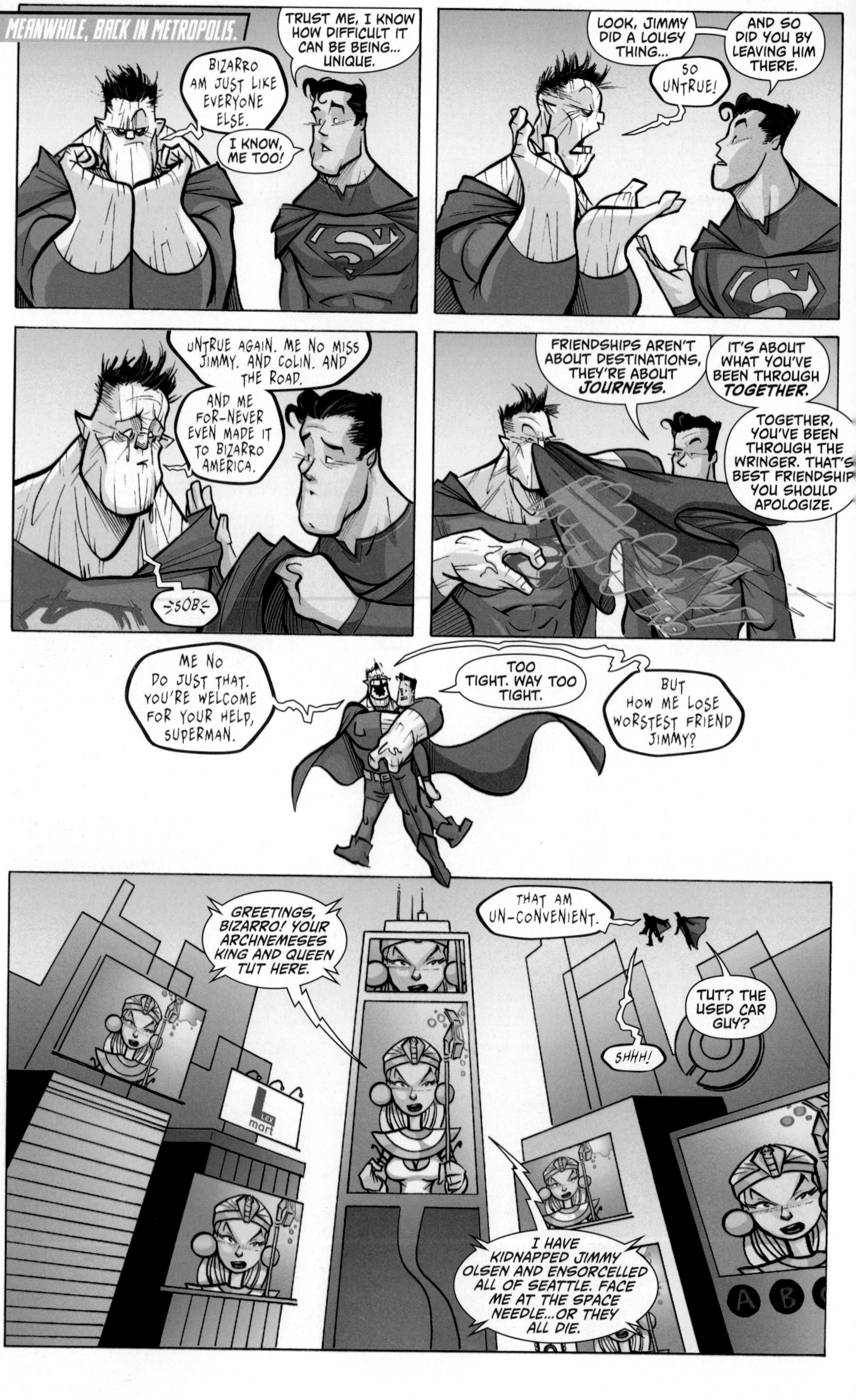
MEANWHILE, BACK IN METROPOLIS.
TRUST ME, I KNOW HOW DIFFICULT IT CAN BE BEING... UNIQUE.
BIZARRO AM JUST LIKE EVERYONE ELSE.
I KNOW, ME TOO!
LOOK, JIMMY DID A LOUSY THING...
SO UNTRUE!
AND SO DID YOU BY LEAVING HIM THERE.
UNTRUE AGAIN. ME NO MISS JIMMY. AND COLIN. AND THE ROAD.
AND ME FOR-NEVER EVEN MADE IT TO BIZARRO AMERICA.
SOB
FRIENDSHIPS AREN'T ABOUT DESTINATIONS, THEY'RE ABOUT JOURNEYS.
IT'S ABOUT WHAT YOU'VE BEEN THROUGH TOGETHER.
TOGETHER, YOU'VE BEEN THROUGH THE WRINGER. THAT'S BEST FRIENDSHIP. YOU SHOULD APOLOGIZE.
ME NO DO JUST THAT. YOU'RE WELCOME FOR YOUR HELP, SUPERMAN.
TOO TIGHT. WAY TOO TIGHT.
BUT HOW ME LOSE WORSTEST FRIEND JIMMY?
GREETINGS, BIZARRO! YOUR ARCHNEMESES KING AND QUEEN TUT HERE.
THAT AM UN-CONVENIENT.
TUT? THE USED CAR GUY?
SHHH!
LEX mart
I HAVE KIDNAPPED JIMMY OLSEN AND ENSORCELLED ALL OF SEATTLE. FACE ME AT THE SPACE NEEDLE...OR THEY ALL DIE.
A B

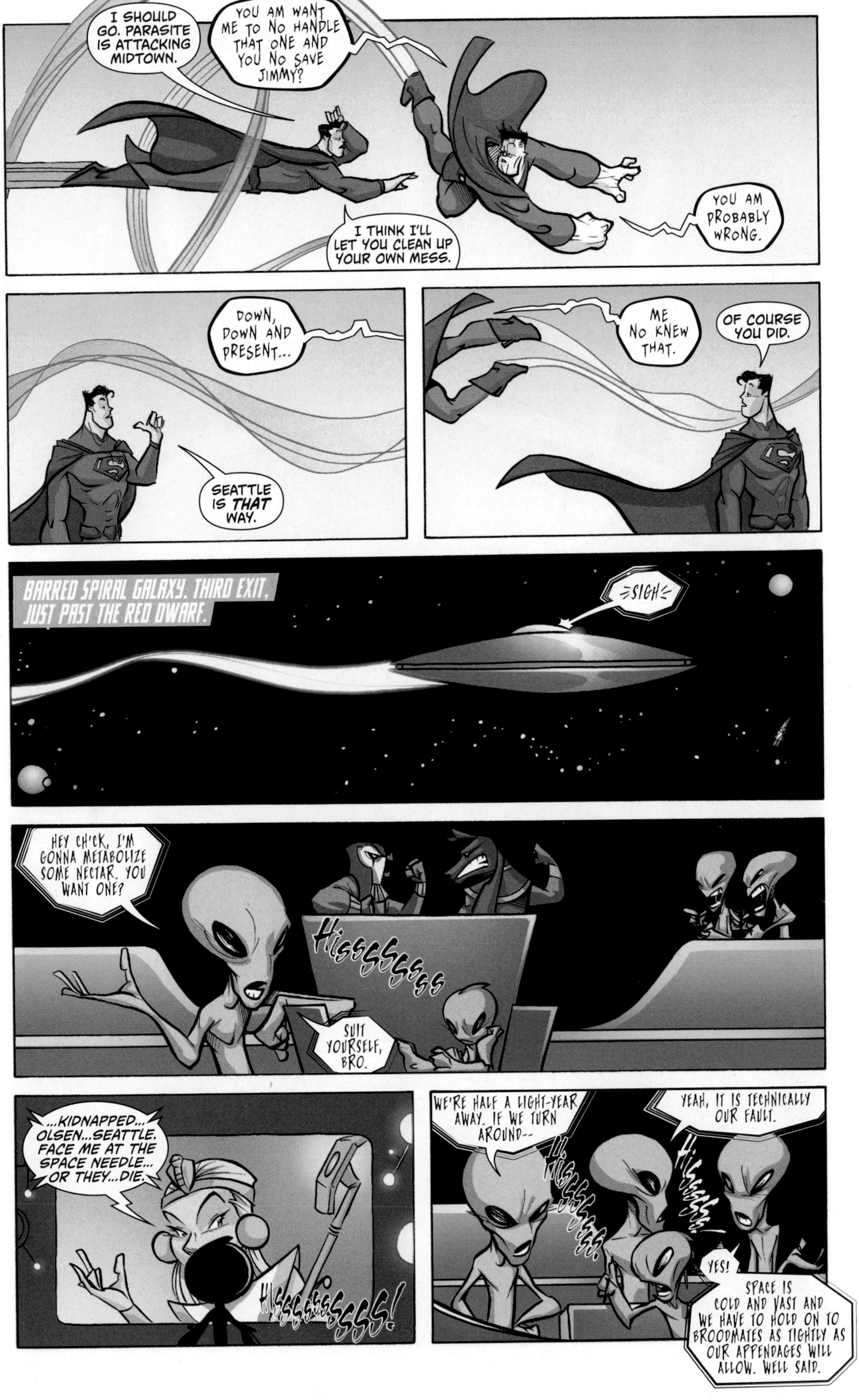
I SHOULD GO. PARASITE IS ATTACKING MIDTOWN.
YOU AM WANT ME TO NO HANDLE THAT ONE AND YOU NO SAVE JIMMY?
I THINK I'LL LET YOU CLEAN UP YOUR OWN MESS.
YOU AM PROBABLY WRONG.
DOWN, DOWN AND PRESENT...
SEATTLE IS THAT WAY.
ME NO KNEW THAT.
OF COURSE YOU DID.
BARRED SPIRAL GALAXY. THIRD EXIT, JUST PAST THE RED DWARF.
SIGH
HEY CH'CK, I'M GONNA METABOLIZE SOME NECTAR. YOU WANT ONE?
HISSSSSSSS
SUIT YOURSELF, BRO.
...KIDNAPPED... OLSEN...SEATTLE. FACE ME AT THE SPACE NEEDLE... OR THEY...DIE.
HISSSSSSSSSS!
WE'RE HALF A LIGHT-YEAR AWAY. IF WE TURN AROUND--
HISSSSSSS
YEAH, IT IS TECHNICALLY OUR FAULT.
HISSSSS
YES!
SPACE IS COLD AND VAST AND WE HAVE TO HOLD ON TO BROODMATES AS TIGHTLY AS OUR APPENDAGES WILL ALLOW. WELL SAID.

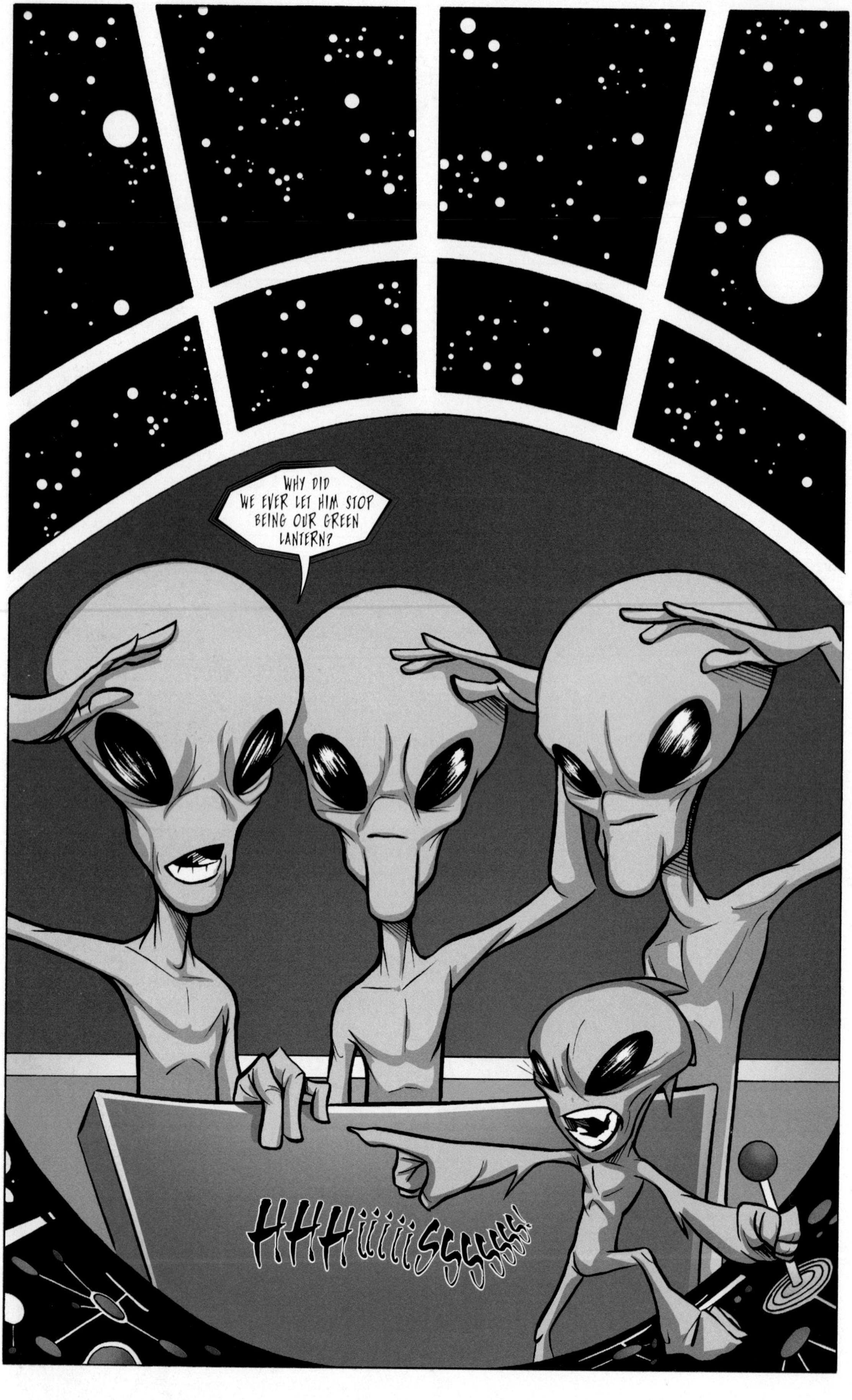
WHY DID WE EVER LET HIM STOP BEING OUR GREEN LANTERN?
HHHiiiiiSSSSSSS!

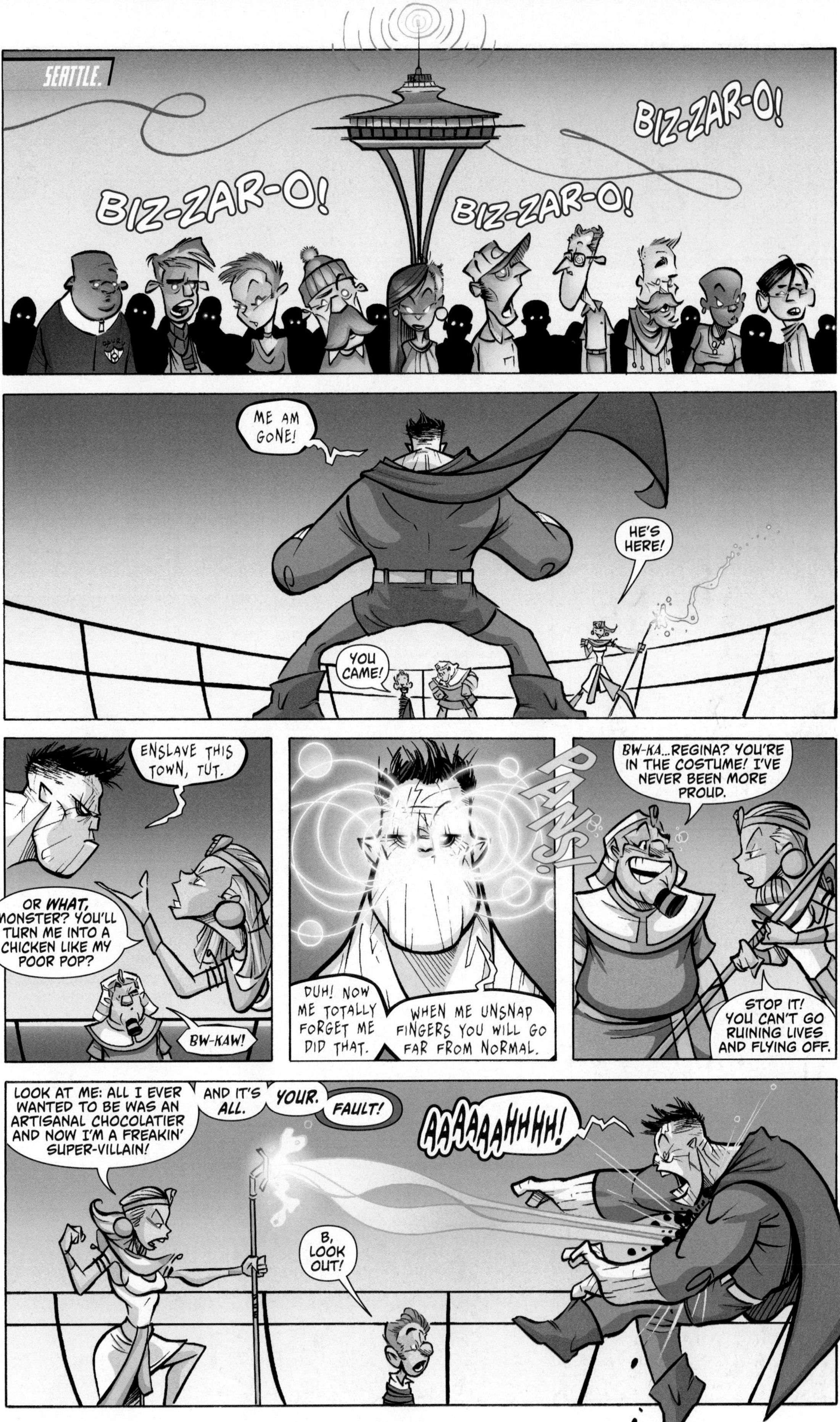
SEATTLE.
BIZ-ZAR-O!
BIZ-ZAR-O!
BIZ-ZAR-O!
ME AM GONE!
HE'S HERE!
YOU CAME!
ENSLAVE THIS TOWN, TUT.
OR WHAT, MONSTER? YOU'LL TURN ME INTO A CHICKEN LIKE MY POOR POP?
BW-KAW!
DUH! NOW ME TOTALLY FORGET ME DID THAT.
WHEN ME UNSNAP FINGERS YOU WILL GO FAR FROM NORMAL.
PANS!
BW-KA...REGINA? YOU'RE IN THE COSTUME! I'VE NEVER BEEN MORE PROUD.
STOP IT! YOU CAN'T GO RUINING LIVES AND FLYING OFF.
LOOK AT ME: ALL I EVER WANTED TO BE WAS AN ARTISANAL CHOCOLATIER AND NOW I'M A FREAKIN' SUPER-VILLAIN!
AND IT'S ALL.
YOUR.
FAULT!
AAAAAAHHHH!
B, LOOK OUT!

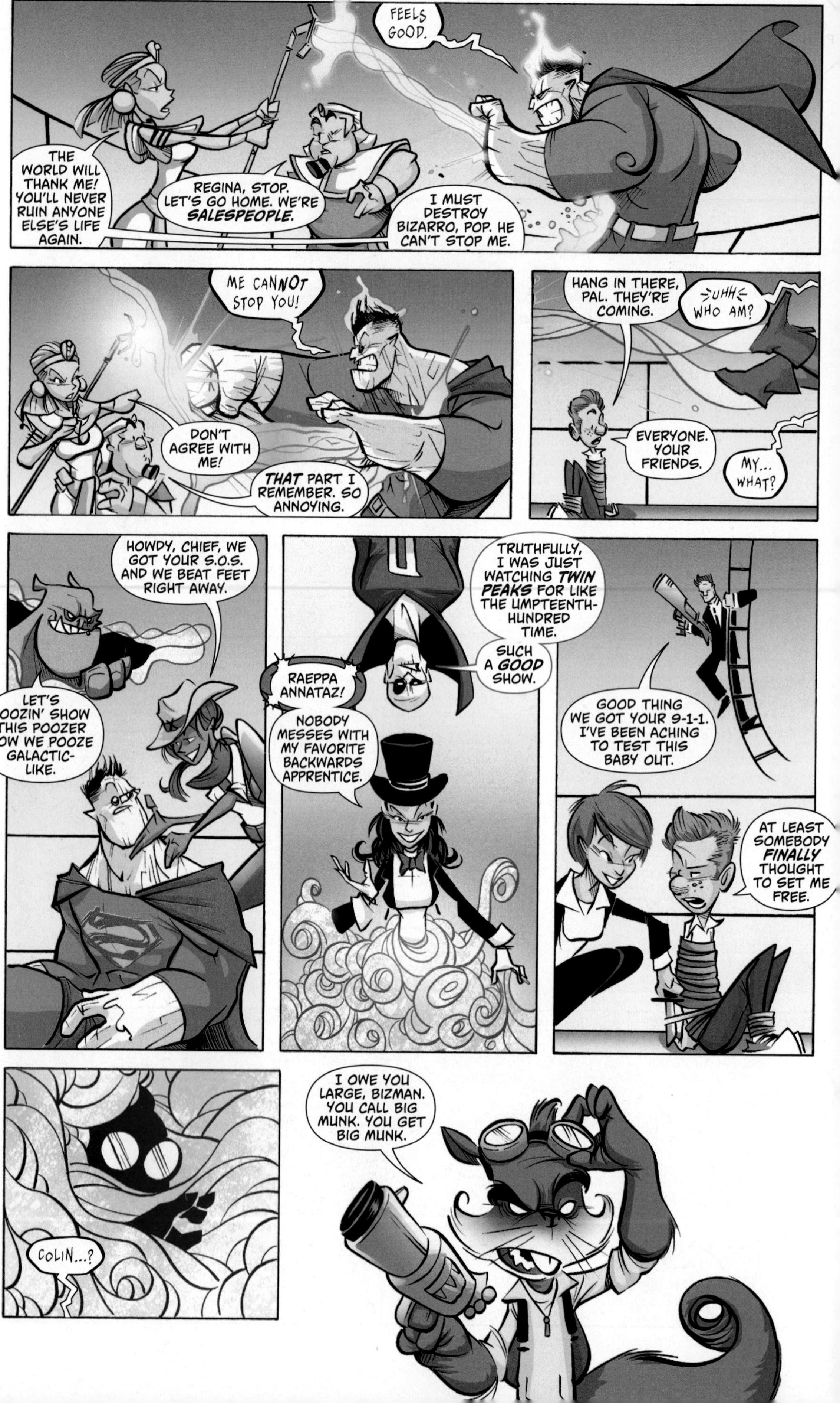
FEELS GOOD.
THE WORLD WILL THANK ME! YOU'LL NEVER RUIN ANYONE ELSE'S LIFE AGAIN.
REGINA, STOP. LET'S GO HOME. WE'RE SALESPEOPLE.
I MUST DESTROY BIZARRO, POP. HE CAN'T STOP ME.
ME CANNOT STOP YOU!
DON'T AGREE WITH ME!
THAT PART I REMEMBER. SO ANNOYING.
HANG IN THERE, PAL. THEY'RE COMING.
UHH WHO AM?
EVERYONE. YOUR FRIENDS.
MY... WHAT?
HOWDY, CHIEF, WE GOT YOUR S.O.S. AND WE BEAT FEET RIGHT AWAY.
LET'S POOZIN' SHOW THIS POOZER HOW WE POOZE GALACTIC-LIKE.
TRUTHFULLY, I WAS JUST WATCHING TWIN PEAKS FOR LIKE THE UMPTEENTH-HUNDRED TIME.
SUCH A GOOD SHOW.
RAEPPA ANNATAZ!
NOBODY MESSES WITH MY FAVORITE BACKWARDS APPRENTICE.
GOOD THING WE GOT YOUR 9-1-1. I'VE BEEN ACHING TO TEST THIS BABY OUT.
AT LEAST SOMEBODY FINALLY THOUGHT TO SET ME FREE.
COLIN...?
I OWE YOU LARGE, BIZMAN. YOU CALL BIG MUNK. YOU GET BIG MUNK.

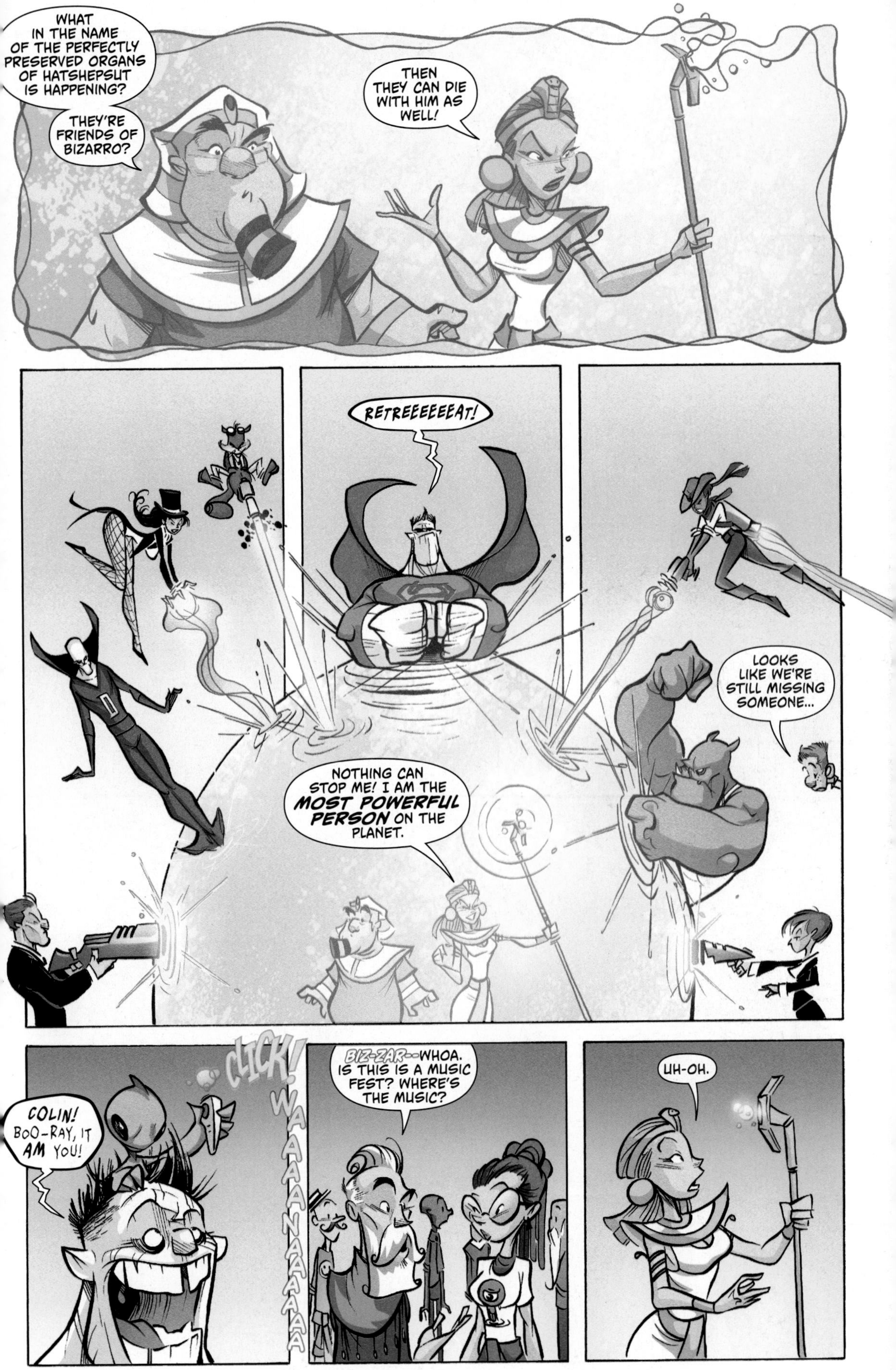
WHAT IN THE NAME OF THE PERFECTLY PRESERVED ORGANS OF HATSHEPSUT IS HAPPENING?
THEY'RE FRIENDS OF BIZARRO?
THEN THEY CAN DIE WITH HIM AS WELL!
RETREEEEEEEAT!
NOTHING CAN STOP ME! I AM THE MOST POWERFUL PERSON ON THE PLANET.
LOOKS LIKE WE'RE STILL MISSING SOMEONE...
CLICK!
WAAAAAAAAAAAAA
COLIN! BOO-RAY, IT AM YOU!
BIZ-ZAR--WHOA. IS THIS IS A MUSIC FEST? WHERE'S THE MUSIC?
UH-OH.

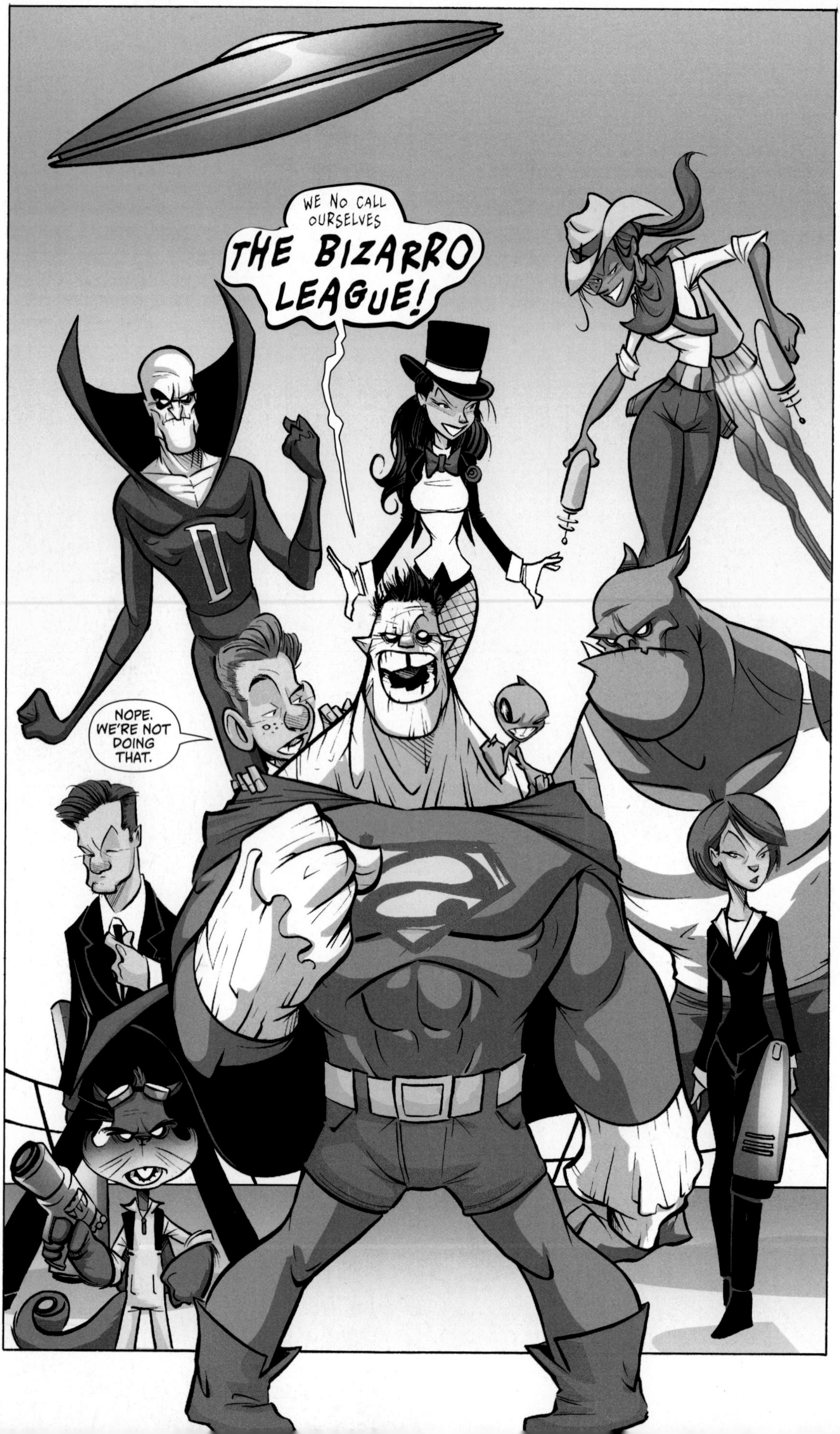
WE NO CALL OURSELVES THE BIZARRO LEAGUE!
NOPE. WE'RE NOT DOING THAT.

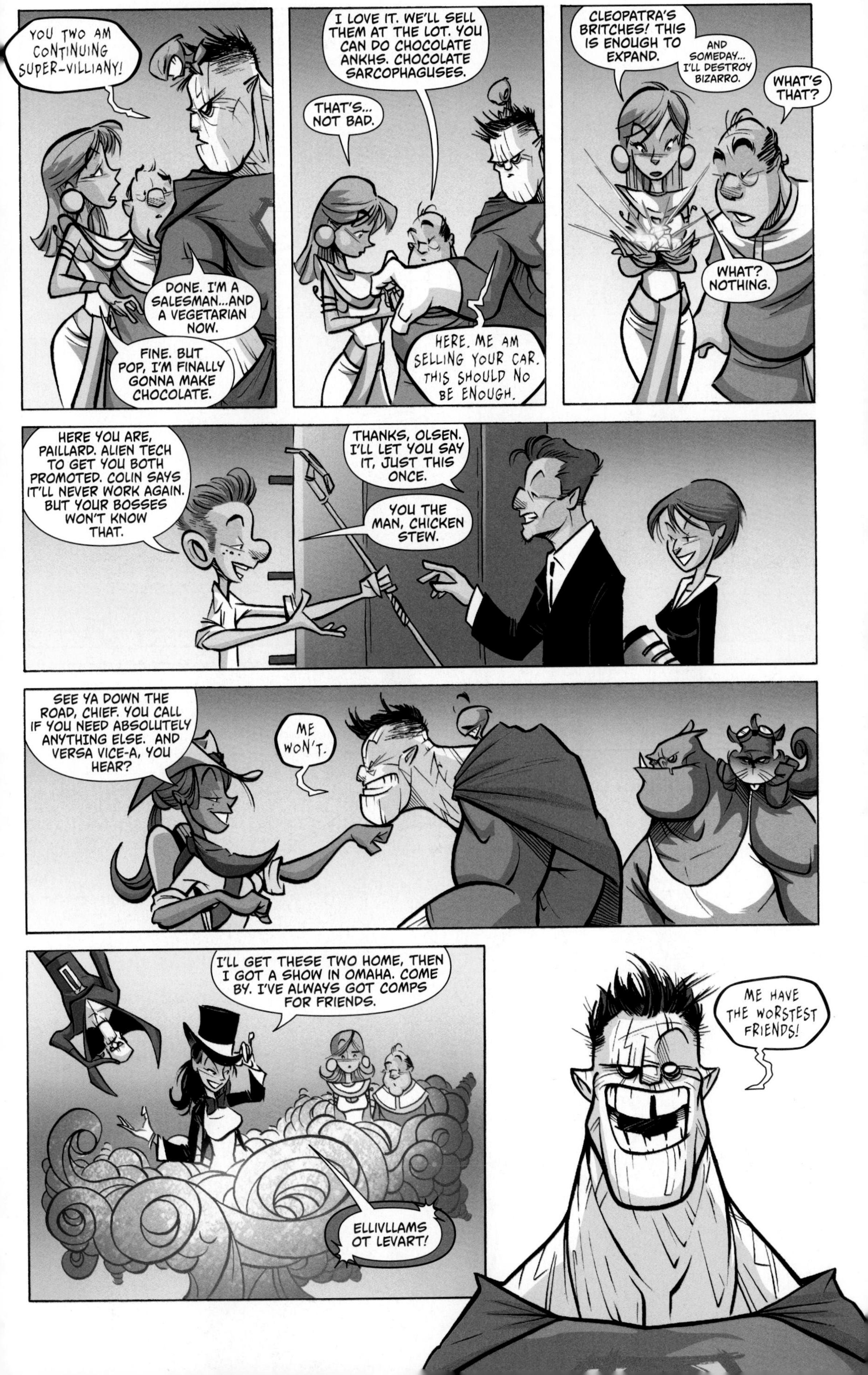
YOU TWO AM CONTINUING SUPER-VILLIANY!
DONE. I'M A SALESMAN...AND A VEGETARIAN NOW.
FINE. BUT POP, I'M FINALLY GONNA MAKE CHOCOLATE.
I LOVE IT. WE'LL SELL THEM AT THE LOT. YOU CAN DO CHOCOLATE ANKHS. CHOCOLATE SARCOPHAGUSES.
THAT'S... NOT BAD.
HERE. ME AM SELLING YOUR CAR. THIS SHOULD NO BE ENOUGH.
CLEOPATRA'S BRITCHES! THIS IS ENOUGH TO EXPAND.
AND SOMEDAY... I'LL DESTROY BIZARRO.
WHAT'S THAT?
WHAT? NOTHING.
HERE YOU ARE, PAILLARD. ALIEN TECH TO GET YOU BOTH PROMOTED. COLIN SAYS IT'LL NEVER WORK AGAIN. BUT YOUR BOSSES WON'T KNOW THAT.
THANKS, OLSEN. I'LL LET YOU SAY IT, JUST THIS ONCE.
YOU THE MAN, CHICKEN STEW.
SEE YA DOWN THE ROAD, CHIEF. YOU CALL IF YOU NEED ABSOLUTELY ANYTHING ELSE. AND VERSA VICE-A, YOU HEAR?
ME WON'T.
I'LL GET THESE TWO HOME, THEN I GOT A SHOW IN OMAHA. COME BY. I'VE ALWAYS GOT COMPS FOR FRIENDS.
ELLIVLLAMS OT LEVART!
ME HAVE THE WORSTEST FRIENDS!

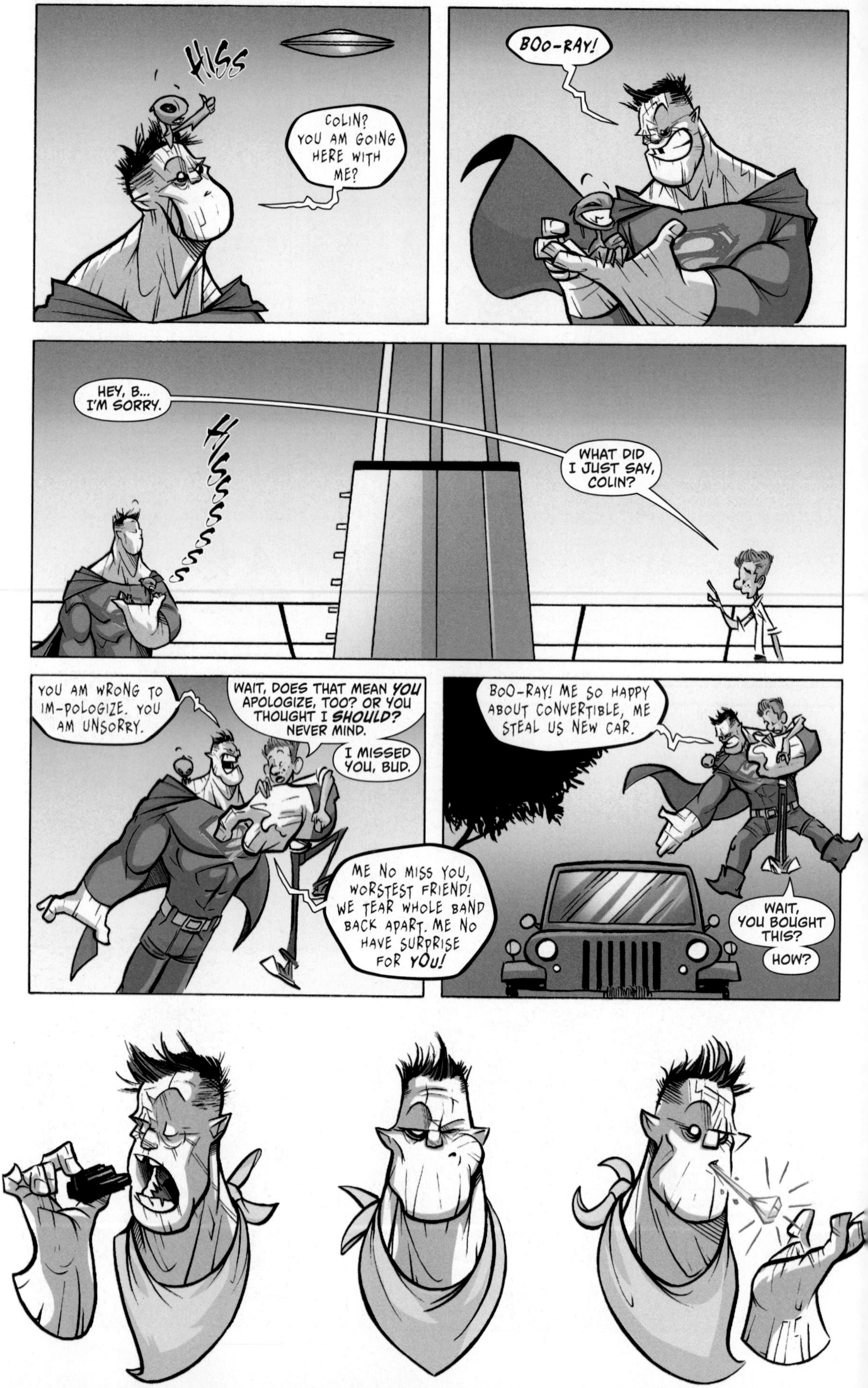
HISS
COLIN? YOU AM GOING HERE WITH ME?
BOO-RAY!
HEY, B... I'M SORRY.
HISSSSSSSSS
WHAT DID I JUST SAY, COLIN?
YOU AM WRONG TO IM-POLOGIZE. YOU AM UNSORRY.
WAIT, DOES THAT MEAN YOU APOLOGIZE, TOO? OR YOU THOUGHT I SHOULD? NEVER MIND.
I MISSED YOU, BUD.
ME NO MISS YOU, WORSTEST FRIEND! WE TEAR WHOLE BAND BACK APART. ME NO HAVE SURPRISE FOR YOU!
BOO-RAY! ME SO HAPPY ABOUT CONVERTIBLE, ME STEAL US NEW CAR.
WAIT, YOU BOUGHT THIS?
HOW?

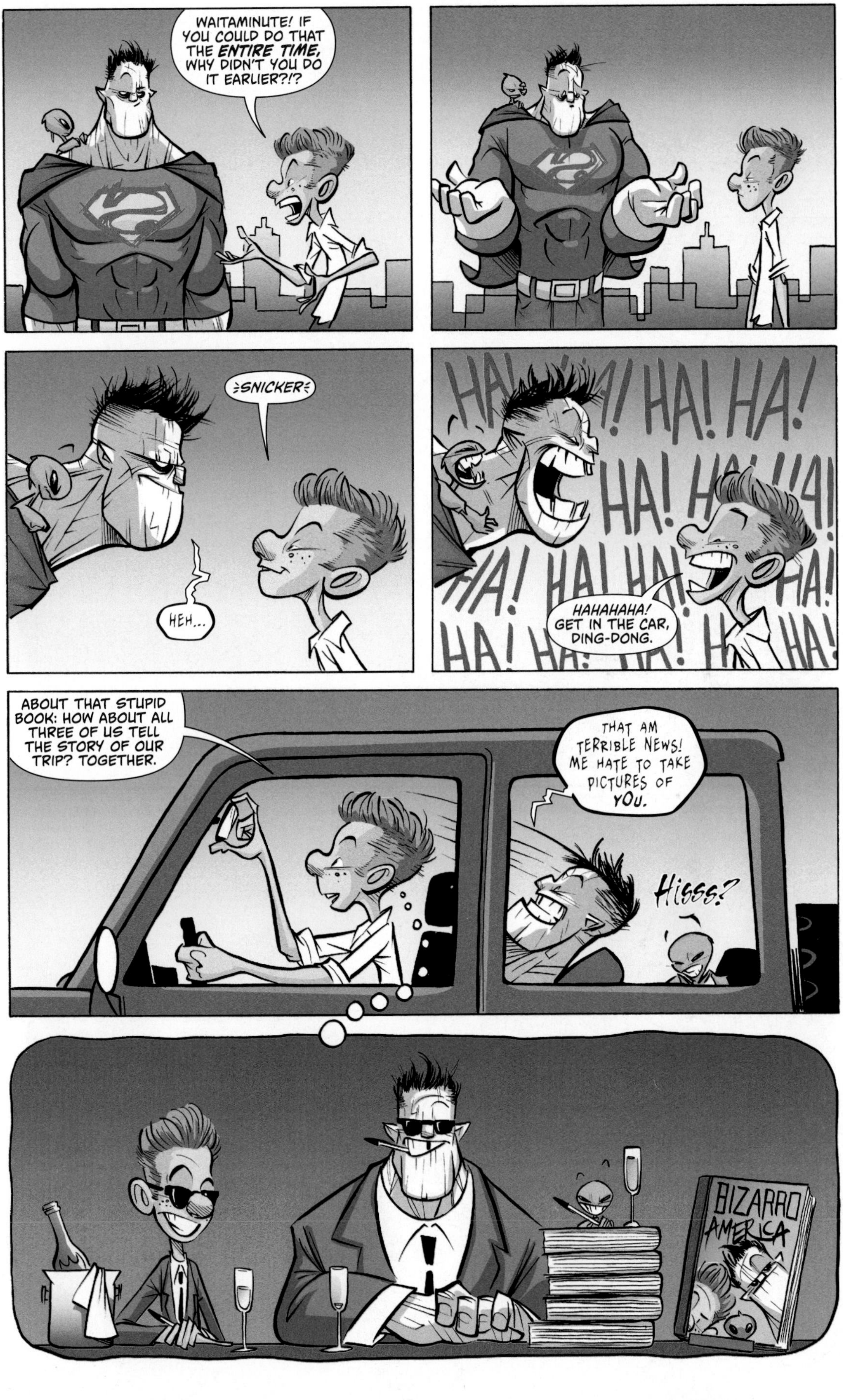
WAITAMINUTE! IF YOU COULD DO THAT THE ENTIRE TIME, WHY DIDN'T YOU DO IT EARLIER?!?
SNICKER
HEH...
HA! HA! HA! HA!
HA! HA!
HA! HA! HA! HA!
HAHAHAHA! GET IN THE CAR, DING-DONG.
ABOUT THAT STUPID BOOK: HOW ABOUT ALL THREE OF US TELL THE STORY OF OUR TRIP? TOGETHER.
THAT AM TERRIBLE NEWS! ME HATE TO TAKE PICTURES OF YOU.
Hisss?
BIZARRO AMERICA

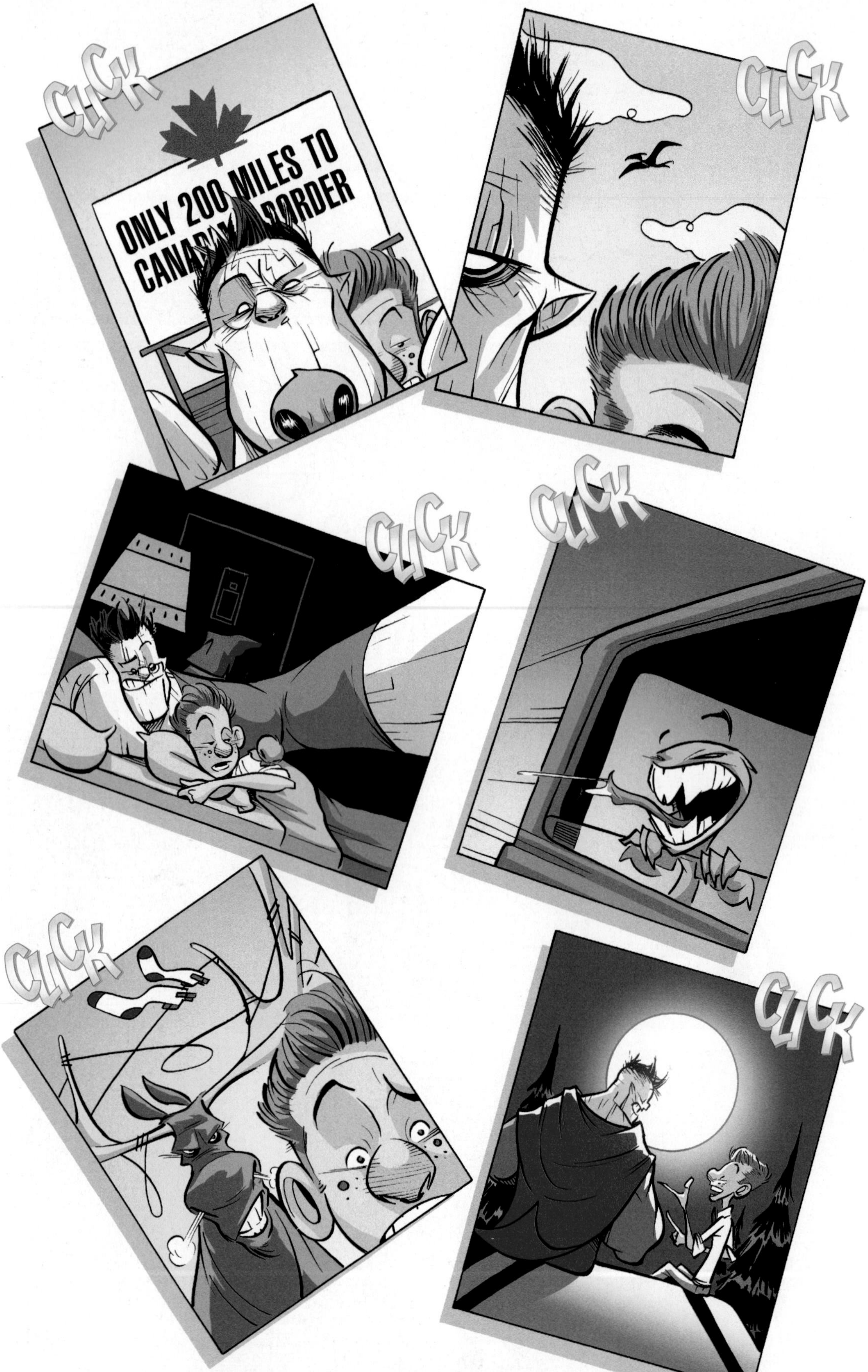
CLICK
ONLY 200 MILES TO
CANAD BORDER
CLICK
CLICK
CLICK
CLICK
CLICK

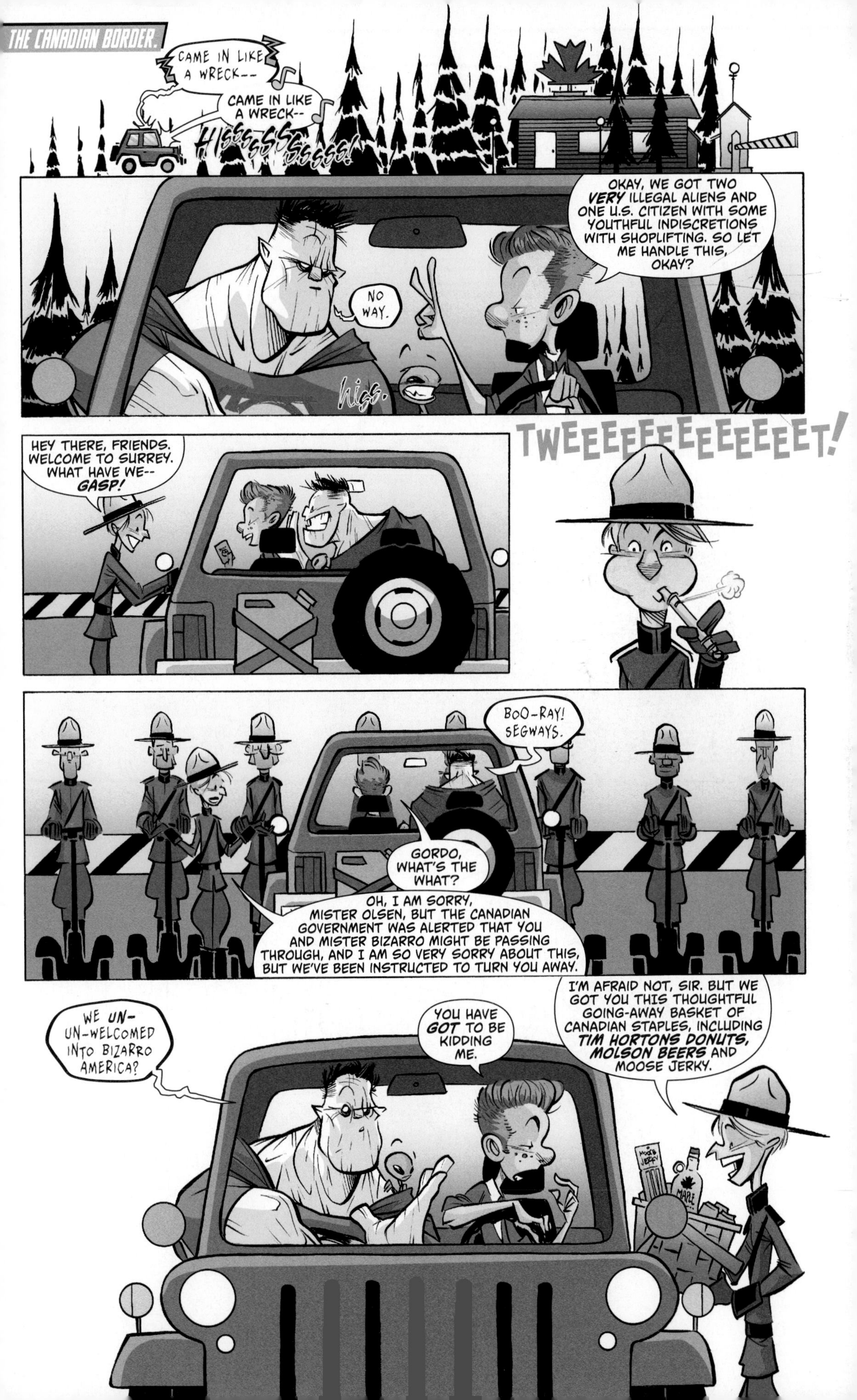
THE CANADIAN BORDER.
CAME IN LIKE A WRECK--
CAME IN LIKE A WRECK--
HISSSSSSSSSSSS!
OKAY, WE GOT TWO VERY ILLEGAL ALIENS AND ONE U.S. CITIZEN WITH SOME YOUTHFUL INDISCRETIONS WITH SHOPLIFTING. SO LET ME HANDLE THIS, OKAY?
NO WAY.
hiss.
HEY THERE, FRIENDS. WELCOME TO SURREY. WHAT HAVE WE-- GASP!
TWEEEEEEEEEEEET!
BOO-RAY! SEGWAYS.
GORDO, WHAT'S THE WHAT?
OH, I AM SORRY, MISTER OLSEN, BUT THE CANADIAN GOVERNMENT WAS ALERTED THAT YOU AND MISTER BIZARRO MIGHT BE PASSING THROUGH, AND I AM SO VERY SORRY ABOUT THIS, BUT WE'VE BEEN INSTRUCTED TO TURN YOU AWAY.
WE UN-UN-WELCOMED INTO BIZARRO AMERICA?
YOU HAVE GOT TO BE KIDDING ME.
I'M AFRAID NOT, SIR. BUT WE GOT YOU THIS THOUGHTFUL GOING-AWAY BASKET OF CANADIAN STAPLES, INCLUDING TIM HORTONS DONUTS, MOLSON BEERS AND MOOSE JERKY.
MOOSE JERKY
MAPLE

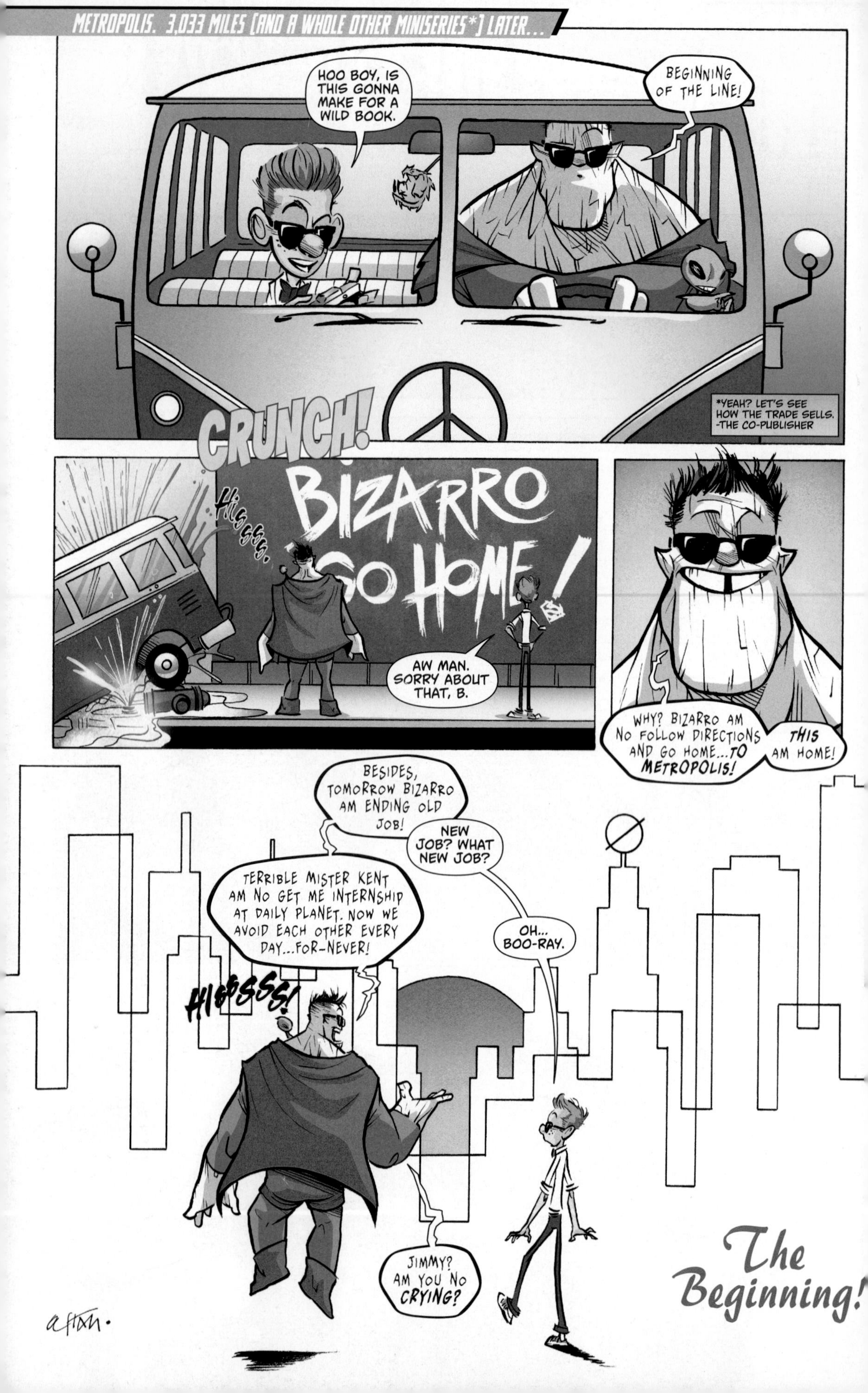

METROPOLIS. 3,033 MILES (AND A WHOLE OTHER MINISERIES*) LATER...
HOO BOY, IS THIS GONNA MAKE FOR A WILD BOOK.
BEGINNING OF THE LINE!
*YEAH? LET'S SEE HOW THE TRADE SELLS. -THE CO-PUBLISHER
CRUNCH!
BIZARRO GO HOME!
HISSSS
AW MAN. SORRY ABOUT THAT, B.
WHY? BIZARRO AM NO FOLLOW DIRECTIONS AND GO HOME...TO METROPOLIS!
THIS AM HOME!
BESIDES, TOMORROW BIZARRO AM ENDING OLD JOB!
NEW JOB? WHAT NEW JOB?
TERRIBLE MISTER KENT AM NO GET ME INTERNSHIP AT DAILY PLANET. NOW WE AVOID EACH OTHER EVERY DAY...FOR-NEVER!
OH... BOO-RAY.
HISSSSS!
JIMMY? AM YOU NO CRYING?
The Beginning!

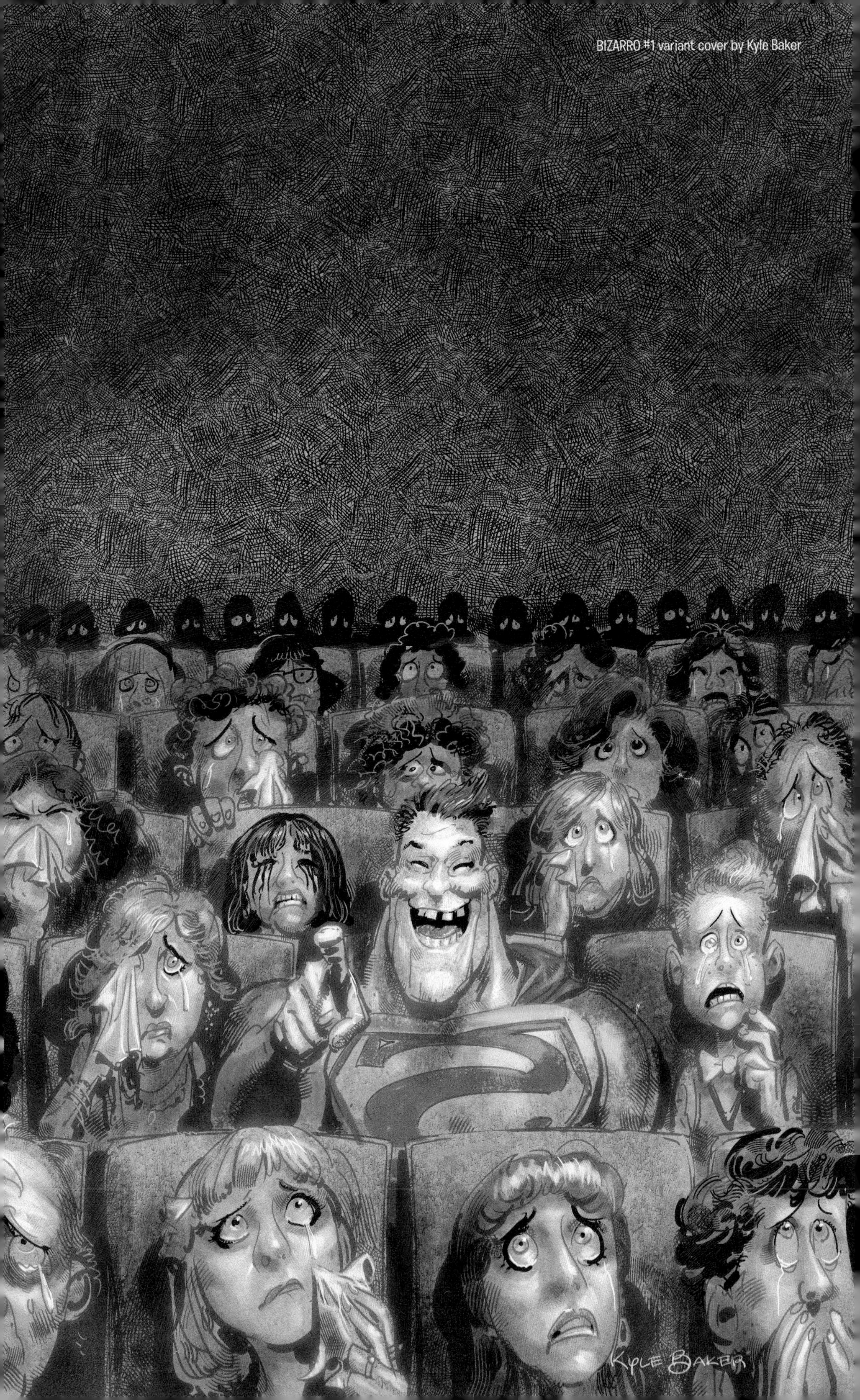
KYLE BAKER
BIZARRO #1 variant cover by Kyle Baker

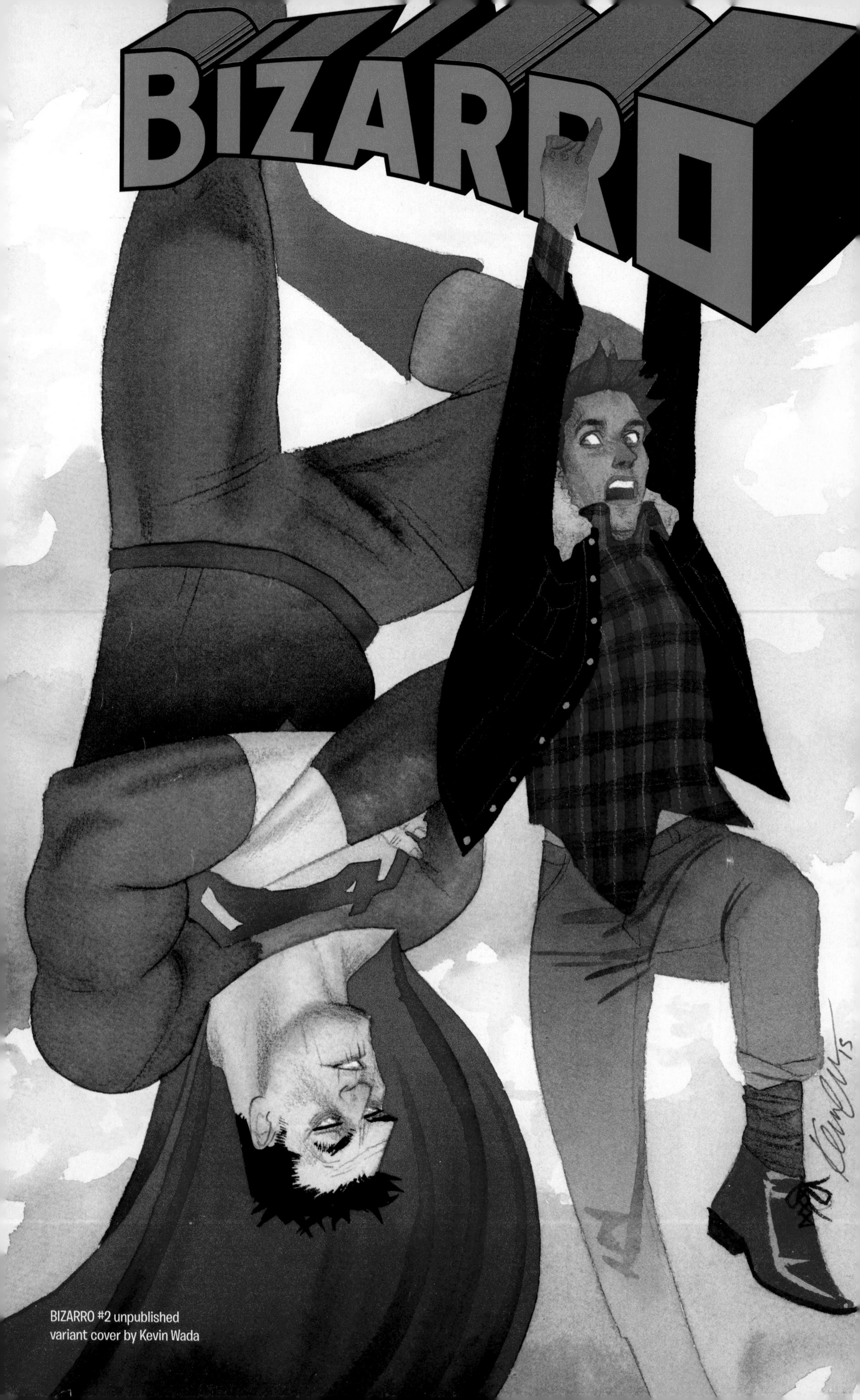
BIZARRO

BIZARRO #2 unpublished
variant cover by Kevin Wada

Bizarro and Jimmy character sketches by Gustavo Duarte

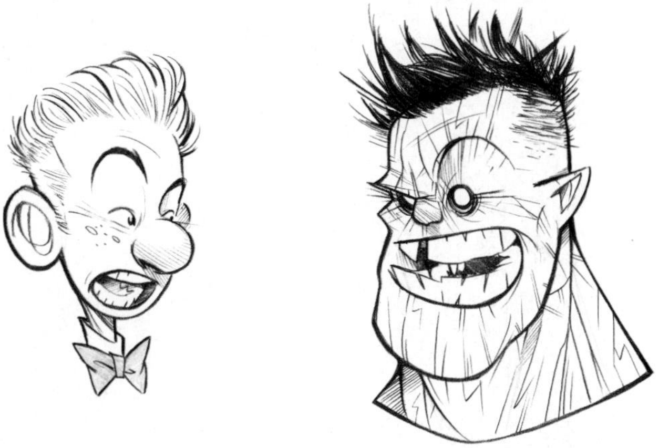

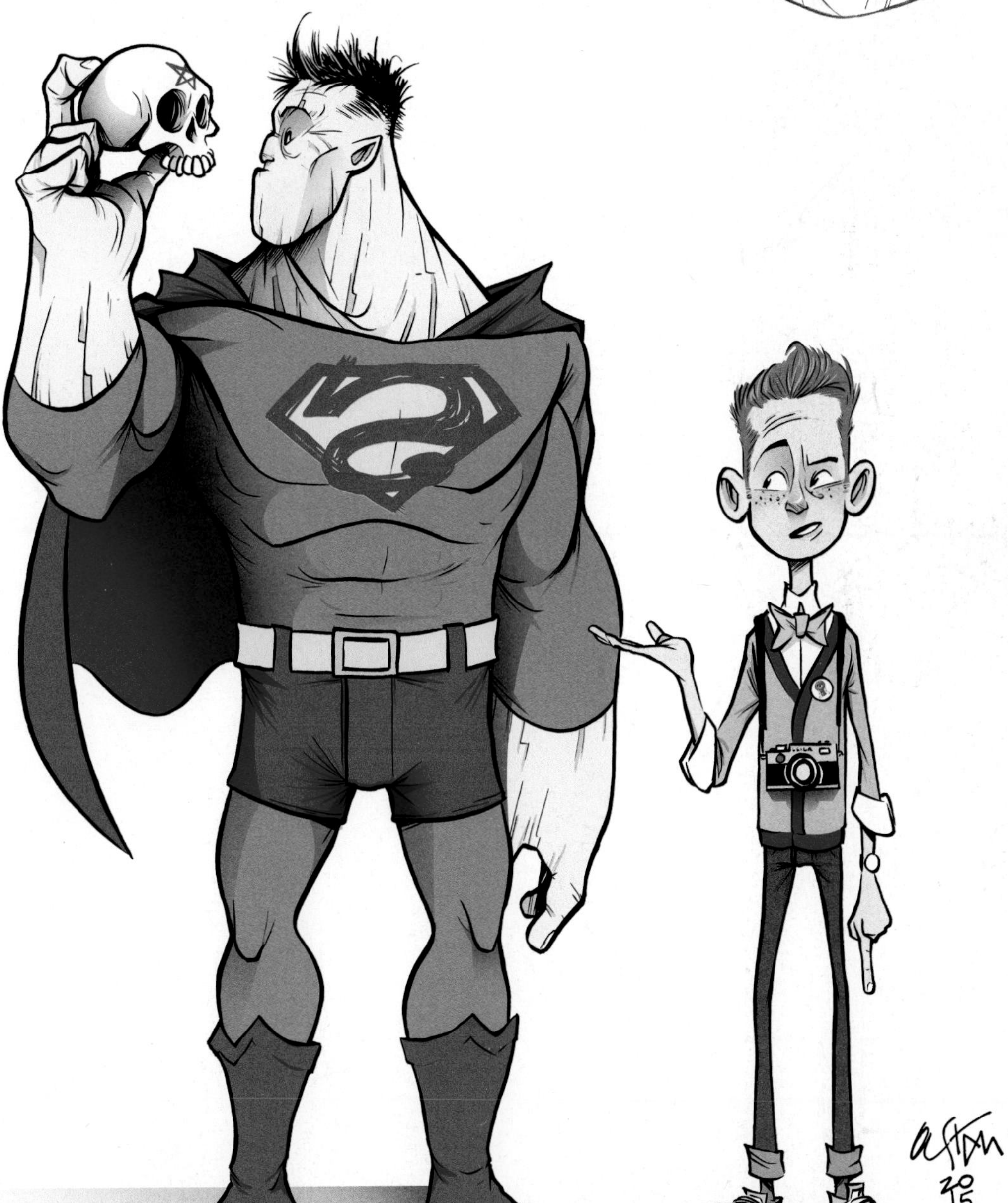

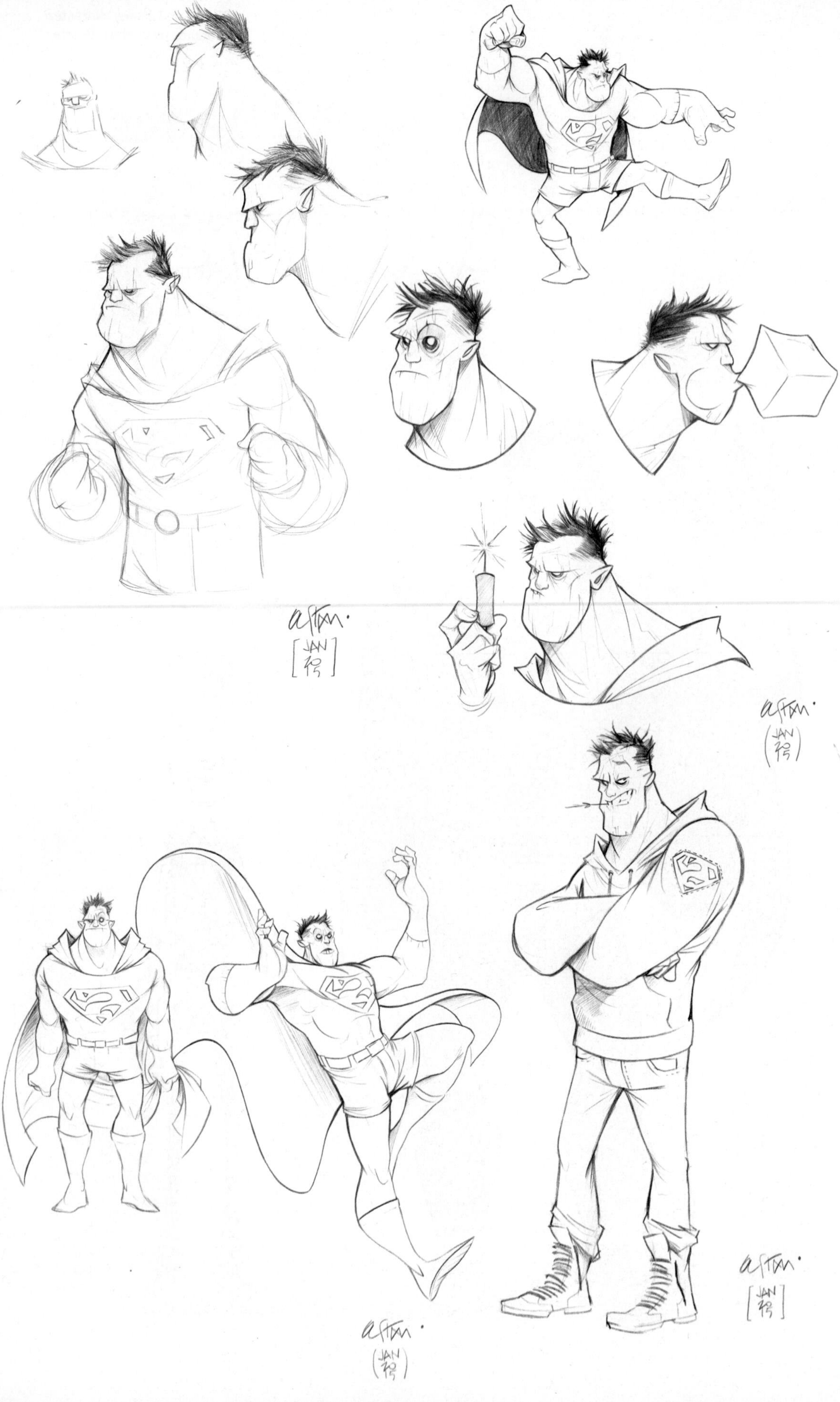

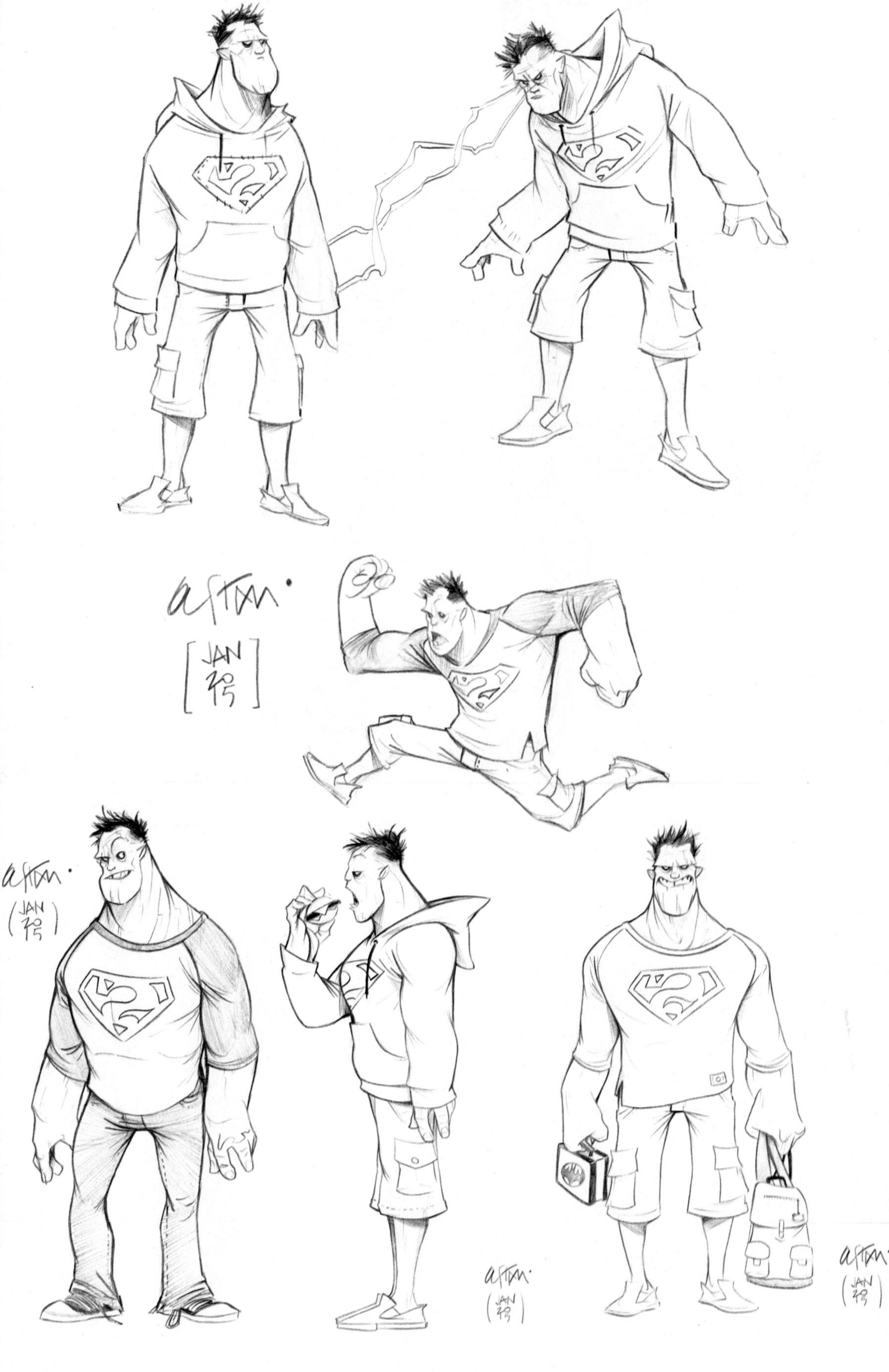

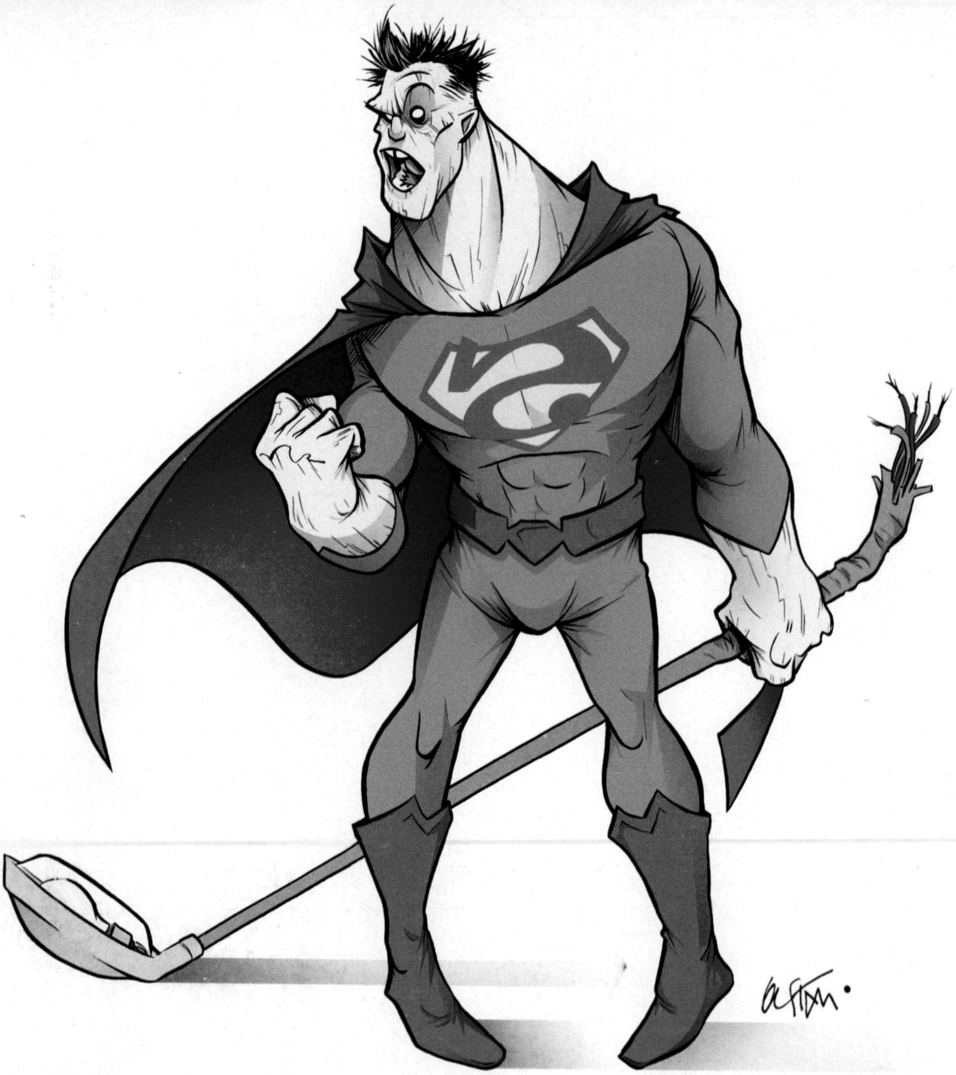

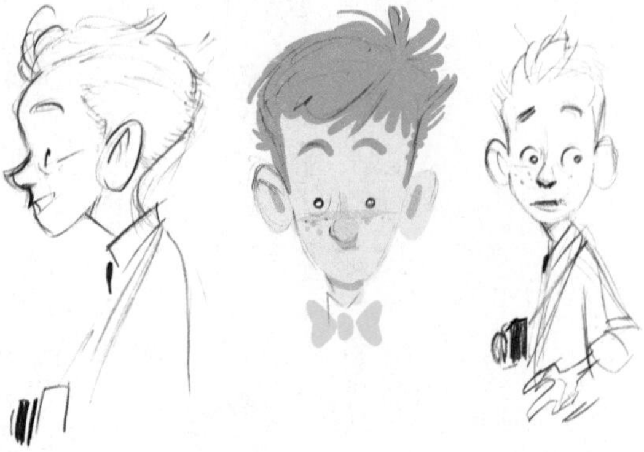

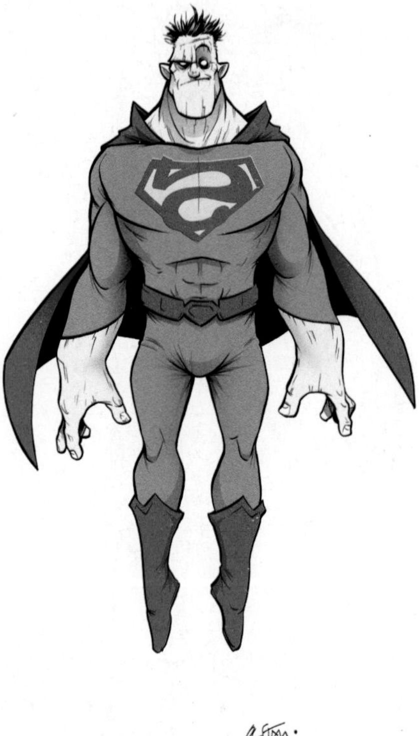